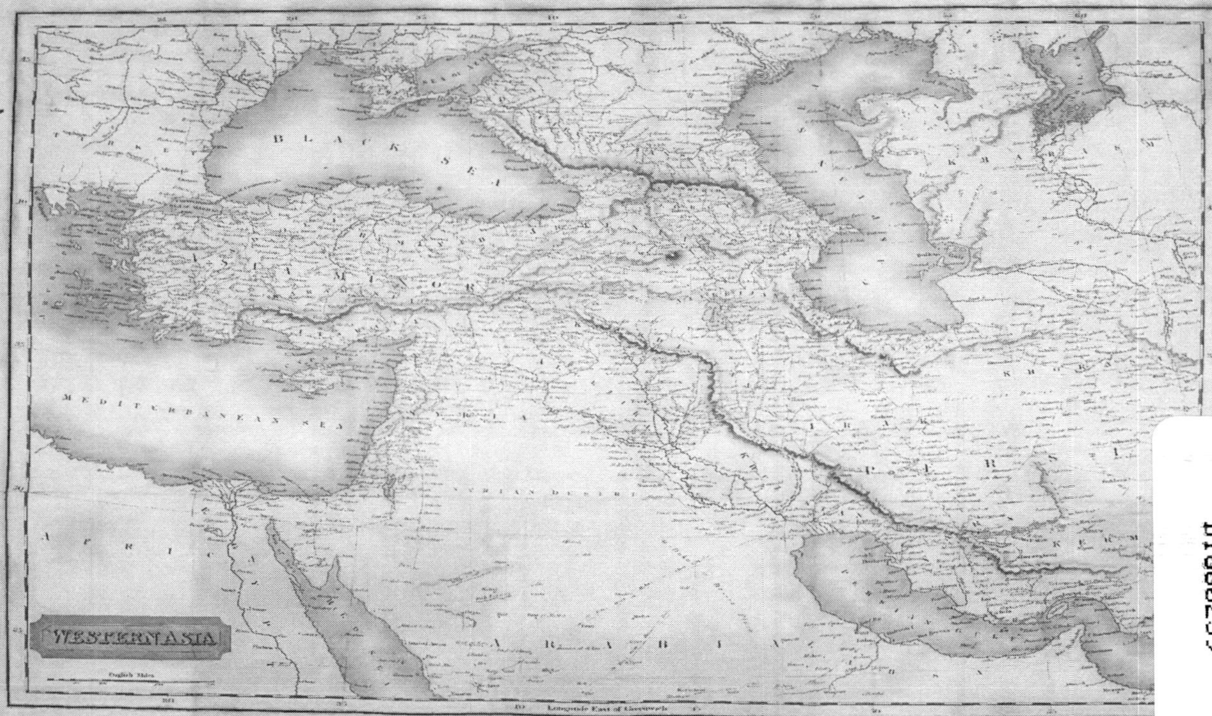
WESTERN ASIA
BLACK SEA
MEDITERRANEAN SEA
ASIA MINOR
SYRIAN DESERT
ARABIA
AFRICA
PERSIA
IRAK
KHORASAN
Longitude East of Greenwich
English Miles

# HISTORICAL ACCOUNT
# OF
# DISVOVERIES AND TRAVELS
# IN
# ASIA

# HISTORICAL ACCOUNT OF DISCOVERIES AND TRAVELS IN ASIA,

From the Earliest Ages to the Present Time.

by

HUGH MURRAY, F.R.S.E.

VOL. III

GYAN

*Published by*

Gyan Publishing House
5, Ansari Road
Daryaganj, New Delhi-110002
Phone: 011-47034999, 9811692060
E-mail: books@gyanbooks.com

*Distribution Network*
gyanbooks.com
India, USA, Canada, UK, Australia, France



ISBN : 978-81-212-6092-3 (Set)
ISBN : 978-81-212-6089-3 (PB)
First Published, 1820

2nd Impression 2021

*Printed at:* Gyan Press, Delhi.



**Historical Account of Discoveries and Travels in Asia, Vol. III**
Author: Hugh Murray

# HISTORICAL ACCOUNT

OF

# Discoveries and Travels

IN

# ASIA,

By HUGH MURRAY, F. R. S. E.

---

VOL. III.

---

---

1820.

# CONTENTS OF VOLUME III.

## BOOK IV.

WESTERN ASIA.

### CHAPTER I.

PERSIA.—EARLY TRAVELS.



### CHAPTER II.

PERSIA.—RECENT TRAVELS AND PRESENT STATE.



### CHAPTER III.

PILGRIMAGES TO THE HOLY LAND.

## CHAPTER IV.

ASIATIC TURKEY.



## CHAPTER V.

ARABIA.



---

# BOOK V.

EASTERN ASIA.

## CHAPTER I.

COUNTRIES BETWEEN INDIA AND CHINA.



## CHAPTER II.

CHINA.—PORTUGUESE AND SPANISH DISCOVERIES.

## CHAPTER III.

CHINA.—EMBASSIES AND MISSIONS.



## CHAPTER IV.

BRITISH EMBASSIES.



## CHAPTER V.

JAPAN.



---

# BOOK VI.

NORTHERN ASIA.

## CHAPTER I.

THE TERRITORY OF CAUCASUS.

## CHAPTER II.

### SIBERIA.—EARLY DISCOVERIES.



## CHAPER III.

### SIBERIA.—RECENT TRAVELS.

# HISTORICAL ACCOUNT

OF

# DISCOVERIES AND TRAVELS

IN

# ASIA.

# BOOK IV.

## WESTERN ASIA.

## CHAPTER I.

### PERSIA.—EARLY TRAVELS.

*Zeno.—Barbaro.—Contarini.—Vicenze Alessandri.—Sherley.—Don Garcia de Sylva.—Herbert.—Olearius.—Chardin.—Bembo.—Fra Leandro.*

THAT vast and varied region, which extends from the Indian Ocean to the Caspian, and from the Euphrates to the mountains and deserts of the Indian frontier, has formed, in all ages, a distinguished seat of Asiatic empire. On the Euphrates were seated those of Babylon and Nineveh, the first which appear to have aimed at the dominion of the world. The seat of the empire of the Great King was transferred eastward to that vast plain which extends from the Persian Gulf to the Caucasian mountains; and the Parthians, in the same position, opposed a limit to the progress of the Roman arms. The successive Arab and Tartar dynasties which afterwards swayed the sceptre of this region, seldom attempted to pass the line of the Euphrates and Tigris.

All the oriental empires are subject to change; but Persia, above all, has been swept by an almost perpetual tempest of war and revolution. Internal rebellion and foreign invasion have never ceased to distract that unfortunate country. An inevitable cause may be found in its physical position. Its vast and luxuriant plains are bordered and deeply indented by ranges of mountain territory, whose fierce and brave tenants are ever observant of the wealth and weakness of the regions beneath. As soon therefore as the energies of the dynasty begin to sink under the pleasures of its voluptuous capitals, a more vigorous hand is always ready to snatch the sceptre which its present master is unable to hold. Thus Persia continually changes its aspect; for the track of these barbarous conquerors is always desolating, while yet the bounties of nature enable it continually to recover from their ravages. There the plough is continually yielding to the sword, and the sword to the plough; the same city is found in one age an opulent and magnificent capital, and in the next a heap of ruins. The picture, though essentially the same, is in all its details and minute features perpetually changing.

Towards the close of the fifteenth century, the Turkish power was in the highest state of energy and activity. Mahomet II. after stripping the eastern empire of its remaining provinces, had wrested from it its last seat, the imperial city. He had thus established a name terrible alike to the East and the West, and was supposed to aim at universal empire. The Venetians, whom liberty, commerce, and naval power, had raised to a high place among the nations of Europe, were the state who viewed his progress with peculiar alarm. They held important possessions, both on the Archipelago and the Euxine; and the interposition of this barbarous and tumultuary power threatened to intercept that intercourse with India, which formed the most valued source of their wealth. In this exigence, there appeared no great power on whose co-operation they could rely, except Persia. The rulers of this monarchy could not view without alarm, the progress of so great a power on their western frontier; yet there was little appearance that, without some powerful impulse, they would venture to contend with such an adversary. The republic had ties with Uzum-cassan, the present monarch of Persia, of a somewhat peculiar nature. His queen Despina was daughter of a Greek prince, who then assumed the title of emperor of Trebisond; the antipathies of religion being extinguished in the two monarchs by their common dread of the power of Mahomet. This monarch had married another daughter to Nicolo Crespo, who, from his wide dominion over the islands, bore the title of Duke of the Archipelago, and was united by intimate ties with the state of Venice. Her potent and wealthy nobles were then judged suitable mates for the daughters of kings. Three of them had married three of the daughters of this insular prince, and became thus, in a certain sense, allied to the emperor of Persia. One of them was CATERINO ZENO, belonging to a family equally distinguished for wealth, knowledge, and enterprise, and who thus, when the republic had determined to send an embassy to the Persian monarch, appeared the fittest person of all others to undertake it. This was a commission attended with considerable danger, in consequence of the hostile and barbarous regions which intervened; but the patriotism of Zeno induced him to attempt it without hesitation. Having landed in Caramania, he made his way, through very serious obstacles, to the Persian court. He was received with overflowing joy and kindness by the monarch; but on mentioning to the attendants his wish to see his aunt the empress, the utmost horror was at first expressed at such an idea. It was stated, that once to allow her face to be seen by him, would be considered an entire breach of conjugal faith. The king, however, on being made acquainted with the ambassador's request, agreed, from respect to the republic, and to his own relationship, that he should have an audience. The queen received him with every mark of joy and kindness, inquired for all her relations at Venice, and on his rising to depart, insisted upon his taking up his residence within the palace. This intimacy was so far from giving any offence to Uzum-cassan, that he entirely shared it. Zeno had free access to their most retired apartments, even while they were together in bed. The queen, it is said, was the most religious of women, and though at the head of this Mussulman court, did not at all abate her attachment to the Christian religion. What is singular, this strenuous difference of belief in no degree affected the harmony of the royal pair. It only made the queen feel thus an additional motive, zealously to second all the views of Zeno against the Turkish power. Uzum-cassan was by no means forward to engage in this contest; but their continual solicitations, joined to some insults which his vassals had received from the Ottoman Porte, at length determined him to try the fate of war. After a temporary promise of success, however, his troops sustained a signal overthrow, and he found his victorious career for the first time checked. Mortified at this disaster, he strongly urged Zeno to repair to Europe, and endeavour to prevail upon its princes to afford that powerful assistance of which he had so largely boasted.

Zeno could not well decline this request, though the road was by no means patent. He found his way to the Black Sea, and embarked in a vessel for Caffa. The Genoese captain, however, learning his character and destination, formed the treacherous design of delivering him up to the Great Turk. Happily a Venetian citizen, resident at Caffa, having learned this felonious intent, came off in a little boat, conveyed away Zeno, and secreted him in his own house. Our ambassador, however, having brought off only his person, found himself under the most extreme want of funds, either for present subsistence, or for his destined journey. In this extremity, his servant Martino earnestly petitioned to be sold as a slave, for the supply of his master's wants; and Zeno was so far wrought upon by the urgency of his case, as to accept this too generous offer. The narrator celebrates it as one of the most illustrious examples of self-devotion ever exhibited by any one in a servile condition. The Venetian senate esteemed it so highly, that they not only redeemed Martino, but granted him a handsome pension for life. Zeno, thus provided with the *needful*, set out on his journey through Poland and Hungary. He prevailed on the king of

Poland, not indeed to make war himself on the Turks, but at least to cease hostilities against Hungary, and thus leave that power at liberty, if it chose, to take arms against the common enemy. News, however, soon arrived, that Uzum-cassan, tired of his unsuccessful war, and complaining that Christians "had many pro-"fessions and words, but few actions," shewed no inclination to renew hostilities. This disposition was confirmed by some domestic incidents, in which he was soon after involved. The Curds, his enemies, chose to circulate a report of his death, which being conveyed to his son, commanding in the south of Persia, that prince, mentioned under the odd name of Gurlumameth, made haste to occupy Schiras, as the prelude to seizing upon the whole of the vacant empire. Learning soon his error, and finding his father inexorable, he went over to Mahomet, who readily supplied him with the means of supporting his usurped claim. Uzum-cassan had then recourse to an artifice, which has been justly considered unworthy of his high dignity. He feigned, first sickness, and then death; whereupon, at his prompting, several of the great lords wrote to the prince, urging him to make haste and take possession of the throne. The unhappy and ever too credulous Gurlumameth hesitated not to obey the summons, but on his arrival was instantly thrown into prison, and soon after put to death.

EVEN before the departure of Zeno, the States of Venice had already sent out another ambassador. JOSAPHAT BARBARO, who had performed a journey to the Crimea, and several parts of Muscovy and Tartary, was selected as one accustomed "to endure and deal with barbarous men," for the mission to Persia. He landed at Curcho (Curco) in Caramania, whence passing through Tarsus and Adana, he directed his route to the Euphrates. He notices nothing remarkable till he crossed that river and arrived at Orfa. His next stage was Merdin, which appeared to him the most extraordinary city in the world for situation. It is ascended by a stair cut in the rock, more than a mile high, at the top of which is the gate; but there is no wall, except the walls of the houses, the defence of the place being trusted solely to its inaccessible site. The Turks hyperbolically assert, that the inhabitants never see a bird flying above them. It contains three hundred houses, and several manufactures of silk and cotton. Barbaro saw here with surprise a personage entirely characteristic of Asiatic manners. As he sat in the caravansera, a man, naked, shaven all over, and covered with goatskin, entered, and seating himself on the floor beside him, opened a little book and began to read. Soon after he drew nearer and asked our traveller who he was; on being told "a "stranger;" he replied, "I too am a stranger, "and we are all strangers in this world." He said he had wandered for many years naked over the world, without being able to find any thing that pleased him; and he had now thought of abandoning it altogether. Then after exhorting his auditor to live well and moderately, and to despise the world, he took his departure.

After some days' travelling Barbaro came to a town which he calls Assanchiph, all the rocks in the neighbourhood of which are excavated so as to form human habitations. The streets are led along the side of high steeps, so that the waggons and people appear to be moving in the air. He soon after began to pass the highest part of the mountains of Curdistan, inhabited by bands of fierce and desperate robbers. The mission fatally experienced their prowess, being attacked by a band at the top of a lofty mountain. What prowess the rest of the party might display is not stated; but our author's efforts were vigorously and exclusively directed to the safety of his own person. He spurred his horse with such fury, as soon left both friends and foes at a distance. Two of his companions afterwards came up, who told the sad tale of disaster; that the Persian ambassador and his own secretary had been killed, they themselves severely wounded, and all their effects taken. It is not said that they ventured any criticism on the speed with which he had carried himself off from the scene of action. After passing the mountains, and approaching the capital, he conceived himself in safety, when he was met by a band of Turcomans, who inquired whether he was destined. Being told that he was conveying a letter to the king, the leader demanded to see it. Our author assures us, that it was in the mildest possible manner that he represented the disrespect which would be shewn to the king, by making such an exhibition of his letter. The Turcoman replied only by raising his fist, and aiming at the jaws of Barbaro so furious a blow, that the pain was felt for four months after. They beat also his interpreter, and left them, he says, very ill content, but without any farther injury.

Having reached Tauris, where Uzum-cassan resided, and announced his arrival, an immediate message came desiring to see him. No one could be worse equipped for such an interview, since all the attire he had left did not amount to the value of two ducats. Having no means, however, of procuring any more suitable vestments, he went in this humble guise. He was ushered through several large courts into a garden, in the midst of which was a lodge, where his majesty was seated on cushions of gold brocade, with a fountain playing before him. He received the ambassador in the most polite manner, told him he knew of the sad disaster, and desired that he would draw out a complete list of all the articles robbed from him, which would be made good. He was afterwards admitted to a more formal interview, and was taken to see the wolf fights at the Maidan. But the exhibition which most gratified him was that of the presents just brought by an Indian ambassador. They included a great shew of rare animals, particularly lions of a peculiar species, which seem rather to be Bengal tigers, and the zirnapha or giraffe (camelopard). He was still more dazzled by the display of jewels, which appear to have been very numerous and valuable. Pre-eminent among them was a balass ruby, weighing two ounces and a half, which the monarch holding up to Barbaro, asked if he had ever seen its equal, and at what price he would value it. The ambassador replied, that it appeared to him indeed without a paragon, and to be estimated not in gold, but in cities. Pleased with the admiration which these sights inspired, the monarch made a full display of all his glittering treasures and possessions; his immense wardrobe, and the large armouries filled with gold and silver ornaments and vestments, to be distributed as prizes at solemn festivals. Barbaro was then entertained by the exhibition first of female dancers, and afterwards of male wrestlers, who carried on their exercise with such force and fury, that death was often the lot of the vanquished. One man of gigantic size and muscular strength, after having bared his limbs for the game, was excused when he stated the number to whom his encounter had proved fatal.

These amusements were interrupted by the intelligence which the king received of the occupation of Schiras by his son, in the manner and on the grounds already stated. He immediately set his army in motion upon that city, marching at the rate of forty miles a-day. Our author declares, that in this immensely rapid march the troops were accompanied by all their families, women, children, and infants in the cradle; yet it was performed in the greatest pomp, and amid an uninterrupted supply of all the comforts and luxuries of life. He declares himself aware of the great peril thus incurred by him of losing all credit with European readers, but he says, "I have seen it, and I know it." In explanation he states, that the infants at the breast were placed in a small cradle fastened over the horse's shoulder, while the mother or nurse sat behind, and held in her left hand the cradle, and also the reins, while the whip was fastened to the little finger of the right hand. The children a little more advanced, were accommodated in baskets, which, as well as the cradles, were worked and adorned in proportion to the wealth of the parents. The females wore a veil of woven horse hair, which at once concealed their faces, and sheltered them from the sun and dust. Although this army did not consist of above 25,000 fighting men, it was attended by 30,000 camels, 25,000 horses, 20,000 asses, and 5000 mules.

Barbaro did not follow the army far, but finding himself indisposed, stopped at Sultania. He afterwards visited different parts of the south of Persia, particularly Schiras, and enlarges much on its populousness, extent, and the vast trade of which it was the centre. He saw also the remains of Persepolis, called by the natives Cilminar, or the Forty Columns; but he does not seem to have any just idea of the period at which, or the nation by whom they were erected. According to a constant tendency both of the Mahometans and of the early travellers, he refers them to a Jewish origin. One conspicuous figure, leaning on an arch, was concluded to be Solomon; while another bearing obvious marks of strength, was supposed to be Samson. There was another with a mitre on its head, and its hand raised in such a manner, that our traveller could not help fancying it the Pope in the act of giving benediction.

After Barbaro had returned to the north of Persia, and was residing at Tauris, Uzum-cassan was taken ill and died. His sons then began as usual their bloody scramble for the empire. That very night, three of them strangled the fourth, and divided the sovereign power among themselves. It was not long before the second killed the eldest, and raised himself to the throne. While such deeds were going forward, Barbaro was seized with a strong inclination to absent himself. Having hired an Armenian guide, he arrayed himself in the poorest clothes, and set out in a very humble guise for Erzerum. He reached it in safety, and, after some difficulty, made his way across to Aleppo, and thence to Venice.

THE states of Venice were indefatigable in their embassies to the Persian court. The next was AMBROGIO CONTARINI, who set out in 1473, passed through Hungary and Poland, then embarking at Caffa, made his way not without difficulty through Mingrelia and Georgia to Tauris. Here he found every thing in the most violent commotion in consequence of the insurrection of the young prince already mentioned, which the king had set out to suppress. In passing through the streets they heard the people exclaiming,

"These are the dogs who come to introduce a "schism into the Mahometan faith, we ought to "cut them to pieces." They reached, however, the caravansera, the director of which received them well, and assigned them good quarters; though he expressed the utmost astonishment how they could have entered the country at a time when the most rigorous orders had been given that no strangers whatever should be allowed admission. He found no one who would undertake to conduct him to Uzum-cassan, and was obliged to keep very close within his caravansera, as whenever he ventured out with his interpreter to buy food, he was saluted by the people with furious cries, which were expounded to signify, that he ought by all means to be cut in pieces. He was relieved, however, by learning the arrival of one of the king's sons, whom he calls Musubey, from whom he hoped to obtain all that he stood in need of. He waited upon him therefore, and presenting a piece of camblet, stated his destination for the king his father, and requested protection and a guide. The prince heard this oration with the most frigid indifference, and scarcely deigned an answer, so that Contarini had nothing left but to return home exactly as he had gone. Matters soon became worse; he learned that the prince was extorting money by all means from every quarter, in consequence of which all the merchants had shut their shops to evade his observation. Under these circumstances, the caravansera appeared much too conspicuous a station, and he was happy to thrust himself into the corner of an Armenian convent, out of which he never durst shew his head. Thus he remained for a long time in heavy durance, till he learned that a great Persian lord named Chadi Laicher, who had been sent ambassador to Turkey, was now returning to Uzum-cassan at Ispahan. He found means to be introduced to him, stated the situation in which he stood, and petitioned to be allowed to proceed in his train. This address being accompanied with suitable presents, was most graciously received, the request granted, and notice being given of his period of departure, Contarini found himself safely on the way to Ispahan. The country between Tauris and that city, was in general arid, and the water often salt, but the fruits excellent. Ispahan was not yet the imperial city of Abbas. No expressions are used to indicate any extraordinary magnitude; and he observes, that it bore marks of the ravages of war, yet that it was situated in a fine and fertile country. He found here his countryman Barbaro, and was well received by the king. The court then proceeding to Tauris, he returned with it thither. Soon after his arrival at Tauris, the king made the proposal that Contarini should return to Europe, and inform the Christian states how affairs stood in Persia, while Barbaro should remain. Our ambassador expressed much mortification at this arrangement, and reluctance to concur in it, so that Uzum-cassan was at last obliged to state his positive will and command to that effect. Contarini being then assured that there remained no further alternative, agreed with the best possible grace, and an amicable parting took place. He proposed at first to return by the way he had come, but was led by circumstances to cross the Caspian to Astrakhan, where he made his way home through Tartary, Russia, and Poland.

The condition of Persia at a subsequent period, under the reign of Shah Thamas, second successor to Uzum-cassan, is illustrated in a report made to the Senate of Venice in 1575 by their agent Vicenze Alessandri, who had resided for some years in Persia. The manuscript has found its way into the British Museum. Ismael, he says, the father of the present monarch, after having sworn fidelity to the son of Uzum-cassan's daughter, obtained the character of a saint; then, "with little fear of God, cut off the said son's "head," and seized the kingdom. His administration, however, was vigorous; he humbled the power of the Turks, and preserved internal tranquillity. His son, Shah Thamas, was then seventy-four years old, of which he had reigned twenty-three. He exhibited all the vices of a weak and tyrannical despotism. He had not quitted the palace for ten years, and thus entirely neglected the duty, always considered incumbent upon an eastern monarch, of administering justice in public. The people murmured loudly; but when they were heard crying day and night at the palace gate, a message was sent out, that they should go to the judges appointed for the purpose; never considering, says the writer, that it was against himself and his ministers that the cries were raised. A merchant having raised a prosecution against some persons who had stolen cloths from him, the judge dismissed both plaintiff and culprits, and kept the cloths to himself. At court the business was entirely hushed by presents to a few of the principal lords. The unfortunate owner got himself mounted on one of the palace towers, where he was within hearing of the royal ear, and continued crying day and night, what the king was doing, and why he paid no regard to the wrongs of his subjects? The only result, however, was to be bastinadoed, and made to leap about by stones thrown at him. At Tauris, the capital, a band of robbers broke into the repositories of a principal merchant, and carried off 6000 scudi, "besides killing him." Some days after they broke into the house of an Armenian merchant, and carried off 4000 pieces of silk, which were publicly sold in the palace. Both were treated by the king as matters of perfect indifference. Another merchant having been handsomely feasted by some *Curzi*, or royal guards, was immediately after robbed of a large sum by persons whom he believed to be in the employ of these his courteous entertainers. By friends and presents he found access to the king, and earnestly entreated that the Curzi should be imprisoned and examined. The king expressed his entire concurrence, provided the merchant would accede to the condition, that in the event of not being able to prove his allegations, his head should be cut off. The merchant did not think it expedient to embark in a contest liable to such a termination. A few days after, however, he obtained certain information on the subject; and having by a new present of four hundred ducats gained fresh access to the king, the money was found in the possession of the Curzi. The king then, imitating the example of his judge, graciously ordered that it should be deposited in his own treasury.

Amid all these irregular doings of this illustrious person, the author describes him to be venerated by his subjects rather as a god than a king. In disease they invoked him oftener than either Ali or Mahomet, vowing, in case of recovery, to make a handsome present, at least to kiss the palace gate. Happy was the house which contained the least scrap of garment worn by him, or a drop of dirty water in which his hands or feet had been washed. These precious relics were carried to the remotest extremities of the empire, to be used as remedies against every disease. He was even supposed, like Ali, to have the power of raising the dead. This awful reverence, however, had marvellously declined in Tauris, the capital, and place of his usual residence. This city was almost entirely in the hands of two furious factions, of whom the victorious one would not hesitate to go to court and massacre all the ministers, and the king himself, if he attempted to resist them. To avoid those unpleasant occurrences, he had begun to prefer the abode of Casbin.

The trade of northern Persia is described by Alessandri as very considerable, but carried on entirely by the way of Aleppo and Constantinople. The expenses, he says, are very great, and the profits very small.. During his stay, an English merchant, whom he calls Signor Tommaro of London, (doubtless one of the company of merchant adventurers, probably Alcocke), had resided for some years at Tauris. He represents him to have met with very little success, and to have been repeatedly in danger of being plundered of his property. He had therefore left Tauris, and was not likely to return.

We now approach the most brilliant period of the Persian annals, formed by the reign of Shah Abbas the Great. A second son, he, according to the custom of the country, waded to the throne through the blood of his kindred; but he afterwards maintained such profound domestic tranquillity, and extended so far the frontier of the empire, as to render his own reign and that of his successors a truly fortunate period of Persian history. No Europeans resided so long, or enjoyed so high confidence at this eastern court, as the two brothers Sir Antony and Sir Robert Sherley. Purchas sounds their praises in a truly lofty key. According to him, they were the hinge on which the affairs of Persia and of the whole East turned. He represents the Shah as destitute, without them, of musketry and artillery; and exultingly proclaims, that if two millions of infidels had cut each others' throats, the Christian world owed this great benefit solely to these two brothers. I must do Sir Antony the justice to say, that, in his own narrative, though written with considerable self-complacency, no pretension is made to these mighty achievements. He states himself to have been the particular friend and *protegé* of the Earl of Essex, "whom he had made the "pattern of his civil life." At his advice he undertook the voyage to Persia, hoping thereby, he says, to promote the glory of God; or if not, even with regard to the humble concerns of trade, "it "might prove a subject to extract great and good "matter out of." He embarked in a Venetian vessel bound to Aleppo; but on the passage to Zante he received notice of a passenger who "used most "scandalous speeches of her Majesty;" whereupon, "not only moved with the dutiful zeal "which a subject oweth to his prince, but even "with that respect which every gentleman oweth "to a lady," he directed his people to bestow on him "a fit reward." What the nature of this recompense might be, is not stated; but "divers "principal merchants" approved it highly, and judged it scarcely adequate to "the sceleratnesse "of the fact." However, "the shippe was all "in an uprore," and notice was given at Zante, that they could have nothing more to do with him. He made his way therefore with difficulty to Cyprus, and thence to Aleppo. He found Syria "a goodly country," but uncultivated; "here and there as it were sprinkled with miser-"able inhabitors, which in their fashion shewed "the necessity they had to live, rather than any "pleasure in living." The English merchants

" were the only gentlemen, or the most benigne " gentlemen that ever I met withall ;" so that though one Hugo de Potso attempted all the injury " which an ill mind and a great purse" could do, he effected his passage safely across the desert. He passed a Bedouin encampment, and was introduced to " Aborisci, king of those Arabies, a poore " king, with ten or twelve thousand beggerly sub-" jects, living in tents of blacke haire cloth." He was honestly and civilly treated, and " the king " gave us good words, without any kind of bar-" barous wondring."

At Bagdad Sir Antony, wishing to pass as a merchant, converted all his property into jewels, but was much dismayed when all these were " stayed by the Bassa." This reduced him to a very serious dilemma, as he had nothing left to maintain himself, a brother, " whose affection to " mee had onely led him to that disaster," and twenty-five other followers, mostly gentlemen, " onely carried with their loves to mee," all of whom were in the power of Turks, a race notoriously cruel, and " addicted to get by all means, " just or unjust." This great train and wealth, moreover, were soon found to have rendered them objects of serious suspicion. A Florentine merchant assured Sherley, that " there was a great " muttering amongst divers great men there, what " I was, and what my designs might be." He was at first very distrustful of this Florentine, but soon found him a most generous friend, who procured him a place in a Persian caravan, and supplied him with money sufficient not only for his wants, but to make a splendid appearance before Shah Abbas. He appears to have passed up the rivers and through Curdistan, and though he professes great resignation to the divine will, cannot help adding, " Yet my frailty gave me a continual " terrour during those thirty daies in which we " wandered with that company of blind pilgrimes " through the deserts." He passed the site of Ninive, but found " not one stone standing which " may give the memory of the being of a towne. " One English mile from it is a place called Mosul, " a small thing, rather to be a witnesse of the " other's mightinesse and God's judgment, than " of any fashion of magnificency in itself." After passing " a great tract of good and ill countries," he arrived at Casbin, then the imperial residence. Shah Abbas was absent on a military expedition; but he was well received by the governor. Shortly after the Shah arrived victorious over his enemies, and made his triumphal entry into Casbin. This auspicious moment was seized by Sherley to present himself. He and his party coming up in the midst of the procession, alighted and kissed the monarch's stirrup. " My speech " was short unto him, the time being fit for no

" other: That the fame of his royall vertues had " brought me from a farre countrey, to be a pre- " sent spectator of them; if there were any thing " of worth in mee, I presented it, with myself, to " his majesty's service." The king replied most graciously, that he had done him infinite honour, that the country was at his service, and only doubted if he would find any thing in himself answerable to so great a report. Next morning Sherley sent a present, and was admitted to an interview. Abbas, he says, put no question about " our apparel, building, beauty of our women, " and such vanities," but directed his inquiries solely to subjects connected with the military art. On being told that Sherley had at home some models of fortifications, " left in the spoile made " of me at Babylon," he went home and spent several hours in carefully perusing them.

Sherley now spent a series of years in the service of the Shah. He seems to have well understood courts, for he says, " So much I know, that " in handling with princes' especial affairs, I ought " not so much to repose myself upon the good " and just property of my proposition, as upon " the direct knowledge of the nature of the " prince." He does not, however, give so full an account of Abbas as might have been expected. He draws a character entirely and vaguely panegyrical, and the transactions narrated are only those public ones which belong to general history. I have already observed, that he makes no pretensions to the immense influence and services which are imputed to him by Purchas. Even the missions with which he was entrusted to European powers, were conferred on his own earnest advice and urgency, the king continuing long to doubt their expediency, and to consider them even as derogatory to his dignity. It was in one of these missions that Sir Antony wrote his narrative, which does not come down to the time of his finally leaving Persia.

A more particular account is given of Shah Abbas by John Cartwright, who visited Persia at the same time with Sherley. The following is the description given by him: "The Prince "is very absolute both in perfection of his bodie "and his minde; of an indifferent stature, nei-"ther too high nor too low. His countenance "very sterne, his eyes fierce and piercing, his "colour swarffie, his moustachees on his upper "lip long, with his beard cut close to his chinne, "expressing his martial disposition and inexora-"ble nature, that at the first a man would think "to have nothing in him but mischiefe and cruel-"ty: And yet he is of nature courteous, affable, "easy to be seene and spoken withall." The morning was spent chiefly among his horses, and the forenoon in his armoury. At three he came to the Meidan, and joined with his courtiers in warlike exercises. He is described as very strict in the execution of justice, often sitting in person for that purpose, and " not sparing to hang up " his chiefe Caddi or judges," in case of notorious malversation. " I have seene him many " times alight from his horse, merely to do jus- " tice to a poore bodie." In this manner, it is said, " the Persian empire hath flourished in sa- " cred and redoubted lawes, the people demean- " ing themselves after the best manner they can ; " —armes, artes, and sciences, doe wonderfully " prosper."

The most curious picture which I have seen of the character and policy of Shah Abbas, is given by Don Garcia de Sylva, in the narrative of an embassy from Goa, then subject to Spain under Philip III. It has not, so far as I know, been printed, but is found in manuscript in the British Museum. One of the most fatal blows struck against the Portuguese eastern empire, was the capture of Ormuz by a combined English and Persian force. Purchas has preserved several narratives of it by Pinder, Wilson, and Monoxe, English officers who were present in this memorable expedition. In November 1621, a fleet of five vessels and four pinnaces was fitted out from Swally roads to cruize against the Portuguese. Near the mouth of the Persian Gulf they received a proposition from Shah Callibeg, the Persian commander, who was about to undertake the siege of Ormuz. He invited them to co-operate, reminding them that the enemy was theirs as well as his, and promising half the booty. After due deliberation by Captains Blithe and Weddell and Monoxe, the Company's agents, it was determined to accede to this proposition. They sailed first to Kishme, where the Portuguese, being reduced to the last extremity, chose rather to surrender to the English than the Persians. Unfortunately, one of the few shots that were fired proved fatal to Baffin, the celebrated northern navigator, who was struck by a ball from the castle, " wherewith he gave three leapes, by report, " and died immediately."

From Kishme the armament proceeded direct to Ormuz, and saw it for the last time in all its glory. " It was of great bignesse, and seemed a " most famous thing to looke upon from the " ships, with steeples and towers: the castle was " the fairest, largest, and strongest, that ever I " saw." The Portuguese, after a slight resistance, evacuated the town, and withdrew into the castle, whence it soon appeared that it would be no easy matter to expel them. Monoxe complains that the Persians were ignorant of the art of war, and expresses his surprise " that " one of the wonders of our age, Shah Abbas, "should send over an army so weakly provided." They sprung mines, indeed, and made breaches, which appeared to the English very good; but Callibeg declined attempting them, and was not even provided with scaling ladders or other means of attack; so that Monoxe began to suspect, "his mining is for gold, not to make "breaches, unless it be breach of promises." He murmurs also, that the Persian commander never admitted him into his counsels when he could possibly avoid it, and shewed very little disposition to abide by his engagements. Meantime certain accounts were received of "the "great wants and weake estate" of the Portuguese garrison. They suffered chiefly in regard to water, which was in small quantity and brackish, while their food was rice and salt fish, "two very good preparatives for a good drinke "if they had it." They were hence seized with a violent flux, which carried off six or eight in a day, besides weakening the rest. It is asserted, therefore, that the Persian general by a vigorous attack might have carried the castle, but he continued only making new mines, "whereof he "hath three in hand, as if he would blow up the "castle wall round about, before he will make "his entrie." At length a breach being made which apparently enlarged the first, an assault was ordered, and the Persians rushed up at first with the greatest fury, but they "run their reso-"lution out of breath," and were repulsed by a handful of Portuguese. He says "they hang in "a cluster upon the breach, just as a swarm of "bees upon a tree or bush that want a hive, or "like a flocke of sheepe at a gappe, where none "is so hardy to enter." These proceedings would have little advanced the siege, had not the internal distress of the garrison daily increased; and the Persians at length carried several of the outworks. Our narrator is then obliged to own one art in which they are "very well "seene,—for I do not thinke there is any hang-"man in all Germany that can go beyond them." When they have taken an enemy, "at one blow "off goeth his head;" the finger is then thrust in at the mouth and out at a hole made in the ear, "in such sort that no butcher in Eastcheap "can do it better." They are not less "cun-"ning" to flay off the skin, and "stuffe it with "straw like a foot-ball." These are then carried in triumph as trophies to their general. The Portuguese being at length reduced to the last extremity, sent a message to the English, earnestly beseeching that the treaty of surrender might be made with them, and not with the Moors. The English, with the concurrence of the Persian general, acceded to a convention, according to which the Portuguese were to give up Ormuz and all that was in it, on condition of a safe personal conveyance to Muscat or India. After this treaty, two Persian deputies waited upon them, and, after a long preamble, submitted the proposal, that the English should deliver the captain and several of the principal Portuguese, whom it would be honourable to transmit as trophies to Shah Abbas; "which vilde and dishonourable motion when I heard, I absented myself, hating my eares for being guilty of the hearing of the same." The Portuguese, therefore, were duly "dispeeded out of the castle," to the number of 2600, who were in a dreadful state from wounds and disease. Monoxe does not come down to the promised division of the booty, but augurs ill as to its fulfilment, from the eagerness with which he saw the Persians seizing the property, and "whole bales of goods, chests, and rupetas, with God knoweth what in them," conveyed over the walls. He inclines to think, therefore, that "we shall be served with what themselves please."

The intelligence of this capture struck the vice-regal government at Goa with the deepest dismay. It was determined to attempt recovering by negociation what they had lost by arms; and an officer of distinction, Don Garcia de Sylva Figuerroa, was sent to demand the restitution of these important possessions. Don Garcia landed at Bandel, where he was received with great demonstrations of courtesy by the governor, but was detained for some days by want of horses; during which time he suffered extremely from the intensity of the heat. He then reached Gombroon, and set out to traverse the plain of Laristan. The land here is dry, salt, and, unless in some particular spots, quite barren. Throughout all this region, water is procured only from wells. The road lay through a plain bordered on each side by mountains composed of a whitish earth without stone, and entirely destitute, as well as the plains, of tree, bush, or shrub. These naked tracts, however, were covered with goats, the largest and finest in all Persia; and forming, in many villages, the sole wealth of the inhabitants. In travelling by day the heat was found quite intolerable, and they were obliged to take the benefit of moonlight. In approaching within a league of Lara, the governor came out and requested them to delay their entrance till next day, when it might be made in state, according to the wish of the king and the viceroy of Schiras. Meantime they were copiously supplied with dates, grapes, and melons. Next morning, about half a league from Lara, the governor appeared attended by numerous grandees, covered with gold, silver, and various coloured robes. They were preceded by 400 troops, and attended by an almost innumerable crowd of spectators; to maintain order among whom, a number of porters brandished large sticks, which, though employed with the utmost vigour, proved scarcely sufficient to fulfil their purpose. At the same time the fields resounded with all the music of Persia, producing, he says, "an incondite and bestial "sound." The noise was tremendous indeed, but without the least harmony. The most prominent instrument was a species of timbrel, resembling a very large sieve, such as he had seen not many years ago in Estremadura, where it must have been introduced by the Moors,—a vulgar and barbarous instrument, but delightful to Persian ears, and its presence indispensable at every ball given through that vast empire. Lara is an ancient city, nearly as large as Ormuz, but not so handsome. Being the seat, however, of a considerable inland trade, it is well supplied with caravanseras. The bazaar, built by Alaverdi Khan when sultan of Schiras, appeared one of the most "sovereign and distinguished" edifices in Asia, and fit to be compared with the first in Europe. It would add lustre to any city, and he could not help considering Lara unworthy of such a display of magnificence.

After leaving Lara, the embassy passed still between the same ranges of mountains; but the scene was not so entirely naked, the road being bordered by shrubs and small trees, planted apparently by travellers for the benefit of their shade. They had now an opportunity of observing the Turcomans, with their nomadic habits and rude appearance, rather Scythian than Persian. On their approach to Schiras, the governor met them with a still more numerous and splendid retinue than at Lara. The crowd was also much larger; but the cane being used with increased diligence, maintained tolerable order. Near the gate, a considerable number of veiled females on horseback formed part of the crowd. Schiras, on entry, did not answer the expectation which its appearance had excited. The gate was paltry, the streets narrow and ill kept, and many of the houses in ruins. From without, it was magnificent and superb; within, poor and miserable; a contrast very commonly presented by the cities of the East. This city was an object of enmity to Shah Abbas, having been the head-quarters of a rebel whom he had reduced by cutting off the water; which circumstance had considerably impaired its prosperity. The environs were truly beautiful, covered with the finest gardens, and watered by innumerable streams, natural and artificial. It is compared to Valencia, and the town to Cordova.

Beyond Schiras, the ambassador came to the spot called Cilminar, celebrated for the mighty ruins which cover its site, the remains of the ancient Persepolis. They were diligently surveyed by our author, who describes them with an enthusiasm which perhaps betrays him into some degree of exaggeration. He dwells on the superb range of columns, particularly those called the "forty minarets," the magnificent stairs by which it is ascended, the vast interior square, 430 feet by 310, and the huge pieces of marble without any apparent juncture. The sculptures were innumerable; and are conceived by him to represent the actions of a race of men prior to any now known, even to the ancient Babylonians and Persians. Yet, though ascending to this vast antiquity, they are so entire, that with the exception of a few fragments broken off, they might seem to have been recently finished. In comparing these with the monuments of other nations, he observes, that the pyramids are mere artificial mountains, while the temples of Greece are in ruins; here only, art and grandeur are united in pristine perfection. The high polish of the marble was amusingly shewn by a mastiff, who seeing his own figure reflected on the walls, was worked up to fury, which was always increased by the view of the corresponding gestures in the reflected image; till the same scene being repeated wherever they came, they were at length obliged to chain and send him off.

At Ispahan the embassy were met by the same retinue and crowd, and were equally stunned by the noise of cymbals and instruments. They saw here a troop of females mounted on horses very finely caparisoned; their faces covered, but their hair hanging down, richly ornamented with pearls and jewels. As they approached, clouds of dust concealed this city. When they entered, it appeared still more wretched and ruined than Schiras; the streets narrow, irregular, and winding; the whole aspect old, poor, and miserable. In short, he indignantly declares it "a thing "most shameful and abominable." From this doom, however, were excepted the edifices erected by Shah Abbas, which were very splendid. They consisted of an excellent caravansera, containing complete accommodation for a great number of merchants; and a bazaar of vast extent, surrounding the caravansera, and filled with the most precious commodities. But the greatest display of magnificence was in the Meidan or great square, on one side of which was built the palace, resembling a tower with gilded virandas. On the top, somewhat retiring, was a square turret most beautifully gilded, whence the sultanas, at a jealousy, could command a view of the Meidan, the gardens, and the whole town. The grounds and harams attached to the palace were shut from every eye. The gardens round Ispahan were fine, but could not rival the extent and beauty of those of Schiras. Shah Abbas had also built a very fine new mosque, the minaret of which was as high as the steeple of Seville, the highest in Spain. When the embassy came in front of the palace, they were desired to fall prostrate; but this appearing to them beneath their dignity, they refused to do more than take off their hats, while the Persian lords dismounted, and threw themselves on the ground.

The next city which the embassy visited was Caxem (Cashan), which they found comparatively small, but pleasant, and the inhabitants mild and peaceable. They were here present at a bull fight, to witness which the whole inhabitants of the town, male and female, were collected. All were gay and animated, except the owners of the bulls, on whose countenances care sat painted; which was changed, however, into triumph, when their bulls had gained a victory. As the fight proceeded, the passions of the multitude warmed; they raised vehement cries, which came at length to blows and bloodshed. The females did not take any concern in the blows; but no effort which the human voice could make was by them omitted. Stunned with this uproar, the ambassador offered them money to go home quietly; but this offer being conceived an insult, turned their indignation upon him, and only added a new source of tumult, so that he was glad to make off with all speed. These bull fights prevail over all Persia; but Cashan is the place where they excite the greatest enthusiasm, and are carried to the greatest height.

The next great city to which the embassy came was Casbin, then the royal residence. Their entrance here was distinguished by greater honours than at any of the other cities. They were met by twelve hundred horsemen most splendidly attired and accoutred, and whose armour glittered with gold and jewels. There was no crowd however, no females; all under pain of death were prohibited to come out. They were handsomely accommodated in a house close to the great mosque; but the ambassador, impatient for his introduction at court, was disappointed on being told that it could not take place for two days. On the appointed morning six hundred men appeared as bearers of the presents, who, it was found, expected to get each something to carry. This rather discomposed the embassy; for though there was enough to divide among the whole, the articles, frittered into so many minute portions, did not make the same imposing appearance as in a collected state. On reaching the palace, they were detained for half an hour at the gate. Indignant, less at the hardship than at the "pride "of these barbarous orientals," Don Garcia announced his determination to return home unless immediate admission was obtained. Hereupon he soon gained permission to enter the royal gardens, and proceeded through an avenue of large and beautiful trees of considerable dimensions, to a lake; in the midst was a summer-house, open on all sides, but covered with a cupola, supported by four columns. The approach was by a small bridge, of which they had passed two-thirds when the train suddenly stopped, and the interpreter called out "the King." Shah Abbas in fact appeared, coming out alone from the summer-house. The first view of this prince subverted every idea which Don Garcia had formed respecting the court of this great potentate. Accustomed to Spanish pomp and parade, exhibited on an augmented scale in its viceregal government at Goa, he seems to have been unable to conceive a court in which its display was not considered as the first privilege of royalty. Nothing therefore could be more remote from his ideas, than one where all parade seems to have been held in contempt, and nothing but real business regarded. Instead of an oriental pageant, blazing with gold and gems, he saw a little man, drest in a paltry robe, such as was worn by his meanest subjects, and a bonnet still shabbier than the robe. His face, not naturally swarthy, was tanned by continual exposure to the air; his hands were rough, coarse, and black, like those of the rudest peasant, whom indeed he in every respect resembled. The ambassador however dropped on his knees, put his hand to his mouth and then to his sleeve. The king received him graciously, asked for the king of Spain, and caused him to be ushered into the apartment, where he promised soon to join him. Don Garcia was led in by two Persian lords, the viceroys of Ghilan and Curdistan, who squatted themselves on their hams upon each side, whereupon he placed himself between them in the same position, though his sword and spear rendered it rather incommodious. As he sat, a person entered in a plain robe, without scimitar or any ensign of dignity. Don Garcia deemed him therefore unworthy of notice, till some one said, "The ambassador of Room," (the name by which the Ottoman Porte is known in the East). There seems to have been something electrical in the impression made by this announcement, which appeared irresistibly amusing to the Persian court. The courtiers burst into loud fits of laughter, and the viceroy of Ghilan whispered who he thought it had been. He frankly owned that he had taken him for a Mollah of one of the poor Arab tribes whom he had seen near the head of the Persian Gulf. This redoubled their mirth; and the king, on entering, being told the grounds of it, enjoyed them greatly, and rallied the Turkish ambassador on the subject. That personage appeared at first somewhat discomposed, but soon resumed his natural dignity and gravity. During this time Don Garcia had remarked a boy in a plain green robe, with his arm round a pillar, standing like a statue, without the least notice being taken of him by any one. It was a new surprise to learn that this was the heir-apparent of the monarchy. He remarked also a lady with a face broader than it was long, seated at a viranda on the bank of the lake. She demeaned herself with an air of majesty, as if all that passed was done only for her amusement; but he does not seem to have taken the trouble to inquire who she was.

Supper was now brought, which agreed as little as any other particular with all the preconceived ideas of Don Garcia. It consisted of rice, mutton and fowl, with a desert of plums half green, radishes, and cucumbers. The fare, in short, was such as might have been expected in the tent of a wandering Arab, rather than at one of the most splendid courts of the East. He talks with derision of such "poor and miserable customs;" and had no comfort unless in observing, that these rude viands were served in dishes of solid and massive gold. The king was courteous; he drank to the king of Spain, and then to the Turkish ambassador's beard. His mind however appeared to be entirely occupied in discussions with the envoy respecting some contested provinces; so that he could afford nothing but courtesy to the Spaniard, who at the proper hour ordered his equipage, and returned home.

Don Garcia fully expected that this ceremonial introduction would be immediately followed by a more private interview, in which he could enter on the business of the mission. The king, however, delayed this on various pretences; and, in the mean time, a rumour spread that the court were preparing to set out for Sultania. The ambassador saw that he was trifled with; and learning that the Shah spent part of every evening at the Meidan or great square, determined to go thither, and force an interview. There, accordingly, he found the king, who seeing, by Don Garcia's action and air, that it was impossible to give him the slip, voluntarily rode up, and invited him to sup in one of the royal gardens. As soon as they were seated, the Shah opened the conference with his own complaints. He expressed great surprise, that the Pope and Spain should not have joined their whole force against Turkey, and that the former, whose power was so generally acknowledged, should not have united all Christendom in a league against their common enemy. Don Garcia represented the divisions and self-interest which reigned among the European states; but urged that Spain had done much with her gallies to check the power of the Ottoman. The king replied, he doubted that was very little, otherwise how could the Turkish ambassador have declared that he never knew till now there was such a country as Spain. Don Garcia vehemently depreciated the knowledge of the ambassador, urging also that he did not fill any military department; but the Shah remarked, that a person in his high official station ought to know every thing connected with the political state of his country. When this topic was exhausted, Don Garcia began to touch upon that of Ormuz. On this point the mind of Abbas was evidently made up. He was fixed and well resolved not to cede an inch of his conquests; but, at the same time, was willing to conciliate the Spaniard by every courtesy and concession which would cost him nothing. In this exigence, he bethought himself of a Catholic monk, whom he had allowed to settle, and establish a small convent, at Ispahan. He had even assumed a sort of semblance of Christianity, to be put on whenever it could answer any purpose.* He

* It appears even that he was at one time formally baptized; an event to which the Jesuits ascribe all the victories with which his arms were crowned against the Turks and Tartars. See " Nouvel Conversion du Roi de Perse, avec la " Deffette de deux cens mil Turcs après sa conversion." Paris,

sent, therefore, to the head of the convent, desiring that he should repair to him instantly, with his sacred book. In the mean time he shuffled and shifted; he asked a sight of the ambassador's sword, and was lucky enough to involve him in a controversy on the comparative merit of Persian and Castilian blades. By these shifts he got over the time till the superior made his appearance. The king instantly started up, took him in his arms, and kissed him, then melted into tears, and rivetted his eyes on the holy page, of which Garcia knew well that he did not understand a syllable. The Spanish retinue, however, were highly edified with the spectacle, and pronounced Abbas the most pious and best of kings. The ambassador, who knew all this to be rank hypocrisy, and saw the Persian lords laughing in their sleeve, deemed it incumbent upon him to say the direct contrary of all that he thought. He expressed his deep admiration of what he saw, and which fully confirmed the report of his majesty's piety, which was already so widely spread over Europe. After this exhibition, a supper, as plain as formerly, was brought in. As soon as it was over, the ambassador judged it time to proceed to business, and began to open the

1606. Also, "Histoire Veritable de tout ce qui s'est faict et "passè en Perse depuis les ceremonies du Baptesme du "Grand Sophy." Paris, 1616.

subject of his mission. The instant, however, that the name of Ormuz was mentioned, the monarch was seized with a paroxysm of holy fervour, far surpassing all that he had yet exhibited. Between every glass, he rivetted his eyes on heaven in inward prayer, and holy tears streamed down his cheek. In this frame of the royal mind, it would have been obviously unbecoming to press the mention of any secular concerns. Don Garcia, therefore, renewed the expression of his admiration; but as the king descended from this high key, and began to enter into common conversation, he made repeated efforts to renew the subject; but whenever the slightest allusion was made to Ormuz, the monarch's eyes were constantly seen raised upwards, and his tears again beginning to flow. The ambassador had the firmness to suppress his almost frenzied rage, and to maintain an outward politeness; but seeing, that any farther mention of the subject could only serve to rekindle in the monarch the flame of piety, he rose and took his leave.

The king, from this time, shewed Don Garcia still more uniform attention, and sent him daily presents of corn, fruits, and game. The ambassador, on the other hand, went nightly to the Meidan, always resolving and hoping to get his remonstrances listened to. Whenever he appeared the king rode up, gaily accosted him, and usually calling for wine, drank the healths of the king, queen, and prince of Spain; then, when he saw the name of Ormuz beginning to tremble on his lips, pretended some urgent business, and rode off abruptly. The time thus passed, till it suddenly became known that the court was to set out in three days for Sultania. Hereupon Don Garcia went to the Meidan, determined to bring the Shah to something. As soon as the military exercise was over, he rode up, and pointedly said that he wished to speak to him on the subject of Ormuz. Abbas could contrive no shift to extricate himself; so that the ambassador had now the opportunity to open the full budget of his wrongs; the capture of Ormuz, of Queixome (Kishme), and of Camaraon (Gombroon) in time of profound peace, from a power for whom he had always professed friendship, and whom his glorious zeal for the Christian faith should make him view as allies, and even as brothers. In this extremity Abbas could think of no excuse, but to say that he had taken them from the natives, to whom they most properly belonged. The ambassador, by appealing to a hundred years' possession, soon shewed the utter futility of this pretext, so that the monarch saw no resource but suddenly to put spurs to his horse, and gallop off. Next day he transmitted a message, that, according to certain information, the

Turks were already besieging Van, which obliged him to set out without the possibility of again seeing the ambassador.

The narrative of Don Garcia here closes; but it would appear that he spent a longer time in Persia, and died in that country. It need scarcely be added, that every future attempt to obtain restitution of the conquests made by the Shah, had the same result with those which we have now commemorated.

In 1633, the Duke of Holstein having formed the design of establishing a silk manufactory, sent an embassy into Persia, to make arrangements for procuring the raw material. A very good account of this mission was written by the secretary, Olearius; but as its period differs little from that of the more full and satisfactory narrative of Chardin, our limits will admit only of a very rapid outline. They were obliged to land near Derbent, in the province of Shirvan. Brugman, the principal ambassador, who seems to have been of a violent and quarrelsome temper, involved himself in a dispute with the governor, on account of receiving a horse, the quality of which did not appear to him suitable to his dignity. Although the circumstance was clearly proved to have arisen entirely from mistake, he sent off the bearers without any present, which is considered in the East as the highest indignity. The governor of Derbent, deeply resenting this treatment, did every thing in his power to annoy them, and withhold the means of proceeding. They were obliged to send a messenger to the Khan of Shirvan, through whose good offices they were at length supplied with the necessary accommodations. They reached Schamachi, where they were received with all due honours. They had an opportunity here of seeing the baptism of the Armenians, of whom great numbers inhabited this city. The whole body went in procession to the river, being protected against the insults of the Mahometans by a strong body of troops. The Khan had a rich tent erected, and the gentlemen of the embassy were supplied with fifteen horses, to enable them to contemplate this pious exhibition. Four men leaped in first, and swam about, breaking a thin coat of ice with which the river was covered. The bishop then stepped forward, and after having read for about an hour, consecrated the water by dipping into it a golden cross. The Armenians then running to the bank, some of them plunged in, others sprinkled their faces with water, while others merely drank a small portion. The Khan checked his attendants, when they attempted to offer any serious annoyance to these devout bathers, but indulgently permitted some of them to caper about, in mimicry of the dances which the worshippers were performing round their bishop.

From Schamachi, the ambassadors proceeded by Ardevil, Sultania, Koom, and Cashan, to Ispahan. They were received and accommodated in a distinguished manner, but were soon involved in a violent fray with an Indian ambassador, who happened to be resident at Ispahan. The quarrel began with one domestic on each side, and soon spread through the whole body of the servants; till the Indians having killed a German, and tied his body to a horse's tail, the warfare became open and violent. Mr Mandeslo killed their chief, of which we have seen that he had afterwards nearly cause to repent; and considerable damage was done by the Germans with their fire-arms. The Indians, however, made holes in the wall, and poured in such clouds of arrows, that our party were in serious danger of being overpowered, when a body of troops arrived from the Sophi for their relief, on whose appearance the Hindoos made off. The Sophi once threatened to cause the Indian ambassador's hands to be cut off, but contented himself with ordering him and his whole train to leave Ispahan. Soon after, the embassy had their public audience, in the ceremonies of which there was nothing peculiar. They were received in the hall of justice by the Sophi, a young man about twenty-seven, plainly dressed, but having near him a scimitar set with diamonds. They had afterwards many private interviews with this prince, whose favour they conciliated by becoming his bottle companions. They were invited as to hunting parties; but if game did not instantly make its appearance, wine was produced, and such a noise soon arose, as frightened away all the feathered creation. Yet they saw also some huntings contrived upon the futile plan of enabling the Sophi to take vast quantities of game without effort. In taking cranes, a long hidden way was made under ground, at the end of which was strewed a quantity of wheat, when the cranes rushing in, were taken with ease, to the number of about eight hundred. The king also chusing to hunt pigeons, went to a lofty tower done up as a pigeon-house, when a great noise being made, the birds flew out, and were readily brought down in vast numbers. Upon the whole, though nothing is mentioned as to the business of their mission, they express the highest satisfaction at the distinguished and courteous manner in which they were uniformly treated.

In the early part of the seventeenth century, Sir Thomas Herbert, a very accomplished English gentleman, visited several countries of the East, and particularly Persia. He wants method, and makes too great a parade of his learning, but he has hit off, in a quaint and lively style, some of the leading features of Persian society. He says, "Now concerning the natives, they are ge-"nerally well limbed and straight; the zone "they live in makes them tawny; the wine "cheerful; the women paint; the men love "arms; all affect poetry; what the grape in-"flames, the law allays, and example bridles." "The Persians," he says, "have been long praised "as of all men the most civil; which disposition "they reserve unto this day." "At meals," adds he, "they are the merriest men alive; no "people in the world have better stomachs, or "drink more freely, yet are harmlessly merry. "At this exercise they sit long and drink sound-"ly, condemning that precept of the Alcoran as "an idle toy." The following feature does not seem to have pleased him so much: "The better "sort are so oft on horseback, that they hate to "see men walk; such they think distempered in "mind." This inference apparently had been applied to himself; hence he tauntingly retorts, "A madder thing to see them ride, though it "were only for half a stone's cast."

In regard to political constitution, Sir Thomas observes, "Under most miserable servitude these "wretched Mahometans do live, happy only in "not knowing what a free subject means." Yet he observes, that justice is administered with great rigour, and that "travellers can scarce find "a more quiet place than Persia." He does not mention having seen the king except once, when he passed accidentally through the court in his English dress. He then received a very gracious salutation from that monarch, who, he states, took particular delight "to see exotiques in their "own country habit."

Among the many travellers who have thrown light on the Persian empire, Chardin has always been considered as the one to whom Europe is most indebted. He devoted his life, as it were, to the knowledge of Persia. He made long and repeated visits thither; he traversed it in length and breadth, from the Caspian to the ocean. He knew Ispahan better than Paris. The only journey, however, of which he has given a detailed account, is that undertaken in 1673. On this occasion he carried a commission from the king of France, to collect a number of valuable jewels, for the purchase of which he brought other jewels, with 12,000 ducats in gold. He proceeded through Poland to the Crimea, embarked at Caffa, and landed at Isgaour in Mingrelia. He found this a mere desert spot, where the traders took up their temporary abode while vessels were lading. They then inclosed a market-place with stakes, and erected a few little wooden huts for their residence. Chardin sent an express to a monastery of Theatines, situated about forty miles up the country, who, he had been assured, would supply him amply with the means of proceeding into Persia. Meantime he was much dismayed to find that there was not a single article of provision to be purchased, nor any thing except slaves chained two and two together. He was obliged to subsist himself and his attendants upon dried fish without bread. A few days after his arrival, news came of the approach of a band of Abcas (Abassi), a Caucasian people, who had entered Mingrelia avowedly as allies against the Turks. The merchants, however, lost not a moment in hurrying on board with all their effects, so as to be out of the reach of these trusty confederates. Accordingly, on their arrival the whole market-place was instantly seen in a blaze, and on landing again they found nothing but ashes.

About a fortnight had now elapsed, and Chardin was longing very much for the arrival of the Theatines, when the Prefect at length made his appearance. Our traveller ran up to him with a joy which he was far from returning. He besought God to forgive any one who had advised him to come into this country; that it was the most barbarous in the world, and the people more wicked than it was possible to conceive. Chardin having boasted that he had a letter to the Prince of Mingrelia, the Prefect assured him that there was not a baser robber in his dominions. As an improvement on the general state of affairs, the Turks and Georgians were laying waste the country with fire and sword, carrying captive all who did not save themselves by flight. He exhorted him, therefore, most earnestly to return by the way he came, without a moment's delay. Chardin, however, courageously determined to proceed. He sailed by sea to Anarghia, and thence to Sipias, the Theatine convent, where he was well lodged. His baggage, when landed, filled eight carts, the fame of which spread over all Mingrelia, exciting an universal wish to obtain some share of their ample contents. The rumour soon procured him the honour of a visit from the Princess of Mingrelia. She had with her eight female attendants, and about ten men, shabbily clothed and mounted. Being waited upon by the superior, she immediately asked for the Europeans, who had brought the baggage; whereupon Chardin was introduced. Her highness put a thousand questions, in reply to which he declared himself to be a Capuchin, in the view of acting which character, he had arrayed himself in very mean attire, hoping thus to obtain credit for some measure of poverty. She put, moreover, other questions, as, whether he had ever been in love? how he could avoid falling in love? and whether he had a wife? On this last question being answered in the negative, she bitterly lamented his case, and undertook to provide one, without paying the least regard to his loud protestations of having no wish to be so accommodated. This train of questions, with the bursts of laughter which accompanied each, greatly discomposed our author, especially as he could with difficulty evade the repeated instances to see the contents of his trunks. He promised, however, to wait upon her highness next day, and bring a handsome present.

Next morning Chardin received from the Princess an invitation to dinner at her residence, which was two miles distant. He was received in a covered space in front of the house, where she and her females sat on a carpet, the guards being placed in a circle on the grass. She was richly dressed and painted, and seemed to have studied every art to heighten the effect of her charms. The present was then produced, seemingly by no means ample, as it had cost only 20s. and could not now be valued at more than L.3; however, no dissatisfaction was then expressed. The dinner consisted of a hog roasted whole, and the Princess offered to kill an ox if he would stay supper; but this was understood to be merely a compliment, which Chardin was far from wishing to press farther than it was meant. All the subjects of conversation were unwelcome. She resumed that of the wife, promised to introduce her very speedily, seemingly to our author's great tribulation. She made specific inquiries for a number of valuable articles; and in receiving always negative answers, became very sensibly out of humour. As he took leave, ill luck decreed, that beneath his mean frock some fragments of a fine linen shirt became visible. Her highness instantly ran up, pulled up the sleeve to the elbow, and exhibited the precious garment in full view. A busy conversation was then heard with her women; and it became evident, that this fatal disclosure had ruined all the faith hitherto placed in his protestations of poverty.

The events of this interview tended to inspire Chardin with the most gloomy forebodings as to the fate of his property. That very night he dug a deep pit, in which he deposited his gold. The two boxes containing the diamonds were then concealed in the thatch of the roof, where it appeared scarcely possible that any one should trace them. These precautions were not superfluous, for in two or three days two *gentlemen* of the neighbourhood were introduced. Being immediately reinforced by thirty followers, they beat and bound all who resisted, and began the strictest search into all valuable articles contained in the house. The instant that Chardin saw the style in which this inquest was to be carried on, he felt, that without some very extraordinary effort, all was over with his diamonds. He hastened up, therefore, before the plunderers, and snatching the boxes, made a leap from the window which in his cooler moments he durst not have ventured; then flying full speed to the foot of the garden, threw them at random among a thicket of briars. On his return, he found them employed upon the trunks, which he was ordered either to open instantly, or have his head severed from his body. Instead of complying, he began to speak; whereupon a soldier conceived him to have accepted the latter alternative, and had his sword already out, but was luckily stopped. Chardin turned away his eyes, that they might not behold the dismal events which now ensued. The gentlemen picked out every thing which appeared valuable and portable; they searched the garden, and even the briars, but luckily did not light upon the boxes. As the subterranean consignment also escaped their notice, the whole damage did not exceed four hundred crowns. Chardin, however, made an appeal to the Prince, who had his castle at fifteen miles distance. The Prince expressed regret, but stated, that, in the present distracted state of the country, it was out of his power to restrain his nobility from such practices. He promised to endeavour to obtain restitution; but his efforts, if made, were fruitless. As to their friend the Princess, they learned, from the very best authority, that a third of the proceeds went into her treasury.

These perils were immediately succeeded by others equally formidable. News arrived that a Turkish army had entered Mingrelia, and was laying all waste with fire and sword. Our author was obliged to fly for five leagues through the mire to a fortress in the woods, where a chief friendly to the Theatines afforded them shelter. They could obtain no lodging, except a miserable bake-house open on every side to the rain, and only preferable to the open court in which the multitude were obliged to crowd. Meanwhile the Turks coming to the house, found nothing which was at once valuable and portable; so that after taking away a few trifles they departed. Fate, however, decreed, that a Mingrelian *gentleman* deemed it prudent to glean such particulars as they had overlooked. Chardin had left his library, not apprehending that Mingrelia contained any person, foreign or native, to whom it could be an object of cupidity. The gentleman's ingenuity, however, found the means of turning these literary treasures to account. Being in want of light to carry on his search, he tore out the paper, and made it supply the place of candles; while the gilt bindings, in which our author was curious, were judged worthy to be carried off as ornaments. Only a few fragments attested to Chardin the fate of this valued portion of his property.

Our traveller felt now a very strong inclination to bid adieu to Mingrelia; but the enemy being in possession of all the passes into Georgia, rendered the journey dangerous; and he complains bitterly of the extravagant love of life which actuated the Mingrelians, and rendered any one unwilling to hazard theirs in serving as his guide. He was obliged, therefore, to take a circuitous route by sea, and landed at Gonieh, where, after some custom-house exactions, he reached the frontier of Mingrelia. He describes in the strongest terms his satisfaction at quitting a country, where, he says, the most direful of human evils, the loss of goods, insult, slavery, *marriage*, had alternately menaced him. With a light heart, therefore, he climbed the tremendous steeps of Caucasus, though the snow at the top was often ten feet deep, and required to be removed by shovels. The lower declivities, however, were well cultivated, and produced excellent wine.

Mingrelia consists of a plain interposed between the Euxine and some of the loftiest steeps of Caucasus, which water it with so many streams as to render the soil excessively soft and moist. Hence the plough is said to be often unnecessary, and equally efficacious when made of wood as of iron. This superabundant moisture is injurious to grains and fruits of every description, except the vine, which is particularly plentiful and excellent. The state of society seems much to resemble that which prevailed in Europe during the very rudest period of the feudal ages. The great lords have absolute jurisdiction over their vassals, which extends even to putting them to death, or selling their wives and children into slavery. They have castles in which all their treasures and valuables are kept, and which serve as a retreat to their vassals in case of invasion. War, theft, and rapine, form their daily occupation. The chief, and even Prince, sits down at the same table with the meanest of his servants, having, however, superior place and food appropriated to him. The men are handsome, and the women possess an ample share of that beauty which is so generally and strikingly characteristic of the Caucasian tribes.

The Mingrelians pretend to be Christians, and to have a church of their own, supposed to be founded by St Andrew. Their Catholicos enjoys very considerable revenues, and even rivals the power of the Prince. Nothing however can exceed the ignorance of the clergy, who do not inculcate on the people the very first principles of religion. They maintain their credit chiefly by pretending to foretel the future, and to cure diseases by supernatural means. Their religious rites are performed in the most irreverent manner. Chardin saw one of them baptizing a child, which he did by reading for a long time out of a half torn volume, but constantly breaking off to speak to every one that came into the room. At another time, while he was asking the road at the door of a church, the priest, who was saying mass, called out, that he would come and shew it. He then came out mumbling the mass all the way; then having put some questions, civilly pointed out the road and returned. With all this, they do not account Europeans Christians at all, because they do not keep so many fasts as themselves, nor pay the same devout regard to images.

After leaving Mingrelia, our author entered Georgia, and spent some time at Tefflis. He does not paint the Georgians in such dark colours as their neighbours. He found them in general civil and friendly, though fickle, turbulent, and mutinous. Their manners are licentious, and they indulge deep in every kind of good cheer. He does not believe there is a country in the world where such good wine is drunk, or so much of it. Eating also is treated in the most systematic manner, and occupies an almost inconceivable time. At one entertainment our author remained three hours, without the course of roast meat being yet brought in. They begin to drink small cups, which as the feast proceeds, wax always larger and larger, till at length the most courageous begin to empty large goblets in honour of their chiefs. Chardin was luckily left to the freedom of his own will; for had he attempted to keep pace with the rest of the company, he must have dropt down dead on the spot. Georgia being placed on the limit between the Mahometan and Christian nations, exhibited a great mixture of manners and population. The Princes affected Mahometanism, as the only road to advancement; but they were supposed secretly to share the feelings of the people, whose attachment to Christianity was so decided, that they would not allow a mosque to be built in Tefflis. There were, on the contrary, fourteen churches, which appeared to Chardin to bear a very full proportion to any measure of piety that he was able to observe.

After some stay in Georgia, our traveller began to pass the lofty mountains which separate it from the Persian province of Aderbijan. The road lay over some of the most lofty and rugged. The houses of the peasantry were chiefly dug out of the earth on the sides of the hills, affording a pretty comfortable habitation, warm in winter, and cool in summer. The higher parts of the ridge were covered with perpetual and very deep snow, which could be crossed only by one beaten track, so narrow that two horses could not pass each other. When two parties were so unlucky as to meet, the strongest compelled the weaker to plunge into the snow at the side, which took the horses above the middle, and there wait till the others were gone by. The hardship was considered so severe, that when there was any approach to equality, a skirmish usually ensued. Our party, however, was in such force as always to oblige its antagonists to take the plunge. A storm of fresh snow, when it occurs in these tremendous heights, often causes the destruction of a caravan.

From these high regions Chardin descended to Erivan, a large dirty city, situated on the brink of a precipice, near a large lake of the same name. The inhabitants maintained, that Noah had resided here both before and after the flood; and they continued to point out, at twelve leagues distance, the mountain on which the ark had lighted, and to insist that it was still there. No one, however, had been so fortunate as to make his way up to it. After leaving Erivan, they came in four days to Nacshivan, where only vast piles of ruins told how great this city had once been. He came then to Julfa, exhibiting a range of rocks cut out into numerous habitations. Barbaro saw it or a similar one inhabited; but Shah Abbas, wishing to interpose a desert barrier between his dominions and those of Turkey, had transported all the inhabitants to Ispahan. A few days more brought them to Tauris, once the capital and still the second city of Persia. It continued the seat of a most extensive trade, and was supposed to contain upwards of half a million of inhabitants. Its bazaars were magnificent, filled with the most precious commodities; and he saw no Meidan or public square in Persia so spacious as that of Tauris. It was the theatre of numerous games for the amusement of the populace, among which the wolf-fights mentioned by Barbaro still prevailed. He passed next through Sultania and Sawa, about nine miles to the east of which latter place are some remains of Rey, described by the orientals as once the greatest city of Asia. It is represented as containing 4600 colleges, 15,000 minarets, and 13,000 caravanseras. It was decorated with the pompous titles of "Spouse of "the World," and "Market of the Universe." He passed next Kom, a great and ancient city, and Cashan, which was then very flourishing. Three weeks from Cashan brought them to the imperial capital of Ispahan.

The court of Persia was found by Chardin to have entirely changed its aspect during the eight years of his absence. All who were then in favour were now either dead or disgraced. The state of things was peculiarly unfavourable to his views. Chekali Khan, a disgraced minister, had just been restored to power, in the following odd manner. The king, who was not deterred by his Mahometan profession from drinking wine to the greatest excess, one evening, in a fit of intoxication, ordered a favourite lute player to have his hands and feet cut off. The officer to whom this mandate was given, judged it a mere burst of drunken rage, which would never be thought of more. The king however recollected his order, and finding it not executed, ordered the disobedient officer to suffer the same mutilation. Another who ventured to intercede for both, was also doomed to share their fate. A strong sensation was excited in the court at a sentence so disgraceful and atrocious. Chekali Khan courageously presented himself before the monarch, and made so able and judicious a remonstrance, that he not only saved the hands and feet of the three victims, but restored himself completely to favour, and was reinstated in his office. Chardin candidly acknowledges, that he was an excellent and upright minister, entirely devoted to the good of the state, and possessed of a thousand good qualities. The aversion he shewed to Christians is admitted to have arisen solely from his strict religious principles, which also made him obstinately refuse to drink wine, though continually urged to it by the king, who in his revels used to throw cups of it in his face. One of his best qualities, but the most fatal to the hopes of our learned jeweller, was his strict economy of the public money, and aversion to every kind of vain ostentation. The Nazir, or agent, to whom Chardin applied, acquainted him with these circumstances, exhorting him to hope in the clemency of God; an advice used by the Persians when they consider all human hope as desperate. Chardin was thus left for a long time with very little prospect of any result from his mission; but at length, through the interest of some great men, he found means to have the jewels submitted to his Majesty's inspection, after which a negociation was opened. It was of very great length, and no means were left untried to beat down the price. Arts, threats, promises, tricks, were none of them spared. They sometimes flattered, and sometimes were like to devour him. They were particularly confounded by his adherence to his first price, which appeared to them an obstinacy quite inconceivable. However, by dint of firmness and patience, he brought the treaty at length to a satisfactory issue.

The Persians are described by Chardin as the most civilized nation in the East, and the greatest complimenters in the world. Nothing can exceed the skill with which they administer flattery; sometimes when they know that a person is passing, they contrive to be overheard speaking his praise. With the exception of the priesthood, they are extremely tolerant to the professors of other religions, even those which they think the most abominable. They allow them even, without any very severe criticism, to be taken up and laid down at pleasure. The stranger who sees them only in a passing manner, would form a most favourable judgment; but an intimate acquaintance soon shews them to be only "whiten-" ed sepulchres." Amid their excess of politeness, generosity is entirely a stranger to them; interest here, as over all the East, is the sole principle of action. So different are their ideas of personal dignity from ours, that they place their glory in receiving presents. Without presents, no inferior can approach a superior, nor any one ask a favour from another. The donation is made in the most public possible place and manner, and is immediately followed by the granting of the petition. The Persians are the greatest spenders in the world, and the persons who least think of the morrow. Suppose the king to give one of them fifty or a hundred thousand livres, in less than a fortnight the whole has disappeared. Furniture, slaves, horses, women, have entirely absorbed it. His funds are then exhausted, and he begins selling them piece by piece, till at length perhaps he sells his very clothes. The greatest license is used in the assumption of titles. Even servants, without blame or scruple, affix to their names those of Duke, Prince, or Mirza. The real grandees, on the contrary, and those who aim at rising in the world, ostentatiously assume the appellation of slave. Slave to the king, slave to Mahomet, are the titles of which they make the highest boast. The Persians view with just horror our custom of common swearing. They never mention the name of the Deity, unless with ostentatious reverence; but they introduce it into their conversation too often, either in exclamations of praise or in confirmation of promises; which last they too probably intend to break. Their devout speeches are apt often to alternate with others, in which indecency and ribaldry predominate.

The government of Persia is a complete despotism. The king, according to the original Mahometan idea, which no violence or usurpation has been able to eradicate, is reverenced as the prophet of God. Unfortunately, no due respect exists for the principle of primogeniture; so that, on the death of a sovereign, his sons, as we have repeatedly seen, immediately begin to attack and massacre each other. The princesses are married, not to men of the sword, but to ecclesiastics, as men who cannot raise any pretensions to the kingdom, and who, it is supposed, will be better trained to that submission which these lofty dames claim as their due. With respect to their families, a system of the most barbarous precaution is adopted. They are entirely at the disposal of the king, who, in some instances, has caused the whole to be put to death; and most usually the sons, on coming into the world, have their eyes put out. The provinces are ruled upon two different systems. Originally they were all subject to hereditary governors or khans, who carried on the whole internal administration, and lived in great pomp, merely paying tribute, and furnishing troops when demanded. Shah Sephi, the successor of Shah Abbas, introduced, with regard to the central provinces, the system of intendants, who are mere revenue officers, removable at pleasure. The amount of revenue was thus considerably augmented; but judicious persons considered it as deeply injurious to the prosperity of the empire. The hereditary rulers felt a permanent interest in the prosperity of the province, which they sought by every means to promote; while the new officers study only to enrich themselves during the short era of their power. The attachment, too, and habits of obedience of the people to their hereditary rulers, were in no degree transferred to these upstart governors.

The weakness thus induced has probably been one main cause of that series of destructive revolutions to which Persia has since been subject.

The military system of Persia is entirely different from that of Europe. They have no idea of tactics or regular evolutions. Their reviews consist merely in the soldiers marching along one by one, and having their arms examined. In making war they fly round an enemy like *voltigeurs*, cut off his provisions and water, and, when they see him thoroughly exhausted, fall suddenly upon him. When threatened with a great invasion, they lay waste the frontier, burying all the provisions so skilfully as not to be discovered; while the dryness of the soil preserves all till their return. In this manner great armies of the Turks have been repeatedly destroyed, without any regular action.

The Persians are a lettered people. The sciences are even considered by Chardin as their ruling passion. The great men pay the greatest attention to the education of their children, which is chiefly conducted at home by hired tutors. Even men with long beards, thirty, forty, or fifty years of age, are not ashamed to be seen at their studies, and even to begin the elements of learning. The three ranks of their wise men are *Taleb*, *Mollah*, and *Moushtehed*. This last is a character far superior to any which letters can confer in Europe. The *Moushtehed* is supposed to understand all the sixty-two sciences, and to be entitled to give opinions upon every subject, which it would be perilous to contradict. This lofty dignity is conferred solely by public consent, and there are few who enjoy it undisputed. Chardin knew only one; and even in his case, the voice of the nation was not quite unanimous. There were many, however, on the road to be Moushteheds. Our author extols much the sciences of Persia, representing them as quite equal to those of Europe, unless in respect of some new discoveries, many even of which, accounted new by us, are old in the East. He adds, that all the Greek authors known to us are translated into Persian, and familiarly read. On this last point Mr Langles observes, that he is certainly mistaken, the Greek translations being confined to fragments of Aristotle, Galen, Euclid, and Ptolemy; they know nothing of the history of the west, nor even of their own country prior to the Mahometan invasion. Alexander with them is the mere hero of poetical fables. In regard to their circle of sciences, when it comes to be specified, it does not make so imposing an appearance as in our author's general assertion. The following is the list, according to the order in which they are studied: Grammar and syntax—theology—philosophy—

mathematics. He who has passed through these is ready to enter on astrology and medicine, which are the prime sciences, and those which alone lead to fortune. Morality in Persia is much studied, though little practised. It is communicated in the old oriental modes of proverb, apologue, and fable. After all, poetry is the great passion of this people; and the Persian bards enjoy a high pre-eminence of fame among those of the East. Poetry is continually quoted in their prose writings and common conversation; their fables, and even their treatises on science, are turned into verse. Their images are of the boldest and most glowing description; so that, according to Chardin, our poetry is scarcely prose in comparison. There are two classes of poets; one whose theme is wisdom and morality; and another, whose lyre is devoted to love. At the head of the former is Sadi, of the latter Hafiz. Their love songs, in consequence of the monotony of oriental manners, cannot exhibit that variety of situation and feeling which fill the amatory poems of Europe. They contain chiefly an elaborate picture of the beauties of the beloved object, the miseries of absence, and the joys of possession. Rigid Mahometans scarcely consider it lawful to peruse the works of Hafiz, unless when interpreted in a spiritual and mystic sense, of which, in many instances, they are very ill susceptible.

Ambrogio Bembo, an intelligent Italian, visited Persia at the same time with Chardin. His narrative, however, remained in manuscript till an abstract was recently given by Morelli. His attention seems to have been chiefly directed to the antiquities; and he surveyed not only those of Persepolis, but others at Besetun and Chermonsac (Kermanschaw). The object at the latter place he describes as a sculptured mountain covered chiefly with huntings. To make drawings of these objects, he employed Grelot, who had come out with Chardin; and Bembo was thus involved in a quarrel with that traveller. Grelot, he asserts, came to him quite voluntarily, declaring that he was tired of travelling, and disgusted with the treatment he received from Chardin. This youth is praised as learned, modest, and very serviceable. Of the two manuscript copies of this journey, one is adorned with his drawings, a selection of which would doubtless be very interesting.

Our next narrative relates to a subsequent period, when a daring adventurer, under the successive names Kouli Khan, Velin Naamet, and Shah Nadir, delivered his country from the yoke of the Afghans, only to rule over it with yet a bloodier sway. FRA LEANDRO de Santa Cecilia, a Carmelite friar, under the combined character of physician and monk, then resided in Persia for a series of years. Ever since the time of Shah Abbas there had been convents at Ispahan, which had been variously treated, according to the disposition of the reigning monarch. Under the capricious and barbarous sway of Nadir, their situation was peculiarly fluctuating. At one time that monarch gave orders for four translations: one of the Gospels by European Christians; of the Epistles by Armenians; of the Old Testament by Jews; and of the Alcoran by Persian Mollahs. He was conjectured as having it in contemplation to make a selection from each, and set himself forth as the founder of a new religion. Such was the zeal of the persons employed, each imagining that the Shah would embrace his own faith, that in eight months all the tasks were completed. They came, therefore, at the same time to present them, and were admitted together into the royal garden. They found here a number of other persons in waiting; who being successively introduced, each came out with a rope round his neck, was immediately strangled, and carried away to be thrown to wild beasts. In the course of an hour eighteen were thus disposed of. It is easy to conceive the dismay and horror of the hapless translators. It is boasted, however, that their minds soon regained their serenity; and that, anticipating now an immediate crown of martyrdom, they disputed with each other on whom it should first be conferred. At length they were all admitted; but the glory so eagerly contended for was not destined for them. The king received them well, asked if they were comfortably lodged, and made them a present of 200 tomans. The books he received without even looking at them, being probably diverted by other plans and occupations from that original object.

The most curious part of our author's narrative relates to a residence of some years at Bagdad, then the seat of an almost independent Turkish state. Achmet, its ruler, having set out to besiege Bassora, all the ladies of the haram fasted for three days and three nights to secure his success. This regimen threw the principal Queen into a violent fever, and her life was despaired of. In this exigence, the medical skill of Leandro caused him to be sent for. He was told, however, that he must cure the disease without even seeing the patient. In vain did he protest the impossibility of so doing; the Sultan was absent, who alone could have relaxed the rigid laws of the haram. As Leandro, however, insisted that he must feel her Majesty's pulse, the Aga and eight eunuchs went to negociate with the ladies upon this subject. The result was, that an eunuch came and took him to a room, the entrance of which was closed by a rich curtain that swept the ground. He was then desired to stoop, and put his hand under the curtain, when an eunuch on the other side applied it to the pulse of the lady, who was lying on the floor. The violence with which it beat, and the difficulty of respiration which she was stated to feel, convinced our physician of the existence of strong inflammation. He directed, therefore, copious bleeding, and that she should be kept constantly awake; a prescription, the aim of which we do not thoroughly comprehend, but on which he seems to have placed very great reliance. He then sat with his eyes constantly fixed on two large books that lay before him, so that in case of failure he might be able to prove, how carefully he had studied the case. The patient began to mend; and though a relapse took place, he found on inquiry that it proceeded from neglecting his prescriptions; which being resumed, a complete cure was effected. The Aga then came to ask what was due for this important service. Leandro replied, that he sought only the honour of serving his Majesty; that he made profession of poverty; and having neither wife nor children, was content if he had bread to eat. The Aga expressed the utmost amazement at his neglecting such an opportunity of improving his fortune, above all when he was in such a miserable condition; and at last took leave, saying reproachfully, "Be poor and proud." Very shortly after, however, this officer again appeared, with a countenance all gay and smiling, and invited Leandro to the haram. Our author never doubted now that he would be admitted to an audience of the Queen; the prospect of which appears to have flattered him exceedingly, as well as inspired hopes of influence at court. He was led to the usual entrance, when there came from behind the curtain an old lady, accompanied by three handsome girls, with their veils turned up. Our author was struck with extraordinary amaze at this spectacle, as there was no appearance that any one present could be the Queen, and the young ladies appeared in such perfect health, that they could not be supposed to be fresh patients. The old lady, however, immediately began a speech, in which she stated the anxious wish felt by her Majesty to reward him for so signal a service, and also her commiseration for the want of a wife under which he laboured. She had therefore sent three of her handsomest female slaves, among whom he had only to make his choice, and he should be amply provided with the means of supporting a family. At the same time the ladies were heard in the other room tittering and whispering to each other, in evident curiosity on whom the choice would fall. Our author describes himself as overwhelmed with utter dismay and confusion at this overture, and at the situation in which he found himself. Having given, therefore, the most positive rejection, he abruptly broke off, and ran home to his lodgings.

However mysterious Leandro's conduct might appear to the ladies of Bagdad, his medical reputation was now established. He was called soon after to Canun Assendi, the King's sister, whom he cured of an obstinate swelling in the neck. He was admitted to the view of this lady, and obtained several important privileges for his Christian countrymen at Bagdad. This favour excited envy, and gave rise to cabals among the courtiers, who so far succeeded in poisoning the King's mind, that he ordered Leandro to be thrown into prison. When this was reported to Canun Assendi, she rent her clothes, and immediately wrote to her brother in such urgent terms, as procured the immediate liberation of our unfortunate doctor. The Queen also, on learning the durance in which he had been held, became anxious to make a grand display of her gratitude. By her direction, a band of Turkish women entered the apartment of our author, who was seized with utter amazement, and, above all, with a dread of some new matrimonial proposition. The principal lady, however, began a speech, stating the deep concern which her mistress felt in his sufferings, and her anxiety to gratify every wish he could form, of which she would now afford a signal proof. If, therefore, he would give in a complete list of the persons by whom he had been injured, he should that very evening be regaled with all their heads. Leandro, struck with the deepest horror, rejected this offer in the most unqualified terms. The astonished ladies departed, but returned next day, repeating the proposal, and conjuring him not to reject so kind and generous an offer. Finding him inflexible, they went away, shaking their heads, and declaring that nothing could be done for him now; that he was evidently one predetermined to reject every thing which could lead either to his own advancement, or the gratification of his strongest wishes.

Soon after this period Leandro was obliged by ill health to quit Bagdad, and return to Paris.

# CHAPTER II.

## PERSIA.—RECENT TRAVELS AND PRESENT STATE.

*Malcolm.—Olivier.—Morier.—Present state of Persia. Its Antiquities.*

PERSIA, as we have seen, has from the earliest ages been exposed in a peculiar degree to the evils of foreign and domestic war. The seventeenth century, beyond any former era, presented a series of uninterrupted calamity, under which scarcely any other nation ever groaned. In an early part of it the inroad of the Afghans carried fire and sword to its remotest extremities, and reduced many of its proudest capitals to heaps of ruins. The bloody reaction produced by Nadir Shah, though it vindicated the independence of his country, scarcely induced a pause in the progress of its miseries. Even the lustre thrown around Persia by his foreign victories was only like a flash of lightning through the darkness, which instantly returned deeper than before. After his assassination, Persia had two disputed successions; one of eleven, and the other of fourteen years; during all which periods this great empire continued incessantly tearing its own vitals. It only enjoyed repose, when a daring usurper, after wading to the throne through oceans of blood, held it during his lifetime with a firm and vigorous hand. The last of these was Aga Mahommed, an eunuch, who saved himself by his energy and cruelty from the contempt which his condition would have inspired; and not only held the throne during his life, but transmitted it to his nephew, Futteh Ali Khan, the present sovereign.

Persia, buried in these intestine dissensions, was almost lost to the recollection of Europe, unless when occasionally a Russian gazette announced a triumph on the Araxes and the Kur. From this obscurity it was drawn by a series of political events either felt or dreaded. The French revolutionary government, inspired with the most imbittered enmity against England, conceived the hope of striking a blow against her through the medium of her Eastern possessions. This could only be hoped by an overland expedition, in reference to which the state of the Persian empire was an object of primary importance. The Directory sent a mission under Olivier and Brugniere to ascertain the precise state of that empire; but they were too busily employed in Europe to take any measures in consequence. The attention of our Indian government was first drawn by events occurring within its own sphere. When it was discovered that Tippoo had sent an embassy to the Shah, another became expedient to counteract it. It was conducted by a native Indian; but neither party drew any result from these negociations. After the subversion of the power of Tippoo, India was thrown into alarm by the irruption of Zemaun Shah, King of the Afghans. This was a power against which Persia was well fitted to create a diversion; with a view to which Colonel MALCOLM was despatched in 1801 on an embassy to Futteh Ali Shah. This mission fulfilled all its objects: the Shah gladly embraced the opportunity to invade Khorassan, and conquered a large portion of it; while his invasion had the effect of recalling this barbarous chief from his Indian expedition. The Persian, on this occasion, concluded a treaty, which was to be binding on himself and his posterity while the world existed; and by which all Frenchmen, under pain of death, were prohibited from entering Persia. Many years, however, had not elapsed when it was learned, that without any regard to the stipulations of this eternal treaty, a French agent, called Jouannin, had been allowed to settle at the Persian court, where he enjoyed the highest favour, and was employed in disciplining the troops after the European manner. It was soon added, that in

1808 the Shah had sent an embassy to Paris. Buonaparte, wholly intent upon foreign conquest, courted this oriental potentate, partly as an auxiliary against Russia, and partly, it is supposed, with a remote view to some future operations against British India. He returned the embassy of Futteh Ali with a very splendid one under General Gardanne, which obtained a distinguished reception, and acquired the entire confidence of the Persian court.

This was a state of things which it behoved Britain, by every expedient, to counteract. Colonel (now General) Malcolm, who had so happily conducted the former mission, was sent again to renew, if possible, the ties which he had then formed. General Malcolm, however, on his arrival at Bushire, found that the French influence was quite paramount in the court of Persia, and that he could not be allowed to proceed to court in the manner which was suitable to the dignity of his official character. He proceeded, therefore, no farther than Bushire; and returning to India, suggested to the government there the plan of overawing Persia, by occupying with a military forçe the island of Kishme, which might command in a great measure the navigation of the Gulf. A force of 2000 men was accordingly placed under his command for this purpose. Meantime a great revolution had taken place in

Persian politics. The entire failure of the French in their promises to procure the evacuation of Georgia, the news of the Spanish revolution, and perhaps the natural caprice of an absolute monarch, had deeply shaken French influence at the court of Teheran. The moment was favourable to Sir HARFORD JONES, who came out from Britain on a direct mission from the King; and who conceived himself justified in proceeding, notwithstanding the failure of General Malcolm. This mission has been well narrated by Mr Morier, and has been improved by Mr Macdonald Kinneir, as the means of collecting much geographical information; so that it has greatly refreshed our decaying knowledge of the state of Western Asia.

The embassy landed at Bushire, and proceeded by the usual route to Shiras. This celebrated capital of southern Persia does not seem to have excited in them quite the usual enthusiasm. It is represented as rather pleasing than grand; and the first impression which the view of it produced was much impaired by the meanness of its streets and ordinary houses. The fineness of its climate, and the beauty of its gardens, are fully admitted. It suffered like the rest amid the desolations of Persia; but its trade has of late considerably increased; and it contains a most magnificent bazaar, a quarter of a mile in length, built by

Kurreem Khan, during the time he made it his residence. The population is estimated at 40,000. In this journey the embassy not only examined the ruins of Persepolis, but discovered those of Shapoor, the ancient palace of Sapor, which had escaped the research of former European travellers. The view of Ispahan from the distance of five miles, with its palaces, spires, and magnificent environs, appeared to them one of the most magnificent prospects in the world, and conveyed no tidings of the dire vicissitudes through which it had passed. These, however, became fully visible when they entered the city, and compared it with the description given by Chardin. Its walls were levelled with the ground; its vast suburbs were almost deserted, and a traveller might ride through its circuit for miles, and see nothing but ruins. The principal mosques and palaces, however, are still standing, and have a magnificent appearance, though in decay. Aga Mahommed Hussein, whose talents have raised him to the place of prime minister, being a native of Ispahan, has erected there a splendid new palace, and has enlarged and beautified many of the former edifices; so that Ispahan is beginning to recover from its downfal. After all it has lost, it is still supposed to contain a population of 200,000 souls. The English passed next through Kashan, one of the many cities which have had their turn as the capital of Persia. Though the greater part is now in ruins, it is still very large and populous, and carries on a great trade with Ghilan. Koom, entirely destroyed by the Afghans in 1722, has been in part rebuilt, but bears still the appearance of a vast ruin.

From Koom the mission proceeded to Teheran, which, so far as the royal residence is concerned, forms the present capital of Persia. It scarcely possesses as yet any grandeur or magnificence worthy of the name. Entirely destroyed by the Afghans, it was rebuilt by Aga Mahommed, who was induced, by strong political considerations, to make it his residence. Without being absolutely a frontier town, its situation was convenient for war against the Russians, now the most formidable foes of Persia; and it placed him in the midst of the wandering tribes from whom he sprung, and who formed the main strength of his armies. Teheran, however, has still the aspect of a new city, and contains no edifice of importance except the *ark*, which combines the character of citadel and royal palace. One great obstacle to its extension is the unhealthiness of the air, which prevails generally through the provinces on or near the Caspian, and is so extreme, that few of the inhabitants remain in the city during the summer months. Teheran, therefore, does not contain a permanent population of more than 10 or 15,000, though the military array of the empire, when present, raises it to 60,000.

The reception of the embassy, from the time of its entrance into Persia, had been very distinguished. Sir Harford had made a skilful display of that magnificence which is peculiarly calculated to dazzle the eyes of this oriental people. He wore a robe appropriated only to princes; and suffered to be seen, on proper occasions, the picture of the king set with diamonds, and other splendid presents which he was bearing to the court. At Teheran his reception was more than ever flattering, though in its narrow streets and miserable buildings he saw nothing indicative of royalty. Every thing rich or splendid seemed collected round the throne, while all around was poverty, either real or affected. The house in which they were lodged, though that of the second minister, afforded accommodations inferior to those obtained at Shiras or Ispahan. The minister soon waited upon him, attended by a person who, in Europe, does not usually adhere so closely to public functionaries—the royal poet. A great part of the conversation consisted in loading this personage with the most extravagant praises, which seem to have been given and received alike without scruple or reserve. All agreed that he was superior to every other bard of the age, and had no equal on earth; while some hesitated not to exalt him above Hafiz and Ferdusi. The king owned his merits in a more solid manner, by giving him a gold toman, or upwards of a guinea, for every couplet; which, after all, does not perhaps exceed what the booksellers of London or Edinburgh have paid to some of our popular poets.

In this friendly disposition between the parties, the ceremonies of introduction at court were easily arranged. One necessary preparation was, that the mission should be arrayed in green slippers and red stockings. The narrow streets, as they passed through, were crowded with spectators. On entering the royal hall, they were led between files of troops disciplined in the European manner, who performed the platoon exercise as they passed. At the end of the hall was a small and mean door, which being opened, introduced them into a dark and narrow passage, terminating in another door worse than that of any English stable. This ushered them, however, into a very handsome court, adorned with canals and fountains bordered with trees, at the end of which sat the king richly dressed. The presents were then delivered to the prime minister, and the ambassador began a speech in English, the sound of which seemed a good deal to startle the monarch; but on a translation being given, his surprise was changed into pleasure. He then inquired for the king of England, and whether he was son to him who had reigned at the time of the last embassy. On being assured that the very same king was now reigning, he was heard to remark, that in this point also the French had told lies; for it seems they had circulated a report of the king of England's death. The Shah was about forty-five; and beneath a large black beard and mustachios, rather an agreeable countenance appeared. He entered into a pretty long conversation on literary subjects, being himself a professed patron of learning.

After this interview, the ambassador began to treat with the ministers relative to the terms of the proposed treaty. This negociation was conducted in a manner very remote from European ideas of decorum. The discussions were sometimes accompanied with violent contention, and at other times were interrupted by loud bursts of laughter. Once, amid the most serious deliberation, the minister broke off by asking the ambassador to tell the history of the world from the creation. Afterwards, when he had promised to send a copy of the treaty fully written out, the ambassador received instead of it a large citron. When this treaty was at length produced, the secretary, who valued himself on being the finest writer in Persia, had so filled it with oriental figures and conceits, that it no longer retained any intelligible meaning. Sir Harford having declared it, in this condition, to bear no official value, the secretary was most reluctantly induced to prune it into something more level to an European capacity. When that minister came finally to apply the seals, the Premier called out, "Strike! Strike!" while all the Persians present were exclaiming, "God grant the friend-"ship between the two nations may be lasting! "God grant it! God grant it!"

Irregularly as the negociation had been conducted, its result was completely auspicious. The British obtained all their demands; while Gardanne received his dismissal, being prohibited at the same time to go by the way of Georgia, lest he should hold communication with Russia. A few days after, his whole train received instructions to follow their chief; and Persia remained entirely subject to English influence. After the departure of Sir Harford, Sir Gore Ouseley went thither as a permanent resident.

Persia, as surveyed by the British missions, presents a sad reverse from the picture of that great empire drawn by Chardin. It never could boast indeed of very high culture. If we except the great frontier rivers of the Euphrates, Tigris, and Araxes, which formed always a precarious part of the empire, and are now entirely wrested from it, Persia consists of an immense, dry, salt, plain.

It would therefore be very little productive but for the ranges of mountains which run through it, the streams descending from which form most beautiful and luxuriant valleys, whose charms are vaunted beyond almost any other spot on earth. These valleys form the only cultivated and highly peopled portions; the rest being inhabited by the Iliats, a race of warlike and wandering shepherds, whose habits belong rather to the Tartar races than to those who inhabit the civilized southern empires. As the husbandman, however, ruined by war and oppression, has deserted his fields, the Iliats have descended from the mountains to occupy his place; and many tracts, bearing traces of former extensive culture, are now covered by these Nomadic hordes. Various spots which were formerly the richest, have been rendered wholly unfit for culture, by the drying up of those artificial canals with which they were irrigated. Often the salt with which the soil and waters are impregnated, has accumulated, and rendered the formerly rich soil incapable of producing any thing but soda and other saline plants. Almost every quarter being now exposed to the *cheepaos* or forays of the wandering tribes, the husbandman nowhere enjoys a moment's security. The power and license of these marauders was experienced by Mr Morier, when, in journeying along the plain of Shuster, he was attacked by a band whom he defeated, and carried one of their chiefs prisoner to Ram Hormuz. The governor of that place, however, declared, that really he did not feel at all inclined to undertake the punishment of so great a person, and that the wisest plan would be to liberate the prisoner, on condition of his escorting him safely through the rest of the desert. Mr Morier took the hint, and set out next day under the guard of banditti, with whom the day before he had contended for his life. In consequence of these disorders, Olivier does not conceive that one-twentieth part of the lands throughout this great empire can be in a state of cultivation. Khorassan, in particular, which was formerly covered with populous and flourishing cities, and the seat of an extensive trade, is now described by Mr Kinneir as almost entirely laid waste, by the continual inroads of the barbarous chiefs who occupy or border upon it. The southern province of Khusistan, the best watered part of the empire, and formerly the seat of powerful dynasties, is now scarcely distinguishable from the bordering deserts. Even the Caspian provinces, which surpass all the others in luxuriant fertility, though these benefits are alloyed by the pestilential air, retain indeed some traces of former culture, yet are subject to such oppression, that the inhabitants are said to long for the arrival of their enemies the Russians. Silk is still produced in the different provinces of Persia, particularly those on the Caspian; but that great export trade which, in the time of Jenkinson, made intercourse with Persia so eagerly sought for, and which Chardin reckoned at nearly six millions of pounds, is stated by Olivier no longer to exist. Wool is produced abundantly, chiefly from the long-tailed sheep, the quality of which is various, but nowhere equal to that of Spain and England. The goats of Kerman yield also a fine species, suited to the manufacture of shawls, and other kinds are afforded by the different species of the camel. Cotton is raised in considerable plenty, but almost solely for the supply of internal manufactures. The sugar cane, in the southern provinces, ripens sooner than in the West Indies, though they do not understand so well the art of refining it. Roses are cultivated with the view of producing that essence which is valued in the East above all other perfumes.

The Persians excel in many manufactures, particularly in works of ornament and splendour, for the use of the great. They surpass the Turks, and perhaps even Europeans, in the brilliancy of their colours. They have taught to the latter that exquisite blue called ultramarine, the material of which, the *lapis lazuli*, is found abundantly in some of the mountains of Khorassan. Those rich carpets, which we call Turkey from the channel by which we receive them, are manufactured by the Iliats, or wandering tribes, in the plains of Persia. The Persians excel particularly in brocade and embroidery; silk, manufactured either by itself, or mixed with cotton and wool, forms their staple. Great works of tapestry, formed of silk and wool, embellished with gold, were carried on at court during the era of its splendour; and the art still exists, if a more fortunate period should enable it to come again into action. Leather, paper, porcelain nearly equal to that of China, and shawls similar though inferior to those of Cachemire, are also enumerated among the manufactures of Persia.

Trade in this empire is at a very low ebb. It has no port on the Persian Gulf except Bushire, and the small marine which it once maintained there is entirely annihilated. The Caspian never was nor could be the seat of any extensive trade; since, besides its difficult navigation, the only country with which it afforded a communication, was the north of Russia. Even this is nearly closed by the attitude of habitual hostility in which the two powers are now placed towards each other.

Amid all these changes, the Persian character, like every other thing in the East connected with social existence, has remained without any sensible alteration. They are still gay, polished, flattering, deceitful, eager in acquiring, lavish in spending. The English call them the Parisians of Asia. The late and present Shah have done all they could to make them a less jovial and merry people than heretofore. The Mahometan prohibition against wine, which was held so cheap by the early Sophis, is now enforced under pain of death. The delicious wines of Shiras serve merely as an article of exportation to India. The love of learning does not seem to have declined, though there is no longer the same number of students, or opportunities of instruction. The attendants on the *Madresse*, or college of Ispahan, are reduced from four or five thousand to as many hundreds. The recent travellers do not notice, so much as Chardin, the general prevalence of private education. The sciences cultivated are exactly the same. Astrology continues the high road to honour and fortune, and poetry is cultivated with the same enthusiasm as ever, though we have not been favoured with any specimens of its recent effusions. The same religious tolerance is still found to exist, unless in respect to the Guebres, or ancient worshippers of fire. This unfortunate race has now been rooted out of all the territories subject to the Persian sway. A few small bodies only have found refuge in the unfrequented towns of Kerman, particularly in

Yeyd, where there are supposed to be about four thousand.

Olivier, who had resided long both among the Persians and the Turks, remarks a striking contrast between these two nations. The former are polite, active, and industrious, while the latter are brutal, slothful, and ignorant. The very dress of the Turk is suited only to shew an indolent movement, while that of the Persian leaves all the motions at liberty. At the same time, turbulent and seditious movements, as well as great crimes, are more frequent in Turkey than in Persia. Meanwhile he allows to the Turk some estimable qualities, magnanimity, self esteem, steadiness in friendship, and gratitude; all which are wanting in the Persian. The Persian ministers are more enlightened, and more attentive to the good of their country, but more intriguing and artful. Had Persia been placed, like Turkey, in close contact with the powers of Europe, it would by this time, he conceives, have been entirely European.

The despotic rule of the Sophi is maintained without any thing which can be called a standing army. Even the royal guards, 10,000 in number, are merely a body of militia, who have lands assigned them around the capital, and are ready to be called out at a moment's warning. A corps of 3000 royal slaves is the best disciplined, and, but for its small number, the most efficient of any in the empire. The Shah's main dependance, however, is in the cavalry of the wandering tribes, whose Khans, when called upon, are always ready to attend the King with a proportion of their vassals. Of this species of force it is said, that, by a great effort, he can raise from 150,000 to 200,000. They receive no regular pay, but in return have ample license to plunder; in the hope of which, many of them are said fully to expect that they shall have an annual campaign. The Persians have no tactics, no system, no generalship. They do not distinguish between the civil and military professions; so that if the King does not take the field in person, the army is commanded by the prime minister, although he never perhaps saw a shot fired. Persia is now, as it has always been, easy to conquer, but difficult to hold. It presents nothing which can make head against the attack of a disciplined army; but the vast bodies of irregular horse which hover continually round the invading force, while traversing the expanse of its measureless plains, gradually wear down, and at length overwhelm the largest army. It was thus that Crassus and Julian experienced the most signal disasters with which Roman armies were ever overwhelmed. If the modern Arab and Tartar warriors have been more fortunate, it is chiefly from making their invasions with a similar force, more highly disciplined and inured to war.

Our recent travellers have been active in exploring the antiquities of Persia. Of these the most remarkable is that huge mass of ruins in the south, which is ascertained to belong to that great palace of Darius at Persepolis, to which Alexander set fire in a fit of frenzy. It is decidedly considered by Mr Kinneir to be one of the most ancient as well as magnificent structures in the world. In point of art, however, it is not supposed to vie with the classic edifices of Greece. According to Persian tradition, this superb edifice was completed in the reign of Humai, the mother of Darius Nothus. To the south of Shiras, about sixteen miles to the east of Kazeroon, are the ruins of Shapour, situated in a wild romantic spot on the banks of a rapid river, and at the foot of a range of rocky and precipitous mountains. The buildings are adorned with numerous sculptures, some of them tolerably executed, representing the exploits of the Sassaman dynasty. Sapor, as its founder, evidently gave his name to the city, but the Persian annals represent another to have formerly existed on its site, and to have been destroyed by Alexander. At *Taki Bostan*, near Kermanschaw, is a mountain in which large excavations have been formed, accompanied with a variety of sculptured figures, some of which would not have disgraced the finest artists of Greece and Rome. They contain inscriptions in the Pehlvi, or ancient language, and appear, like the sculptures of Shapour, to celebrate the exploits of the Princes of the Sassaman dynasty.

After all, it is on the banks of the Euphrates and Tigris, that the eye of the traveller wanders in search of the mightiest monuments of ancient grandeur. It is there that we must find all that remains of Nineveh and of Babylon, those first capitals of the world. Desolation covers alike them and the once magnificent country in which they were situated. "The humble tent of the "Arab now occupies the spot formerly adorned "with the palaces of Kings; and his flocks procure a scanty pittance of food, amid the fallen "fragments of ancient magnificence. The banks "of the Euphrates and Tigris, once so prolific, "are now for the most part covered with impene-"trable brushwood; and the interior of the pro-"vince, which was traversed and fertilized with "innumerable canals, is destitute of either inha-"bitants or vegetation." The site of Nineveh appears to be ascertained at the village of Nunia on the banks of the Tigris, opposite to Mosul. Here are found a rampart and fosse four miles in circumference; but Mr Kinneir believes these to belong to a city founded subsequently to the time of Adrian; so that of the ancient Nineveh there exists not now the slightest trace.

About sixteen miles to the south of Bagdad, on the opposite side of the Tigris, are the remains of the Greek city of Seleucia, and the Persian capital of Ctesiphon. All that remains of the former is the rampart and fosse; but Ctesiphon is still distinguished by the *Tauk Kesra*, or palace of Chosroes, presenting a front of 300 feet in length, 160 deep, and 106 feet high.

On the Euphrates, almost due west from Seleucia, travellers have observed with wonder remains which seem clearly ascertained to be those of Babylon. The place of this proud capital of the ancient world is marked only by four or five masses, or rather mountains, of bricks, earth, and rubbish, piled over each other. They have been observed by several travellers; but the late survey of Mr Rich is so peculiarly diligent and minute, that it may supersede every other. The greatest number of ruins are on the eastern bank of the Euphrates, immediately north of the town of Hillah. Here is found a mass called the mound of Amran, 1100 yards long, 800 broad, and 50 or 60 feet high, consisting of earth formed from decomposed brick, and strewed with various species of fragments. On the other side of an intervening valley is an edifice, called by the natives the Kasr, or palace, forming a square of

700 yards. It contains several walls in a pretty entire state, eight feet thick, and ornamented with some remains of painting and sculpture. The bricks are of the finest kind, and cemented with lime; a material not observed by any former traveller, but which was found to be much more efficacious than the usual cement of bitumen. A mile to the north of the Kasr is another mass considerably loftier, called the Mujelibe. It is an irregular oblong, the sides being from 200 to 136 feet, and the height 141 feet. The summit is covered with innumerable fragments of pottery, brick, bitumen, pebbles, shells, and sundry other substances. It contained many dens of wild beasts, and its cavities are filled with bats and owls. Two long galleries, containing coffins in the highest preservation, were extracted; and it was conceived that the same recess, if explored, would have been found entirely filled with them. This last feature, which forms the most conspicuous object of all these remains, has by most travellers been supposed to be the Tower of Belus, the most lofty and conspicuous of all the edifices which were the boast of ancient Babylon. Next to it was the Great Palace, which might have been found in the *Kasr*, had it not been described to be on the opposite side of the river. To solve this difficulty, it has been supposed that the Euphrates has changed its course, as in fact

it does take a sudden bend eastward after passing the Mujelibe. There is, however, another still greater ruin ; but which being situated six miles south-west of Hillah, can scarcely be supposed to have formed part even of the vast *enceinte* of Babylon. It is a conical mound, 762 yards in circumference, surmounted by a brick pile, which raises it to 235 feet. The bricks are of the finest kind, strongly cemented with lime, and containing inscriptions. The ground to a considerable extent round is strewed with ruins. Mr Rich at the first sight of the *Birs Nimrod*, as this pile is called, could not help exclaiming, that it, if any, must be the Tower of Belus. He could not reconcile such an idea with the ancient description, or with the supposed limits of ancient Babylon. There seems, therefore, some impenetrable mystery, which must render it for ever impossible for us to harmonize the picture of what Babylon was, with those vast and shapeless monuments, which alone attest to the eye its former existence.

# CHAPTER III.

## PILGRIMAGES TO THE HOLY LAND.

*Arculfus.—Willibald.—Bernard.—The Crusades.—Bouldesell. Brocquiere.—Breidenbach.—Baumgarten.—Georgewitz.—Aldersey.—Sandys.*

THROUGHOUT all the East, and in Europe during the middle ages, one of the most important and meritorious religious duties was pilgrimage. Doubts may be raised if it has not been too strongly condemned by the severe reason of modern Europe. The view of a spot which has been the theatre of heroic actions, or even the abode of genius, inspires always strong emotions in the susceptible mind. Much deeper must be the feelings of the pious visitant in beholding scenes dignified by the presence of beings so much more exalted, and events affecting the highest destinies of himself and his species. Pilgrimage, too, affording almost the only motive for which, at such a period, distant journeys are undertaken, may be the means of opening the minds of men, and enlarging the sphere of their ideas. It even opens new channels to commerce, of which these holy places usually become distinguished *emporia*. The greatest evil attendant upon the practice is not only the high merit which it is supposed to secure, independent of any inward piety or virtuous conduct, but the expectation that it will of itself wipe away every sin, however enormous, of which the pilgrims have been guilty. Nay, with such confidence, it is said, do they look forward to this wiping off all their iniquities, that they do not hesitate in their journey to add to their list. Multiplied accounts represent the deportment of these visitants of the holy shrines to be by no means of that edifying complexion which their object would indicate.

The tales of these peregrinations are almost innumerable; but whatever edification they may have afforded to those engaged in them, they yield little to gratify the profane inquirer. Father Noe even carefully inculcates it as the first duty of a pilgrim, to quench all spirit of vain curiosity, otherwise he will return without any benefit to his soul. These travels, however, are the earliest of any performed in modern times; and by very diligent search we may glean from them views of the state of society, and of the human mind in those remote periods, which we should vainly attempt to draw from any other source.

About 705 Jerusalem and its holy places were surveyed by Arculfus, from whose report Adamnan drew up a description of them. From the introduction it appears, that Jerusalem, like Mecca and Haridwar, combined an extensive trade with its pilgrimage. The 15th of September was the era of a great fair, when the holy city was crowded with an innumerable multitude buying and selling their various commodities. The multitude of camels and other animals, with which the streets were thronged, caused an accumulation of filth which became extremely offensive, and rendered walking difficult. Then, however, a miraculous rain took place; and this "inundation of celestial waters," collecting all the mire, carried it down the steep and sloping streets by the valley of Jehosaphat into the brook Kedron. Jerusalem, he says, contains many splendid edifices; but he carefully avoids describing any, except the temple of Calvary and the holy cross. It was supported by twelve pillars of wonderful magnitude, and had eight gates looking to the different quarters of the city. In the interior was a smaller edifice, entirely covered with marble, surmounted by a gold cupola, at the top of which was a golden cross. Within was the tomb, seven feet in length, not divided into two by a fragment of rock, as it seems had been reported, but simple, and in which twelve lamps, in honour of the twelve apostles, were kept burning night and day. Close to this was the church of Constantine, distinguished as the place where the true cross, with those on which the two thieves were crucified, had been miraculously discovered under ground. In these places our pious traveller saw sundry objects, which all Jerusalem constantly flocked to handle and kiss with the profoundest reverence. Such were the cup used at the last supper; the sponge on which the vinegar was poured; the lance which pierced the side of Christ; the cloth in which he was wrapt; also another cloth woven by the Virgin Mary, and in which were represented the figure of the Saviour and the twelve Apostles. From Jerusalem Arculfus went to Jericho, where he found nothing except the roofless walls of Rahab's house; all the rest was planted with corn and vines. He proceeded to the Jordan, to view the scene of Christ's baptism, on which a church had been erected. He describes the waters of the river as white like milk, in consequence of the salt with which they had been impregnated. His next visit was to Bethlehem, where he viewed the scenes of the nativity, particularly the water in which the holy infant had been washed, and which during so many ages had never dried up or diminished. He proceeded north to Damascus, which appears always as the metropolis of this part of Asia. It is described as a great and royal city, surrounded with a wide circuit of walls, strengthened with lofty towers. He then returned into Europe by the way of Constantinople.

About 786 another Benedictine, Willibald, a Saxon by birth, raised himself by pilgrimage to a distinguished place in the Romish calendar. From his infancy he had been distinguished by a sage and pious disposition; and on emerging from boyhood was seized with an anxious desire to "try the unknown ways of peregrination,— "to pass over the huge wastes of ocean to the "outer bounds of earth." Rome was the spot which appeared to him placed at this mighty and fearful distance. On disclosing the project to "his carnal father," he was most earnestly dissuaded from it, and entreated not to forsake his country and all his friends, to whom, from so remote a region, he could have little hope of returning. "The warlike soldier of Christ," however, persevered, and at length extorted the consent of his reluctant parents. He set sail from a port which he calls Hamela Mutha, and after a long voyage arrived at Lucca. Thence, crossing many plains and lofty mountains, he found his way to Rome. After paying his devotions at the shrine of St Peter, he was seized with a desire to extend his pilgrimage, and to visit "the delight-

" ful and desirable city of Jerusalem." Taking ship at Rhegium, and touching at Sicily and Samos, he was landed at Ephesus in Asia Minor. He employed himself here in visiting the tomb of the Seven Sleepers, and the cave in which St John wrote the Apocalypse. Hence he proceeded with a companion to Emesa, distinguished by a great church built by St Helena. Here they fell into the hands of the " Pagan Saracens," who threw them into prison, not knowing whence they were, and suspecting them as spies. An old man, however, having examined them, and being told their object, courteously observed, that all men did well to fulfil their law. Yet they remained in prison; but a merchant and a Spaniard treated them with great kindness, took them to the bath and to church, where curiosity attracted a great crowd of spectators. At length these two friends brought them before the King, who inquired, " Whence are these men?" The answer was, " From the western region of the " world, where the sun sets, and beyond which " we know of no land, but only water." The King replied, " Wherefore should we punish " them, they have committed no fault against us; " give them life, and suffer them to go." The pilgrims were therefore allowed to proceed without molestation to the Holy Land. They visited Nazareth, Cana, Tabor, and the Jordan, which rises, it is pretended, from two fountains, *Jor* and *Dan.* Willibald then proceeded to Jerusalem, and gives a catalogue of the holy places similar to that of Arculfus; but it were greatly too much to expect from so eminent a saint any notice of earthly objects. We shall therefore leave him, without further notice, to depart and embark at Ptolemais (Acre).

A third visitant of Palestine at this very early period was BERNARD, who proceeded thither in 878. He came first to Barre (Bari) in Italy, which it seems was then under Saracen dominion. He found a prince, by name *Suldanus* (Sultan), who, on receiving a due consideration, gave him letters, which he assured him would secure a free passage through all the countries that lay on his way to Jerusalem. Bernard proceeded to Tarentum, where he embarked and landed at Alexandria. Here, however, his letters proved of less avail than he expected, the prince having professed a very slender knowledge of the Bari Suldanus, till his memory was refreshed by a donation of thirteen denari. Unluckily it was a maxim here to weigh every thing which could be weighed; a process which, in consequence of the state of the Italian coinage, reduced six denari to three. From Alexandria our pilgrim proceeded up the *Geon* (Nile) to Babylon, the name still borne by the modern Cairo. The king's name was Abdelhachman, who, without paying the least regard to the recommendation of his brother of Alexandria, ordered Bernard to be thrown into prison. In this extremity he asked counsel of God, whereupon it was miraculously revealed to him, that thirteen denari, such as he had presented at Alexandria, would produce here an equally auspicious effect. The celestial origin of this advice was proved by its complete success. Abdelhachman not only liberated the pilgrim, but gave him letters, which he assured him would secure against all farther exaction; and accordingly none is afterwards mentioned. Bernard now descended the *Geon* by Sitimulh, Mohalla, and Damiate, to Thanis, where he found many Christians, and was treated by the monks with what he considers as even an excess of hospitality. Many camels were kept here for the supply of the caravans crossing the desert to Palestine. "Well, says he, may it be called a desert," presenting neither herb nor fruit, and recalling to his memory Campania when covered with snow. He then reached Jerusalem; in describing which he goes through the usual routine, and, leaving it, embarked for Rome.

During a subsequent age, the Holy Land became the object of only too frequent and crowded visitation. It is not here the place to inquire into the character and effects of those extraordinary expeditions known under the name of Crusades. They have furnished an ample theme of narration to numerous eye-witnesses; whose narratives, however, relate too entirely to scenes of blood, and to the successive triumphs and defeats of the Christian armies, to leave them much attention to bestow on those more humble but interesting objects of which we are now in search. Leaving these events, therefore, to general history, of which they form so prominent a part, we shall take up the thread of the peregrinations which took place, from the time when these regions became again subject to the Mahometan power.

The earliest of these narrations which I have met with, and which does not seem to be generally known, is one written in 1331 by William de Bouldesell, who seems to have been endued with an ample share of that credulity to which these early pilgrims were liable. He proceeded first to the monastery of St Catherine at the foot of Sinai. He was hospitably received by the monks, and entertained at free cost for several days. Above all, he was favoured with the view of the marble tomb of that Saint, which the monks opened, and shewed him the bones lying piled confusedly together. They even, by hard beating, brought out a small portion of blood, which they presented to our pilgrim as an especial gift. What particularly astonished him, though it would have removed all surprise from a less believing mind, was, that the blood had not the appearance of real blood, but rather of some thick oily substance; so that upon the whole it appeared to him the greatest wonder that was ever seen in the world. On proceeding to Jerusalem, he met with a woful disappointment. The Saracens, it is true, instead of profaning the holy places, viewed them with the deepest veneration; but, for that very reason, they considered Christians as "heathen dogs," unworthy to behold such revered objects. Bouldesell was therefore obliged to depart, entirely disappointed in the main object of his journey. He proceeded to Damascus, and viewed its splendid gardens, said to be 40,000 in number, whence he returned to Europe.

In 1432, Bertrandon de la Brocquiere undertook his pilgrimage. He sailed from Venice to Jaffa, where, he says, begin the "pardons" of the Holy Land; an expression which too clearly betrays the idea which was uppermost in the mind of these pious travellers. At Jerusalem, now returned under the sway of the infidels, he found only two French monks, who were held in the most cruel thraldom. There were a considerable number, however, of Jacobite, Armenian, and Abyssinian Christians. He made an excursion by Hebron and Gaza across the desert to Sinai. After his return to Jerusalem he went to Acre, which he found almost ruined by the dreadful conflicts of which it had been the theatre. It did not now contain more than 300 houses. He proceeded thence to Damascus, where he made a considerable stay. He found Christians held in the most deadly hatred. The two first persons whom he met, attacked and knocked him down. Brocquiere, rising, drew his sword to take vengeance; but his hand was retained by his companion; a fortunate circumstance, as thirty or forty Saracens immediately came running up to support their companions. The Christian merchants were locked into their shops every night by the Saracens, who opened the doors in the morning at such an hour as seemed to them good; yet the love of gain induced many to make it still their residence. He says, a man in this country ought to appear neither bold nor cowardly, neither rich nor poor. Wealth excites cupidity, poverty contempt. Damascus had been destroyed by Timur in 1400, and part of it was still in ruins; but the portion rebuilt formed a very great city. He states the population at 100,000 men ; but whether in this he includes women, or even male children, is uncertain. During his stay, a grand era was formed by the arrival of a caravan from Mecca, containing upwards of 3000 camels. Its entry into Damascus employed two days and two nights. The Alkoran was carried in front, wrapped in silk, and borne on a camel covered with silk trappings. A number of persons round it were brandishing naked swords, and playing on all sorts of musical instruments. The governor, with the whole city, came out to meet the procession, and to worship the sacred ensign which they carried in front. Brocquiere found the greatest veneration entertained for any one who had been once at Mecca, and was positively assured by an eminent Mollah, that such an one could never be damned.

From Damascus Brocquiere determined to return home by land, though he was warned of the dangers to be incurred by such a route. Accordingly he assures us, that there was no conceivable evil which he did not encounter, except that of denying his faith. His guide was a Mameluke, who obliged him, during the whole time, to sit cross-legged upon mats. He stopped at Balbec, but without bestowing any attention on its magnificent ruins ; and, travelling through Armenia and Asia Minor, arrived at Cyprus.

Towards the end of the same century, the Holy Land, with the wilderness of Sinai, was surveyed by Dean Breidenbach of Mentz, whose work, from its antiquity, and the ample details into which he enters, has acquired considerable celebrity. As these, however, relate almost entirely to the different spots visited by pilgrims, they do not contain much on which we could dwell with advantage. More curious particulars are contained in the journey of Martin Baumgarten of Kuffstein in 1507.

Baumgarten left Cairo on the 15th October, being deposited with his companions in paniers carefully poised on the sides of camels. They were " most barbarously treated by the Saracen " boys, who pelted us with dirt, brick-bats, stones, " and rotten fruit." At Alcanica they found a large caravan preparing to cross the desert, whose members united to protect each other against the Arab robbers. They scarcely dared to eat or drink; and, " as if we had been closely besieged, " slept and watched by turns." They were sometimes awakened at night by a frightful cry, which proved to be for the purpose of scaring Arab assailants, who were thus obliged to make off with the little they could lay hold of. The travellers then came to the bay, through which, he says, the children of Israel passed; and he declares, that the tracks of Pharoah's chariot wheels were still distinctly visible; nay, if any impious hand deface them, they are forthwith miraculously restored. Water became scarce, but they luckily bought some from an Arab, who, on receiving a *mayden*, run it through his wife's ear, whereupon the lady "fell a skipping and "dancing in a strange manner." They found on this road many prickly trees, the blossoms of which put forth a most delicious smell. Their worst adventure was, when they had to traverse a narrow valley of a mile in length, planted with dates, and forming a pass between trackless mountains. The inhabitants, on hearing they were Christians, "came flocking out of their "holes," knocked them down five times, and would be satisfied with nothing but money, which it seems proved always the only effectual mode in which they could be dealt with. As they approached their journey's end, the guides advanced a claim for more than the stipulated sum, and, on refusal, ran off, and "left us in that vast "and dreadful desert all alone." It was incumbent, therefore, to call them back by unconditional submission.

At length the pilgrims arrived at the monastery of St Catherine; and on being shewn into an apartment, imagined their troubles at least suspended; but a band of Arabs found admission, and in a barbarous manner demanded *thus*, which it seems was money; "with which having stopt "their hellish mouths, and greased their ugly "fists," our pilgrims were at length left to repose. They chose a moonlight night to ascend Horeb. The ascent was laborious, though facilitated in many parts by artificial steps, amounting in all to 700. At a certain point the guides presented their swords, and would neither allow them to move back nor forward without a liberal promise of money. At the top they found a church, on the cold floor of which they spent a very comfortless night. Next morning they descended the opposite side into the plain between Horeb and Sinai. Some refreshment was obtained at a monastery called the Forty Saints, once actually containing that number, all of whom had been massacred by the natives; and it was at present served by two monks detached from St Catherine. Their task was now to ascend Sinai, which proved much more difficult and laborious than Horeb. Besides being steep, it was composed of loose stones, which yielded beneath the feet, and when a large one was displaced, others followed, till a torrent rolled down. The heat was at first intense, but on ascending they were refreshed with a cooling breeze; and at length, amid a number of high tops which rose before them, the guide pointed out the highest pinnacle of Sinai. Their energy redoubled, and they were enabled to struggle against ever increasing labours; till at length, "through sharp and hanging rocks, through clefts and horrible deserts, "pulling and drawing one another, sometimes "with our staves, sometimes with our belts," they reached the second summit. The view was most extensive, Sinai raising its head high above all the neighbouring mountains. The Red Sea, though at the distance of three days' journey, appeared beneath their feet, while beyond stretched the mountains and deserts of the Thebais. They saw also "Althor, that famous port," forming then, it seems, the emporium of Indian commodities, which were conveyed thence on camels to Alexandria.

From Sinai our pilgrims returned to the monastery of St Catherine, where they were kindly received, though the tenants "appeared skeletons rather than men." Our party made arrangements for their departure in the quietest manner possible, and set out by moonlight, hoping to elude the covetous vigilance of the Arabs; but scarcely were they mounted when the latter were seen gathered round, "just as a flock of "vultures used to do about a carcase." In the course of the journey they were repeatedly interrupted by bands of them raising hideous cries, and loudly demanding money; on obtaining which, they went away "like a company of dogs, "when their barking is stopt by throwing them "a piece of bread." At length our party left "those horrible mountains," and came to a more agreeable country, situated on the Red Sea, where they joined an Indian spice caravan bound for Egypt. They lost now all fear of the Arabs; but this security involved them in fresh dangers; for travelling day and night "we could not avoid "falling off our camels, while we were half sleep-"ing, half waking. A thousand strange dreams "and fancies came into our heads whilst hungry "and weary, and we sat nodding on our camels." In five days they reached Cairo, where they made some stay. They found that city cruelly tyrannized over by the Mamelukes. A Saracen whom they met in the streets crying bitterly and beating his breasts, informed them, that having just completed an excellent house, a Mameluke taking a fancy to it, had thrust him out, and occupied it without the smallest ceremony. Baumgarten saw here the pyramids, which appeared to him "a "prodigious piece of work, especially in a sandy "country." He was surprised on looking out one morning by the view of the ziraphus, "the "tallest creature that ever we beheld." Another remarkable animal was the musk rat, which "be-"ing made angry, voided a sort of perfume "valued at its weight in gold." The mode of hatching chickens in an oven was also observed. They set out on a new pilgrimage, the object of which was the Holy Land. At Belbes they joined a caravan going to Damascus. After passing "Salheyo and Cattia," they entered upon a desert of deep and loose sand, which sunk beneath the feet. "We could see nothing but the "heavens above, and sand below; nothing green, "no tree, or the least shrub." Near a ruined cottage they beheld 10,000 sheep, goats, and asses, lying all dead, and emitting a stench almost intolerable. A minister of the Sultan of Egypt had forced these from the unfortunate inhabitants of Judea in the room of a poll-tax which he was sent to levy; but in their route through the desert they all perished for want of water. Soon after they came to a large bay, where were very extensive salt pits, said to yield to the Sultan the annual revenue of 100,000 seraphs. At midnight of the same day they reached Laritch (El Arish); and in a few days Gaza, still a great city, larger than Jerusalem; and there they were shewn the ruins of a large edifice, believed to be the temple of Dagon. They now began their journey to Jerusalem, passing over very high and rugged mountains, and in constant dread of robbers; but amid these steeps they plucked "very wholesome and pleasant "herbs, the smell being mighty refreshing."

They then reached Hebron, described as now more like a village than a city; but near which they were shewn the field "where it is said, or "at least guessed, Adam was made." The neighbourhood produced a reddish earth, used in the manufacture of prayer beads. The next stage was Bethlehem, the church of which he describes in the loftiest terms, declaring his belief, that in its glory it had not its equal in the world. It had been built of the finest marble, and supported by forty pillars, eighteen of which had been sacrilegiously carried off by the Sultan of Egypt.

From Bethlehem the pilgrims went up to "the "holy Jerusalem." He was received into a monastery of Franciscan friars, who treated him with the utmost hospitality, and gave the most accurate directions as to every thing to be seen and done; "but the *holy penny* must not be forgot." A mode of catching birds was observed, by pouring water upon the rocks, which as soon as the birds, parched with thirst, beheld, they hastened to it as to a bait, and were easily taken. An anxious wish was felt to enter Solomon's temple, now converted into a magnificent mosque. They even made the attempt, but were "violently "hindered and pushed back again after we were "half up stairs." It was well they were; for it seems every Christian who entered it was offered the alternatives of abjuring his faith, or being cut in two. It was called by the Saracens the holy sanctuary; two thousand lamps were kept constantly burning within it; and it was surrounded with a square pavement of white marble, "so "bright, that the beholders can no more look on "it than they can on the sun itself."

From Jerusalem Baumgarten proceeded to Jericho, which he found, like Arculfus, to consist of one solitary house, now, however, converted from the abode of Rahab into that of Zaccheus. Our pilgrim also visited the Dead Sea, "that "frightful and horrid place." In the approach, every thing looked black, and as it were scorched with lightning; and the ground was full of holes, in which the mules were continually stumbling. A recent shower of rain also had rendered the earth so soft and spongy, "that if any "chanced to fall, the ground giving way receiv-"ed, and as it were hugged him in its bosom, "and he had much ado to get up again." At length, tying their horses to some bushes, they came to the shore; where "the suffocating stink, "the melancholy and hellish aspect of the place, "the shore full of reeds and rotten trees, the "unwholesome saltness and binding quality of "the water, which is bitter as gall, represented "to our eyes the dreadful vengeance of an of-"fended God."

The pilgrims having now returned to Jerusalem, proceeded by the Jordan to Damascus; and thence taking ship at Tripoli, passed by several of the Greek islands on their way to Venice. Baumgarten thence proceeded by land to Kuffstein, his native place.

Among the visitants of Palestine, a conspicuous place is held by Bartholomeo Georgewitz of Cracow, who obtained the title of the Pilgrim *par excellence*. No one has given such full directions as to the course to be followed by the traveller into the Holy Land. He recommends first of all to make his will, " like one going not to " the earthly, but the heavenly Jerusalem." The next task is to chuse his route. He may go by the Greek islands to Constantinople, and then through Asia Minor, seeing in his way the ruins of great cities of the Greeks. On reaching Damascus, a journey of a hundred miles carries him to Jerusalem. Another road is by Hungary, Bosnia, and Poland, but this is more dangerous, being full of murderers and assassins. Both involve great expense, a period of six or seven months, and the danger of being killed. A much more eligible plan is to take ship at Venice, whence he may be conveyed in twenty days to a port of Palestine. A gentleman must put in his pocket 300 sequins of good gold, but if he does without a servant, only 200. The poorer are encouraged by an assurance that their expense will not exceed half that of the rich, and that plentiful alms may be expected. As no beds are furnished on ship-board, he recommends a box, which may serve at once for keeping clothes and sleeping upon. Some good wine, as well as a little comfort in case of sea-sickness, is not to be overlooked. On landing at Joppa or Berytus, the captain gives notice to the monk guardian at Jerusalem. That person hires a Moor, who, with several others, comes down to the ship and takes charge of the pilgrims. There are no inns on the road, but they are lodged in the monasteries. A very short time may suffice for seeing all in and about Jerusalem; but the pilgrim must pay his guides pretty high, if he wishes to view the Jordan. Should he aim at visiting the remoter parts of Judea, he must remain for many months or a year, till opportunities occur to join caravans or parties going to these quarters.

Our pilgrim gives a sad picture of the fate of Europeans who are carried into slavery by the Turks; a catastrophe produced chiefly by the fortune of war. The armies of that nation, in making war against the Christians, were followed by slave traders, carrying chains, with which fifty or sixty were bound in a row together, leaving only two feet between to enable them to walk. The hands were manacled during the day, and at night the feet also. The most miserable fate was that of men of rank, or those belonging to the learned professions. These having no handicraft art or trade, were employed in the lowest labours of the field. He never saw them, however, yoked in the plough. Escape was extremely difficult, particularly for those transported into Asia, in consequence of the great rivers and arms of the sea which they had to cross. It was frequently attempted, however, particularly in autumn, when the ripe corn promised to afford the means of concealment.

In 1581 Laurence Aldersey departed from London, and went across Germany to Venice. This city is "very faire and greatly to be commended." His only dissatisfaction was with its women, of whom he says, "they be rather "monsters than women." The ground of this severe censure is, that "every shoemaker's and "tailor's wife will have a gowne of silke: if a "stranger meete one of them, he will surely "thinke, that he meeteth a ladie." Aldersey set sail on Midsummer day for Palestine. They were soon overtaken, however, with a contrary wind; in the midst of which a Turkish galley came in sight, and caused a great alarm. The master "being a wise fellow, began to devise

" how to escape the danger; but while both he, " and all of us, were in our dumps, God sent us " a merrie gale of wind." As they approached Candia, a violent storm came on, and the mariners began to reproach our author as the cause, " and saide, I was no good Christian, and wished " that I were in the middest of the sea, saying " that they, and the shippe, were the worse for " me." Aldersey humbly replied, " I thinke " myself the worst creature in the worlde, and " consider you yourselves also." At the same time a long sermon was preached, the tenor of which was, " that we were not all good Christians, " or els it were not possible for us to have such " weather." A gentleman also told him the surmises that were on board on account of his not joining in the *Salve Regina* and *Ave Maria*; but Aldersey told him, " that they that praied to " so many goe a wrong way to worke," and made no alteration in his conduct. The friars observing this, and determining to bring the matter to a point, sent round the image of our lady to kiss. Aldersey, on its approach, endeavoured to avoid it by going another way; but the bearer " fetched his course about," and presented it. The proffered salutation being then positively refused, " there was a great stir;" but at length two of the more respectable friars " travelled " with the patron in my behalfe, and made all

" well againe." On the 2d August they arrived at Cyprus; of which he says, " The people there " be very rude; and like beasts, and no better: " they eat their meat sitting upon the ground " with their legs acrosse like tailors." On the 8th they arrived at Joppa, but did not land till next day, when they were permitted by the great Basha, " who sate upon the top of a hill to see us " sent away." Aldersey was mounted before the rest, which displeased the Basha, who sent a servant to dismount and beat him; " whereupon I " made a long legge, saying, Grand mercye, " Seignior." This seems to have procured his pardon; and being " horsed upon little asses," they set out through the wilderness. That very night they arrived at Rama, and found lodging in a house, which they could only enter by creeping on their knees, and had no provisions except what they bought; " drinke we drue from the " well." The town he describes as " so ruinated, that I take it to be rather a heape of stones " than a towne." On their way to Jerusalem they were often stayed and troubled by the Arabs, whose extortions cost them in all twenty shillings a-piece. " They that should have rescued us " stood still, and durst doe nothing, which was " to our cost." On approaching Jerusalem they knelt down and gave thanks; it then behoved them to dismount and to enter the town on foot. The superior met and courteously received them; but he complains that the door of the convent was very low and narrow, and the entry very dark; however, "they were dieted of free "cost, and fared reasonable well." He then begins the catalogue of the holy places, in which there is nothing worthy of record; nor did any remarkable events distinguish his return home, which was by the same route that he came.

Of English pilgrims to the Holy Land, the most intelligent was George Sandys, who journeyed thither in the year 1610. He sailed through the Greek islands to Constantinople, then to Egypt, from Egypt to Gaza. He found that city in a state of visible decay, "the build-"ings meane both for form and matter." The best were of rough stones; some only of mats and hurdles, others of mud; but "amongst all "not any comely or convenient." After all, it seems there were "some reliques that testifie a "better condition." Handsome pillars of marble supported "divers simple roofes;" and broken fragments of them served to ornament the thresholds, doors and windows, "almost of every "beggarly cottage." The castle was "now not "worthy that name." He describes the oppression endured by the Greeks from their Turkish masters as almost intolerable. Their doors are made low, purposely to retard somewhat the sudden irruption of these tyrants; their corn is buried under ground; and though they have "certain small vineyards," yet both the presses and the wine are kept carefully concealed.

Sandys having joined a caravan destined for Jerusalem, passed through Hebron, which he found "utterly ruinated;" but on its site a little village, adorned with a goodly temple erected by Queen Helena. The country here was "the most pregnant and pleasant valley that ever eye beheld." It extends for about twenty miles inward from the Mediterranean, "full of flowery hills ascending leisurely," and looking down on the most luxuriant valleys. Yet this most fertile region is almost uninhabited, containing only a few pitiful villages; "the grass waste-high, unmowed, uneaten, and uselessly withering." They passed through Ascalon, "now a place of no note;" *Cane Sedoe*, "a ruinous thing," but where the caravan "lay in deep pastures without controulment." They then came to Joppa, formerly the only port of Judea, and now the common place of landing for pilgrims, though the accumulation of sand rendered its port much less convenient than formerly. Here the pilgrims pay a sum to a Greek, who serves them as a guide to and from Jerusalem; and conducts them in perfect safety, "being in fee with the Arabians." After leaving Rama, the country rose continually, and at length became very mountainous. The road appeared as if paved with rocks, and often there was no passage, but such as seemed to have been worked by a winter torrent. At length they reached the summit of the mountains, whence they surveyed all those which they had left behind them. The road was now tolerably level, and diversified on each side with hills, with ruins perched on their summits; and "valleys, such as are figured in "the most beautiful landskips." At Jerusalem they were well received by the Pater Guardian, "a reverent old man of a voluble tongue;" though they consider a hundred dollars as rather a heavy charge for eight days' entertainment. The monks make thus considerable profits by the pilgrims; none of whom can with any safety remain, unless within the walls of the monastery. The making of the knights of the Sepulchre was also a source of revenue, as each paid thirty sultanies; and though a rigorous qualification was formerly required, "now they will except against "none that bring money." Many complaints were made, however, of the violence of the Turks, who extorted money on the most trifling pretexts; "which losses they use oft to rehearse as "motives unto charitie." Sandys was led carefully through all the holy places, though he was warned, that the omission of the Salve Reginas and Ave Marias would deprive him of every hope of that indulgence for his sins on which a true good Catholic might securely reckon.

# CHAPTER IV.

## ASIATIC TURKEY.

*Eldred.—Biddulph.—Pococke.—Chandler.—Wood.—Clarke. Macdonald Kinneir.—Skeetzen.—Burckhardt.*

THE portion of Asia of which we are to treat in this Chapter, is, as to its present state, perhaps the least interesting of any. It is tyrannized over by a brutal despotism, which has seated itself above the ancient inhabitants, without imbibing any portion of the genius or arts for which they were distinguished. Hence this region excites our curiosity rather by the traces of what it was, than by any thing that it now is. It is filled with the mighty monuments of former greatness; vast structures erected by the ancient kings of the world, and in which oriental splendour and magnitude are combined with the exquisite art and materials of Greece and Rome. Even the depth of its deserts exhibit the remains of edifices eclipsing those which adorn the most splendid seats of modern empire. A sublime and tender melancholy is inspired by viewing this height of human glory fallen; and the degradation of the present race serves only to render more conspicuous the greatness of those whose place they have occupied.

In the reign of Elizabeth, commerce rather than curiosity was the motive of those journeys which extended to all parts of the world. It was with this view that, on Shrove Monday 1583, John Eldred, "with six or seven other honest merchants," set sail from London. They arrived at Tripoli in Syria, where the English had a consul, and a factory called *Fondeghi Ingles*. Tripoli was the greatest port in the Turkish dominions, about the size of Bristol, and defended by a strong citadel. Its chief annoyance arose from a bank of moving sand, which "every yeere increaseth, and eateth "up many gardens;" which set at defiance all attempts to stop its progress, and, according to a current prophecy, was ultimately destined to overwhelm the city. From Tripoli he proceeded to Aleppo, which, he says, "is the greatest place "of traffick for a dry towne that is in all these "parts." From Aleppo he went in three days to Birrah (Beer), on the Euphrates, where that river "is first gathered into one channel," instead of those numerous branches, which in its early course procured it the name of "the thousand "heads." The stream is here about the breadth of the Thames at Lambeth, and running almost as swift as the Trent. They hired a bark to sail down. In their way the Arabs came to them with provisions, the women swimming out with milk upon their heads. "Their haire, apparell, "and colour, are altogether like to those vaga-"bond Egyptians, which heretofore have gone "about in England." Eldred had proof of their thievish disposition, by the stealing from under his servant's head of a casket, "with things of "good value in the same." In twenty-eight days they arrived at Felugia, where they landed the goods, and placed them on a hundred asses, to be conveyed across Irak Arabi to New Babylon (Bagdad). On the way he passed "the olde "mighty citie of Babylon, many olde ruins where-"of are easily to be seene by daylight, which "I John Eldred have often beheld." He notices in particular the Tower of Babel, which he describes as a quarter of a mile in circuit, and about the height of St Pauls, "but it sheweth much "bigger." It was built of very large sun-dried bricks, cemented by courses of "mattes made of "canes," as entire "as though they had been "laid within one yeere." I do not know of any earlier notice of these remarkable ruins. New Babylon was still a great city, through which an extensive commerce was carried on between Aleppo and the East Indies. He mentions a peculiar mode of bringing provisions from Mosul, upon rafts buoyed up by inflated goat skins. At Bagdad they use the rafts for fire-wood, " let the " wind out of their goat skins," and carry them home by land. From Bagdad he proceeded to Bassora, where the Turk maintained his dominion by a garrison of 500 Janissaries, and 25 or 30 well armed galleys. The vessels which came to this port were from 40 to 60 tons, and, to his surprise, had their planks fastened with cords instead of nails; a mode of construction which has always been used by the Arabs of Oman.

Wishing to return to Europe, Eldred again repaired to Bagdad, but spent 44 days in ascending the stream. He then joined a caravan going to Aleppo. Passing the Euphrates near Hit, he saw " a valley wherein are many springs throwing out " abundantly at great mouthes a kind of blacke " substance like unto tarre, which serveth all " the country to make staunch their barkes and " boates," (bitumen). He adds, " these springs " make a noise like unto a smith's forge in the blow- " ing and puffing out of this matter, which never " ceaseth night nor day. This vale swalloweth up " all heavy things that come upon it." They effected their journey well along the desert, paying to the King of the Arabians 40s. for every camel. Our author's curiosity led him to make an excursion into the different parts of the Holy

Land, "of which places, because many others "have published large discourses, I surcease to "write." In 1588 he returned to London in the Hercules, "which was the richest ship of mer-"chants' goods that ever was known to come into "this realme."

In 1609 there was published at London, "The "Travels of certain Englishmen into farre coun-"treyes;" of which Englishmen, the chief appears to have been "Master William Biddulph." He begins with the warning, "Reader, read the "preface, or els read nothing;" in disregard of which, we shall proceed directly to the matter of his narrative. Sailing from Cyprus, he touched at Tripoli; whence he set out for Mount Libanus, to see the cedars for which it is celebrated. The mountain district was found inhabited by Maronites; a people simple and ignorant, but civil, kind, and courteous. On reaching a certain point, he found twenty-four tall cedars, equal to the largest oaks, and the branches "stretching "straight out, as though they were kept by art." These, and a few at another place, are represented as the only remnant of the forests of Lebanon. Touching on his return at the principal village of the Maronites, all the inhabitants of every age and sex came running out to meet him, and "gave a joyful shout altogether jointly, to express

" their joy at our coming; giving God thanks " that he had brought Christian Frankes of such " farre countries to visit them." The old men invited our travellers to enter; and they were introduced to the patriarch, who entertained them with excellent wine, and conversed on all subjects, except religion and learning, on which points his knowledge appeared to be very limited. Good cheer was the prevailing system; and " their " manner is, when they feast, to sit from mid-day " to midnight, and sometimes all night." Our author, however, remarks, that the four villages on this mountain are now the only places in the world where the Syriac is spoken native. He was also much edified by hearing set forms of prayer in the vulgar tongue, " that the people " might have something to say amen to;" and earnestly recommends the example to England, where it had not yet been established. He found also in these mountains " Drusies," whom he supposes to be the posterity of the first Crusaders, though they have forgotten all Christianity, except baptism and eating swine's flesh. He viewed likewise, with much approbation, the Turcomanny, a " kinde and simple people, dwell-" ing always in the fields, borne and brought up, " living and dying in tents." The men keep the flocks and herds, while the women are busy at home spinning, carding, and knitting, " not spend-

" ing their time in gossiping and gadding abroad " from place to place, from alehouse to wine " taverne, as many idle huswives in England " doe."

Biddulph set sail from Joppa for Scanderoon, the air of which he describes as very pestilential, and strongly advises all mariners to remain close on shipboard. " Making haste to be gone from " this contagious and pestiferous place," they found a caravan, which was in three days to arrive at Aleppo. On the mountainous part of this road they met the Coords, of whom he only states, that they worship the Devil, alleging, " that God is a good man, and will doe no man " harme, but that the Devil is bad, and must be " pleased." At Aleppo he was much gratified with the respect in which he was held as a minister, even of a hostile faith. He never met with any wrong except from his own countrymen, and chiefly those who were most bound to protect him. In general, he cannot help pointing out the respect with which the ministers of religion are treated, not only over all the East, but in every country except England, " where there " is a more learned ministerie than in any nation " in the world." He is obliged to own, however, that the objects of this reverence are not always very happily chosen. Thus dumb men and madmen are here reputed eminent saints. Our author saw one of the latter, who went always naked, with a spit in his hand, while the devout hovered round with rings, into which they thought themselves too happy when this spit was thrust. "The "like account they make, if he take any thing "from their shop-boards, or box them, or any of "their house." There were seen also "idle "fellows whom they call Darvises," distinguished by wearing green, a colour accounted so sacred, that if a Christian is observed dressed in it, "they will cut it from his backe and beat him;" nay, one had his shoes carried off for only being tied with a green string. Their food is very simple, and with the poor consists chiefly of herbs and fruits. Several drinks were observed that appeared new to the English; among others sherbet, composed of water, sugar, and honey, cooled with snow. Another was *coffa*, seemingly not then known in England, but which appeared to them "more wholesome than toothsome." The Turks "drink it off by leasure," sitting either in the coffee-houses, or, which they rather prefer, in benches by the side of the street, "being full of idle and alehouse talke." Another drink was *bersh* or opium, "which maketh them "forget themselves, and talke idly of castles in "the ayre." The water, he says, is lighter than with us, and "goeth down more delectably, as "if it were milke rather than water."

Biddulph saw at Aleppo a number of Bedouin Arabs, of whom he says, " They live in huts, and " are here to-day, and many hundred miles off " within a few days after. They are a base, beg- " garly, and roguish people, wandering up and " down, and living by spoyle, which they ac- " count no sinne." Their kings, however, content themselves with levying a regular tribute from the caravans, and plunder none who quietly pay it, with perhaps a little additional exaction. " These Arabian kings never keepe any money " in their purses, but spend it as fast as they " find it; and when they want, with their sword " they seeke a new purchase." A certain number of Arabs, however, seek employment in the cities as porters, grooms, and scullions, when " their lodgings are on some dunghill or other, " or odde corner of the city, with some silly tent " over their heads." Their women, also, " be- " ing skilful in mourning and crying by arte," are frequently hired to bear a part in the noisy lamentation of eastern funerals.

Biddulph draws a gloomy picture of the ferocious despotism which oppressed this fine country. He says, " The grand Seignior only is free; " all the rest are borne, brought up, live, and die " his slaves." The highest are in no degree exempted. If but a Coppagie appears, " with a " greate seale in a blacke box," the greatest

Vizier or Basha dares not make any resistance, but " suffers this base Coppagie to strangle " them." While Biddulph was at Aleppo, a Basha, surrounded by a hundred followers, on seeing the approach of this herald of doom, merely asked time to say his prayers. In return, these Bashas, while they remain in power, tyrannize in the most barbarous manner; strangling, beheading, and sometimes " putting into terrible tor" tures those who offend, yea oftentimes without " offence, only because they are rich." A Sheriffe, or descendant of the prophet, being emboldened by this high descent to offend the Basha, had his limbs broken at the door of his own house, where he lay, no one daring to afford him either relief or food, till his friends, by paying a sum of money, obtained permission to cut his throat. Divers other tortures are familiarly employed; so that, on the whole, he concludes, " This misery abroad will make us love our own " country the better; and that is the best lesson " I have learned in my travels."

WE shall now proceed to Dr POCOCKE, whose work may be considered as the most elaborate and standard of any relating to this part of the continent. We do not deem it necessary, however, to follow him through the Holy Land, but shall begin where, proceeding through Saphet and Acre, he entered Syria. In viewing the territories of Tyre and Sidon, he could not help remarking with surprise, that of the plains which formed the territory of these two mighty states, neither exceeds twenty miles in length, and four or five in breadth. So limited was the territory which commerce alone raised to the utmost height of power and greatness. Tyre, now called Sur, is situated on the island to which the Tyrians retired and made their last stand, when besieged by Alexander. A few remains were still to be seen of the old walls, and of a strongly fortified harbour. There was a large Syrian church, but no edifices bearing the stamp of a very high antiquity. The inhabitants were extremely few, including two or three Christian families. Sidon, called Saida, was a more considerable town, the residence of a Pasha, and containing a number of newly built houses. The next considerable city was Berytus or Bairoist. Till of late its government had been given by the Porte to the Prince of the Druses; and one of them called Feckerdine, who resided a considerable time in Italy, had adorned it with several handsome edifices, which gave it a classical aspect.

The mountains along this waste were inhabited by the Druses, a Christian people, who live nearly independent under a prince of their own.

Pococke, like Biddulph, fancies they may be the descendants of European Christians engaged in the crusading expeditions. They have a patriarch, bishops, and monks, who, however, are much more employed in the tilling of land than in studious exercises. They have also nunneries, which seem to be rather hospitals, almost all the ladies contained in them being aged and decrepid. The people are upon the whole more simple and honest than is usual among the inhabitants of those countries. Dr Pococke arrived next at Tripoli, the residence of a Pacha, and situated in a delightful valley, eight miles from the foot of Lebanon. He ascended to the convent of Cannobine, situated high up this celebrated mountain. The freshness of the air, the picturesque hills, and beautiful cascades which surrounded it, rendered this a delightful residence, above all when compared with the parched plains beneath. About an hour's ascent from the convent brought them to a large plain almost on the top of Lebanon, at one corner of which was the remnant of the famous cedars. They formed a grove of about a mile in circuit, and were mingled with pines, from which the young cedars were scarcely distinguishable. Stunted cypresses occupied here a higher elevation than any other tree. The natives of Lebanon, though drinking liberally of snow water, are not liable to goitres.

Our traveller now went to survey the ruins of Baalbec; his observations upon which we shall incorporate with those subsequently made by Mr Wood. Thence he proceeded to Damascus. This affords almost a solitary example of a city which, existing in the earliest antiquity, has continued through all ages, and under every vicissitude, to be great and flourishing. Even when destroyed by barbarous conquerors, it has risen instantly from its ashes. This species of permanency appears derived from the extreme felicity of its situation, and the numerous waters by which it is irrigated. Pococke gives the usual account of its gardens, though these, he observes, are merely orchards, through which foot-walks and meandering streams are conducted. As usual in Asiatic cities, the interior is by no means distinguished for beauty, the streets being narrow and dirty, and the most magnificent palaces presenting outwardly only a mass of dead wall. This city no longer contains the numerous Christian merchants observed by Brocquiere, though there is still a street called "Franks'-street." The Christian inhabitants are, however, supposed to amount to 20,000, but bear a worse character here than in other places; and the Turks also are said to indulge to a greater extent than elsewhere the vices for which they are infamous.

From Damascus Dr Pococke proceeded through Hems, the ancient Emesa, splendidly adorned by several of the Roman emperors; and Hammah, the ancient Apamea, which seems to have risen to greatness during the middle ages, and is now in a very flourishing state. He then reached Aleppo, which has been long pre-eminent among the cities of Asiatic Turkey. It is better built than most of the others, of hewn freestone, and with several magnificent mosques and *kanes*. The trade with Persia, which has always been its staple, had already begun to decline.

From Aleppo Dr Pococke went on an excursion to Beer, Roumkala, and other places on the Euphrates. After his return he set out for Antakia, the ancient Antioch, under Seleucus and the emperors the voluptuous capital of the East. Its limits may still be distinctly traced, the whole circuit of the walls being clearly visible. Some part of them, which there is reason to believe was built by Seleucus, are still perfectly entire, and equally distinguished by strength and beauty. This city, after remaining long in the possession of the Crusaders, was taken, in 1269, by Bibars the Sultan of Egypt, and totally destroyed. Its churches, said to be the finest in the world, were then rased to the ground. Dr Pococke could only guess where the site might have been of those edifices which were once the boast of Asia. Aleppo took its place as the emporium of Syria; and Antioch is now a poor ill built place. The only remains of its ancient grandeur are the aqueducts, which, from their subterraneous position, have escaped the eye of the destroyer.

From Antioch our traveller proceeded to Baias or Byas, which appears to be the same with Issus, that celebrated pass from Asia Minor into Syria, where the empire of Asia was decided between Darius and Alexander. Dr Pococke believed he could trace the strait between the hills and the sea, into which the latter seduced his imprudent antagonist. He even discovered in the heart of a thick wood the remains of a triumphal arch, seemingly erected to commemorate this battle. From Baias he proceeded to Scanderoon, which, though the port of Aleppo, he found miserably poor, and gives precisely the same account as Biddulph of its pestilential climate. He went thence to Kepse, the ancient Seleucia, a most extraordinary fortified city, built on a rock, which overhangs on one side the sea, and on the other a mountain torrent. It is supposed to have been built by Seleucus as a retreat, in case of not being able to defend Antioch. There are very few ruins except those of the walls. The women of Kepse have a singular fashion of covering their head-dress with pieces of silver, among which there are many coins and medals of the Seleucide; so that "the head of a lady of Kepse is "often a very valuable piece of antiquity."

Dr Pococke embarked at Tripoli, and the rest of his Asiatic journey relates to Asia Minor. This quarter, however, was afterwards more diligently surveyed by Chandler, and the rest of the Dilletanti mission, in whose company we shall prefer to visit it, though without losing sight altogether of our present author.

There are few individuals to whom we are more indebted for exploring the most splendid antiquities of this part of Asia than Mr Wood. He was invited to join in an expedition for this purpose by two friends, Mr Dawkins and Mr Bouverie, who appeared to possess all the requisites for this delicate and arduous undertaking. A good draftsman was also engaged. Their main object was Palmyra, which, situated in the depth of the Syrian desert, and beyond even the rude jurisdiction of the Turkish Pachas, set at defiance the approach of ordinary travellers. They attempted to reach it first from Aleppo, and then from Damascus; but the governors of both places declared their inability to secure their safety in a tract so exposed to Arab incursion. At Damascus, however, they learned, that Hassia, a village situated four days' journey to the north, was ruled by an Aga whose power reached to Palmyra. At Hassia accordingly they met a cordial welcome, usually given by chiefs occupying these remote situations; and though the object of their journey appeared to him wholly incomprehensible, he furnished them readily with an escort of horse in order to effect it. They passed through Sudud, Houarein, and Kariatein, poor villages; in which were often seen fragments of finely sculptured marble, rudely put together in the erection of cottages. From Kariatein to Palmyra is a plain about eighty miles long, and ten miles broad, in which there is neither a blade of grass nor a drop of water, yet where some fragments of ancient buildings may be occasionally observed. At the end of that space, the hills enclosing the valley opened, and they beheld suddenly bursting on the view the most extensive and magnificent mass of ruins they had ever beheld. Range behind range appeared of Corinthian columns of white marble, standing entire after the walls and solid buildings, to which they were attached, had yielded to time. All around, appeared nothing but an immense and flat desert, extending to the distant Euphrates. As soon as they had recovered from the first impression of vague astonishment, they began to take a more minute survey. On the left appeared the most entire monument, consisting of a long range of wall with twelve noble windows, belonging to the temple of the Sun, the ruins of which rise above it. After a few Turkish edifices, mixed with some fine detached columns, begins a magnificent colonnade, extending for nearly a mile, through the intercolumniations of which are seen other superb structures. Further to the right are the ornaments belonging to two other temples; and at some distance in front are four grand columns, belonging to some edifice, of which there remains now no other vestige. The whole plain for three miles round is covered with columns in all the shapes and shades of ruin; some extended entire along the ground; some with broken capitals; while others present merely the scattered stones of which they were composed.

Palmyra is still inhabited by a few Arabs, whose wretched huts fill the court of the great temple; while every spot of ground intervening between the walls and columns is laid out in plantations of corn and olives, enclosed by mud walls. There are two rivers, the waters of which, judiciously distributed, doubtless conduced greatly to the comfort and subsistence of the ancient inhabitants, but are now allowed to lose themselves in the sand.

Palmyra does not occupy any part in history corresponding to the superb monuments which it now exhibits. It appears to have been founded by Solomon, bearing then the name of Tadmor; but it was doubtless at a subsequent period that these wonderful Grecian edifices were erected. Its greatness could only arise in consequence of becoming the entrepot for the Indian commodities brought up the Persian Gulf, and across the desert to Syria. As a state, it became illustrious only for a short period, through the courage and virtues of Zenobia; and by Longinus, in whom the classic genius of Greece for a moment revived. After their fate, Palmyra sunk back into the same deep obscurity from which it had emerged. Its very existence was nearly forgotten, till its site was explored by modern curiosity.

Our travellers surveyed also the ruins of Baalbec, the ancient Heliopolis. The great temple here, dedicated to Baal or the Sun, is generally considered as almost unrivalled among the remains of Grecian art. Little more remains than nine columns supporting their entablature, which, as well as the portico, is covered with the finest sculpture. The ornaments are formed of a beautiful stone, which Pococke describes to resemble white marble, and which Wood conceives to be a coarse species of it. The magnitude of the stones employed appears truly enormous. The shaft of each column is composed of three, joined together by iron pins, without any cement. One of these stones was seen in the quarry, where it had probably remained for ages, 70 feet long, 14 broad, and 14 deep, and estimated to weigh about 1135 tons. The Turks have made incredible efforts to demolish these fine remains of antiquity. They have chipped and undermined the stones in every possible manner; but the strength of the fabric has in a great measure withstood them; and even when they have overturned the columns, they have been unable to remove the fragments. Besides the great temple, there are two smaller ones in better preservation, though not possessing the same original magnificence.

Baalbec, like Palmyra, does not make a figure in history equal to its remains. Tradition ascribes them, like every thing else here, to Solomon; but a more probable account refers their construction to Antoninus Pius. Mr Wood justly remarks, that these deserts of Syria and Arabia form the country of all others where the worship of the heavenly bodies was likely to originate. Nowhere do the heavens present so many objects to the admiration of mankind, or the earth so few. To the wanderer over these boundless and dreary plains, the celestial bodies alone occur to guide and enliven his route. The custom too of sleeping on the tops of the houses, where, during every interval of slumber, they strike upon the view, must cause them to fill the mind of the inhabitants of a tropical, much more than of a temperate climate.

The observations and drawings brought home by Mr Wood and his companions, combined with other circumstances in exciting throughout this country an ardent zeal to explore and illustrate the remains of ancient architecture. With this view, the Dilletanti Society determined to appropriate L.2000, to be employed in an excursion through Asia Minor. Dr Chandler, a learned antiquary, was placed at its head, accompanied by Messrs Revett and Pars, who acted as draftsmen. The result of this expedition appeared in the work entitled, " Antiquities of Ionia ;" in a collection of valuable inscriptions published by Dr Chandler, and in his narrative of the tour.

The party landed at Smyrna, which had been fixed upon as their head-quarters. This distinguished capital of Asia Minor was founded by Alexander, whose choice of situations has been peculiarly happy. It was accounted the most beautiful of the Ionian cities, and was extolled by the ancients under the pompous titles of " the " lovely, the crown of Ionia, the ornament of " Asia." According to a very usual Grecian system, its principal public buildings were erected on the face of a hill fronting the sea. The hill supplied marble, while its slope afforded a place for the seats, rising gradually above each other, in the stadium, or great theatre for the exhibition of games. This city being one of the chief theatres of contention between the Ottoman Porte and the Greek empire, was nearly ruined; and after being in some degree restored, it was taken and plundered by Timur in 1402. The consequence is, that almost every trace of the ancient city is obliterated. The vaulted foundation of the stadium remains, but its area is sown with grain. There are only a few vestiges of the theatre; and the castle which crowns the hill is chiefly a patch-work, erected by John Comnenus upon the ruins of the old one, whose walls, of immense strength and thickness, may still be discovered. Smyrna, in the course of its revolutions, has slid down, as it were, from the hill to the sea, close to which it is now situated. Under the Turkish empire, it has completely regained its populousness, and has become the centre of the commerce of what is called the Levant. Its mosques, bezerten, and other buildings, are also very handsome, being built chiefly from the marble of the ancient structures.

In an excursion from Smyrna, the travellers, searching for the ancient Clazomene, came to Vourla. The place was considerable, but could not be Clazomene, for any thing that could direct them to which they inquired in vain. At length they recollected the mole thrown across by Alexander from the shore to the island on which it was built; and by careful examination they traced "this monument of that great mind, which "delighted in correcting or subduing nature, by "filling up or forming paths for the deep." It was about a quarter of a mile long, and thirty feet broad. They crossed it, not without difficulty, the swell being high, and the waves washing over it. They found it entirely deserted, and could only trace some faint vestiges of the walls and theatre. They next visited Teos, near the modern Sevri-Hissar. They could trace its walls, five miles in circumference, and delineated the remains of the temple of Bacchus, one of the most celebrated structures of Ionia. The place was entirely deserted; the site presented only a field of barley in ear, buffaloes ploughing heavily by the side of prostrate edifices, and fences of stones and rubbish, covered with illegible inscriptions.

The travellers now set out on the grand object of discovering Ephesus, the second city of Asia Minor. They had to pass over a road infested by the wandering Turcomans, who "overspread "without controul the vast neglected pastures of "this desert empire." The country appeared accordingly covered with the innumerable black booths of these Nomades, with their cattle and poultry feeding round. At length they reached

Aiasaluck, where, amid some miserable cottages, they saw large ruins, a huge castle and mosque. There was no beauty, however, unless in the single stones; and Aiasaluck, even in its glory, had evidently not been Ephesus, but only patched from its fragments. At a little distance, however, the ancient city was at length discovered. Considerable remains of the theatre, odeon, gymnasium, and other structures, were found; but the temple of Diana, the pride of Ephesus and of Asia, had not left the slightest trace of its existence. A few wretched Greeks now seek shelter here in the vaults and sepulchres.

The next grand object was to visit the site of Miletus, distinguished by the remains of a truly immense theatre, built on the face of a mountain which overhangs the city. It had been 457 feet long, and faced with marble, but only a few of the seats, with the vaulted foundation, remain entire. The whole site is covered with rubbish, fragments of wall, and broken arches. This city, once pre-eminent for power, commerce, and learning, was distinguished even in antiquity as fallen; but how much more would this character apply to it now? They discovered also a temple of Bacchus and other ruins, distinguishing a place called Myus, the inhabitants of which had, by the sudden irruption of a body of water, been driven to Miletus. Some doubts, however, have been raised by modern inquirers, whether the spots in question really belong to these ancient cities. Near Kelibesh they found, among the ruins of Priene, a temple of Minerva Pallas, which, as a remain of Ionian elegance and grandeur, was judged well worthy of delineation.

Dr Chandler examined also the following ancient cities: Laodicea, distinguished by considerable remains of a vast amphitheatre, a thousand feet in extent; also of an odeon, the seats of which remained, though the proscenium or front lay in a confused heap. It was of marble, and covered with sculpture, but the style savoured less of Grecian taste than of Roman magnificence.—Hierapolis, now Pambouk, distinguished by an amazing structure, destined either for baths or for a gymnasium; the huge vaults of the roof could not be viewed from underneath without horror. The theatre was also large and sumptuous, and the least ruined of any yet seen.—Philadelphia, now Ala Shehr. This place, notwithstanding the multiplied earthquakes that have shaken it, remains still a mean, but considerable place. The only trace of the ancient city mentioned consists of the walls, many remnants of which are standing, though with large gaps.—Sardis, near a poor village called Sart, presents a number of ruins confusedly scattered over a verdant plain. Some of the most remarkable are of brick, so strongly cemented, that the author could not, without extreme difficulty, detach a single specimen. These structures are attributed to Crœsus ; and it is supposed that, without some very positive violence, they would last for ever. Magnesia is still a large and flourishing city, situated in a beautiful plain, and containing two fine mosques of marble. Pococke mentions the remains of a very grand temple, supposed to be that of Diana Leucophryne, which ranked only second to the Ephesian temple. There are also very imperfect remains of a theatre. Dr Pococke surveyed likewise Angora, the ancient Amisa, capital of Galatia, but found no antiquities, except a few remarkable pillars and inscriptions. The town was very large, and estimated to contain 100,000 souls.

This part of Asia, unlike some others, has been visited more frequently than in proportion to its importance. Passing over, therefore, a host of minor, and even some respectable travellers, we shall traverse some of its most interesting portions in company with Dr Clarke, whose strong powers of observation, with his eloquent and animated pictures of the objects both of art and nature, have raised him to so high a rank among modern travellers. His profound skill in antiquities peculiarly qualified him for exploring a region, of which they form the prominent feature.

Dr Clarke embarked at Constantinople, and sailed down the Hellespont. Nothing, he observes, could be grander than the opening into the Aegean sea, bordered by the vast mountains of Imbros and Samothrace. He then landed and took a careful survey of the plain of Troy and its bordering mountains. Our limits do not allow us to plunge into the depths of the Trojan controversy. Since the doubts of Bryant, and the hypothesis of Chevalier, it has exercised the pens of many learned writers, whose works must be studied in order to judge of the many minute points upon which it depends. To my own mind there never appeared any doubt on the general question. That Homer should not have founded his narrative upon some real historical events, and should not at all events have given an accurate view of the spot on which he represented them, seemed quite inconsistent, both with his own topographical knowledge, and with the state of society at the period when he wrote. Dr Clarke, in fact, observes, that whatever difficulty may exist as to the minutiæ, all the prominent features of Homer's picture are incontestably visible—the Hellespont—the island of Tenedos—the plain—the river still inundating its banks; and the mountain whence it issues. He observes, that a fertile plain, and a mountain abruptly rising from it, are two features which usually combine in the site of ancient cities. From the one the citizens drew their subsistence, while the other became the citadel, to which they retired on the approach of danger.

Entering on the plain of Troy, there occurred first the Mender, which its name, and every circumstance, seemed clearly to fix as the Scamander. Dr Clarke found also the Thymbrius, under the modern appellation of Thymbroek, though other inquirers conceive it to be the Simois. This last he believed himself to recognize in the Callifat Osmack, which rolls to the Scamander, though by a sluggish stream, through an extensive plain, which thus becomes that of Simois, on which were fought the great battles recorded in the Iliad. Strabo had mentioned, that New Ilium, the city existing in his time, was situated nearly four miles in a certain direction from the original city. In this distance and direction Dr Clarke discovered two spots marked by ruins, which, from different circumstances, seem very likely to have been Old and New Troy. The grandeur of the scenery viewed from this plain is said to be almost indescribable: Samothrace on one side, rearing behind Imbrus its snow-clad summit, shining bright on a cloudless sky; while on the other side Gargarus, the highest of the chain of Ida, rises to at least an equal elevation. The descriptive powers of the bard became more strongly felt; and the steps of his deities, while they swept from mountain to mountain, could be distinctly traced.

Dr Clarke ascended to Bonarbashy, where Troy, and the sources of the Scamander, had been idly placed by Chevalier. Instead of two fountains, one hot and one cold, as had been reported, he found them numerous, and all warm, raising the thermometer to 62°. They did not form the source of the Scamander, which lies forty miles in the interior, and which Dr Clarke determined to visit. He passed through grand rocky defiles resembling some of the passes in the Tyrol. Shepherds were playing their reed pipes among the rocks, and herds of goats and sheep browzing. A wild mountaineer race, distinguished by sandals of undressed bulls' hides, occasionally shewed themselves. He came to a town called Æne, suggesting the name of Æneas, who is said to have retired and reigned in the mountainous district above Troy. After passing through the beautiful and highly cultivated district of Beyramitsh, he came to Turkmanle, where the most hospitable reception was experienced. Hence he ascended, with difficulty and danger, across narrow ridges of ice and snow, the loftiest summit of Gargarus. From this point, all Asia

Minor and European Turkey appeared as if modelled on a vast surface of glass. He afterwards went to visit the source of the Scamander, which he found in a grand natural amphitheatre, amid craggy and pine-clad rocks, alpine summits, and roaring cataracts. In descending, he had a view of the ruins of Alexandria Troas, and was particularly struck by their colossal character; so that though materials have been drawn from them for the ornament of all the neighbouring cities, they continue still very extensive. The theatre, and the baths, were in particularly good preservation.

Dr Clarke viewed also the ruins of Telmessus, in the Gulf of Glaucus, on the coast of Caramania. The most conspicuous object was the theatre, built as usual on the side of a hill, along whose slope the seats were disposed. They were in twenty-eight rows, and in front extended a noble terrace, to which a magnificent flight of steps conducted from the sea. One of the most remarkable features was a large vaulted apartment hewn in the solid rock, on one side of which was a hollow recess, of which no trace appeared externally. This is supposed to be an oracular cave, where the priest, concealed within the recess, uttered a sound believed to be supernatural. The whole face also of a large rock fronting the sea was cut out into magnificent tombs.

The remainder of Dr Clarke's travels in Asia was chiefly employed in a visit to Jerusalem and the principal places in its neighbourhood. These scenes of the great events of scripture history were surveyed by him with just devotional warmth, and without any of that blind credulity which beset the early pilgrims. With him, therefore, we shall gladly survey the present state of these celebrated spots, as we endeavoured to glean from the others their condition at an early period.

Dr Clarke landed at Acre, rendered again celebrated by the events of the French expedition, and now the residence of Djezzar Pacha. This extraordinary barbarian, who had held his power for twenty years, accounted himself now independent of the Porte, and undisputed master of Syria and Palestine. His name signified butcher, which he was not unwilling to have understood. The approaches to his palace were guarded by persons from whom, on any displeasure, he had ordered the arm, nose, eye, or other member to be cut off; "marked men," as he called them, and who were held ready to perform the same office for others. His haram was secured by three massive doors, which he every evening opened and locked with his own hand, and provisions were introduced into it by a turning wheel, so constructed that nothing was seen of the person within who received them. The females introduced into it were never more heard of, nor was it ever known whether they were dead or alive. Our author found him in an apartment destitute of all furniture, except a coarse earthen vessel for cooling water; he wore a plain Arab dress, and apologized for having a poignard set with diamonds, as being a necessary ensign of office. He received them with very little ceremony; and during the interview employed himself in cutting paper into various shapes, and in tedious and idle tales, parables, and truisms. On their expressing wonder at the magnitude of his preparations against the Druses, he asked why a pismire should be permitted to creep upon your cheek; and expressed deep indignation at Sir Sidney Smith's interference in behalf of that unfortunate race. It was even confidentially owned by his secretary, that he intended to kill Sir Sidney if he ever had him in his power.

Dr Clarke having obtained permission to visit the Holy Land, set out with a party of his friends, being furnished from Dsjezzar with an escort, and an order to supply him with whatever he wanted. He passed through a fine country, rendered almost uncultivated by the tyranny of its ruler, to Sepphouri, formerly the capital of Galilee, but now a miserable village. It was distinguished by the ruins of a Gothic church erected over the supposed house of St Anne, and where Dr Clarke in fact made the curious discovery of some very ancient pictures, similar to those which are worshipped in Russia. He found himself now in the region of indulgences, relics, and pious frauds of every kind. He laments, that of the numerous Christians who reside in the Holy Land, there are scarcely any who are not a disgrace to their profession, from their ignorance, and often their disorderly lives. Many well meaning persons had been so disgusted with their follies and impositions, that they considered the whole as a trick, and went away worse Christians than they came. Our author, however, determined to regard nothing but the Bible itself; and on comparing carefully its narrative with the actual features of the country, he was alike edified and astonished at the exact correspondence between them.

Nazareth was found reduced to a deplorable state by the tyranny of Dsjezzar; yet the terror of his name procured to the travellers an immediate supply of all they wanted. In this early residence of the holy family, the trade of wonders and relics was carried on upon a still greater scale, and several pretended miracles were even exhibited, the cheat of which was easily perceived. From Nazareth Dr Clarke proceeded to view the Lake of Tiberias, called also Gennesareth. He was particularly struck by the grandeur of its scenery, and the lofty mountains by which it was bordered. The summit of Libanus appeared to the north, covered with deep snow even at this hot season. The party were very desirous to ascend Tabor; but were assured of its being occupied by so strong a body of Arabs as to render the attempt quite unsafe. They passed through the plain of Esdraelon, the scene of encampment to numerous armies, and the most fertile part of Judea. This was attested, even in its present uncultivated state, by the rich verdure which clothed it. Returning through Nazareth, he proceeded to Naplous, or Napolose, the ancient Sichem, capital of Samaria. The aspect of the country presented here a happy change. This territory was subject to the Pacha of Damascus, who appears to have adopted a much more beneficent system of government than the tyrant of Acre. The surrounding district was not only fertile, but in the highest cultivation; and several caravans stationed round shewed it to be the seat of a considerable inland trade. The governor regaled them with all the magnificence of an eastern sovereign. Here were found, fixed seemingly by sure tradition, the tombs of Joseph, of Eleazer, and of Joshua, spacious sepulchres hewn in the living rock.

The journey from this place to Jerusalem presented a striking feature of high cultivation. The limestone hills and stony valleys were covered with plantations of figs, vines, and olives; and even the most rugged mountains were rendered productive by being formed into terraces. He views it, in short, as "the Eden of the East;" and conceives it clearly to shew, that the Holy Land, if everywhere equally improved, would be indeed a land of abundance. Strong emotions were felt by the party as they approached the spot where they were to obtain the first view of Jerusalem. After two hours of earnest expectation, a Greek of the party exclaimed *Hagiopolis!* and threw himself on his knees. They were struck with the grandeur of the spectacle. Instead of a wretched and ruined town, as some had described it, they beheld a flourishing and stately metropolis; domes, towers, palaces, and monasteries, shining in the sun's rays with inconceivable splendour. In honour of Dsjezzar Pacha, they were honoured with a public entry; during which, some of the inhabitants welcomed, others abused them as dogs and infidels. The Franciscan convent of St Salvador, a large building like a fortress, was thrown open, and admitted their whole cavalcade within its vast portals, which were immediately closed. They were then welcomed by monks, whose ample size and rosy countenances would have done honour to the best endowed house of Spain or Italy. The accommodation and fare were good; they were even supplied with tea, a luxury to which they had been for some time unused.

It was now time to visit the grand object of pilgrimage, the church of Calvary and of the sepulchre. Its outward appearance resembled that of any handsome Catholic church. Over the door was a very ancient *bas relief*, representing the Messiah's entrance into Jerusalem. On entering, a slab of white marble was shewn as the spot where his body was anointed. In the middle was a dusty fabric, compared to a huge pepper-box, on entering which they were shewn the sepulchre, with the stone on which the angel sat. To Dr Clarke, who had particularly studied sepulchres, this did not present the slightest appearance of one; it was not, like all others in the East, cut out of the rock, but the sides formed of fine verd-antique marble; and the stone did not fit its mouth. They were then led into a room above, and were shewn an altar stated to be Mount Calvary, and exhibiting the marks of the three crosses, though within a space wholly inadequate. The whole aspect of the place satisfied Dr Clarke, that this supposed site of the crucifixion and entombment rests wholly in the imagination of Queen Helena, the fair founder;

and stands supported by no argument, except the accidental rent in the rock, which is shewn as that miraculously produced at the crucifixion. Calvary besides was without the limits of the ancient Jerusalem, while the church is within the contracted bounds of the modern city. Our author was therefore led to make a diligent search in a glen or dingle without the walls, separating the present city from an opposite hill. He found both sides of it covered with tombs, hewn after the manner of the ancients out of the solid rock, of various forms and dimensions, but some truly magnificent. Here it appeared to him that both Calvary and the tomb were certainly to be found, though it was difficult to fix on the precise spots. Several inscriptions, with some striking ruins, seemed to point out the opposite hill as Mount Sion, the celebrated and sacred citadel of Jerusalem: in which case, the eminence called by the moderns Mount Sion, will form merely part of Mount Moriah, and the modern city will be built on that hill alone. In some of the tombs around Jerusalem paintings were found, similar to those which adorn the walls of Herculaneum and Pompeii. The most distinguished tombs are those known by the name of the sepulchres of the patriarchs, of the kings, and of the Virgin; though there seems much doubt as to the persons by whom, or in whose honour, they were really erected. The most magnificent edifice in this city is the mosque of Omar, built upon the site of the ancient temple of Solomon. The lofty Saracenic pomp which characterizes the structure, its numerous arcades, capacious dome, and area paved with the choicest marbles, joined to the sumptuous costume of the devotees passing to and from the sanctuary, render it altogether one of the finest sights which the Moslems have to boast.

The population of Jerusalem is estimated, on vague conjecture, at 20 or 30,000 inhabitants. The houses are lofty, and the streets cleaner than those of any other city in the Levant, though, like all of them, very narrow. The only manufactures are beads, crosses, and shells; the two former of which are made partly of a species of hard wood, and partly of the black fetid limestone of the lake Asphaltites.

Our analysis of Dr Clarke's narrative having extended to so considerable a length, we shall omit his return by the common route of Bethlehem and Jaffa.

Mr Macdonald Kinneir, whose exertions have contributed so much to extend our knowledge of Western Asia, performed a series of journeys through Asia Minor, which form the best account we now possess of the present state of this part of the Turkish empire. After leaving Constantinople, the first place of importance at which he arrived was Nice, once the capital of Bithynia, and the seat of several general councils. It is now much decayed, but contains a number of striking ruins, particularly some Roman walls, which have acquired the solidity of rock. He came next to Eskishehr, situated in a great plain, having a dry and parched appearance, where Godfrey of Bouillon defeated Sultan Soliman. This was found a wretched place, exhibiting nothing worthy of notice, except a few inscriptions. Here, while Mr Kinneir was sitting in his lodgings, one of those Dervishes who, from being mad, are reverenced as sacred, came in, struck him with the end of a lance, and loudly protested against the indignity of an infidel entering the habitation of a holy man. It really appears to have been his own house, which seems to make his conduct not quite so presumptuous as it appeared to Mr Kinneir, who hastened to the Aga, demanding his punishment. The Aga, however, replied, that it would not be prudent to deal severely with a person so much respected in the city, but held out some evidently delusive expectation of chastising him at some future period. Mr Kinneir, therefore, returned to his lodgings; where the insults of this person still continuing, he was advised to decamp, as in case of a quarrel the whole town would have taken the part of his holy antagonist.

Mr Kinneir now passed through Sever Hissar and Yerma, where he found ruins; but this part of Phrygia was anciently so covered with cities, that it is difficult to identify any particular place. The inhabitants smiled when he asked for ruined places, assuring him the whole country was overspread with them. The agriculture here is wretched; the plough often is not even shod with iron, and is drawn sometimes by ten or twelve oxen. The harrow is merely a large bunch of thorns, with a stone laid across to increase the pressure. The grain is threshed by cattle, wind being chiefly relied upon for separating the chaff. A great part of the country was covered with the roving Turkmans, a boisterous and ignorant race, but much more honourable and hospitable than the inhabitants of the towns.

Mr Kinneir now reached Angora, the capital of an extensive Pachalic, and the scene of the great battle between Timur and Bajazet. It contains 20,000 inhabitants, chiefly Armenians, and is distinguished by the ruins of a temple erected in honour of Augustus. The Pacha seems to be a brutal tyrant, who monopolizes all the necessaries of life in his dominions, and retails them at high prices; so that the people are compelled to emigrate in great numbers to the neighbouring government of Chapwan Oglu. The travellers soon entered the territory of that chief, the most powerful in Asia Minor, maintaining an army of 40,000 men, and almost entirely independent of the Grand Seignior. Ooscat, where he resides, has been almost entirely created by him, and contains now a population of 16,000. He has built a very extensive palace, and lives in great pomp. He had a dignified deportment and a long white beard; made many inquiries about the politics of Europe, and particularly about Buonaparte, of whom he expressed a vast admiration. Our traveller passed through Cæsarea, the ancient capital of Cappadocia, a mean dirty city, but containing 25,000 inhabitants, and a considerable trade in cotton, produced abundantly in its neighbourhood. He then proceeded to Tarsus, the celebrated capital of ancient Cilicia, but was surprised, after a stay of eight days, not to discover a single inscription or monument of art. It is situated, however, in a fertile country, has 30,000 inhabitants, and a pretty extensive foreign trade. Mr Kinneir then surveyed the pass into Cilicia, and the scene of the battle of Issus. Pias or Byas, which corresponds to that ancient place, had lately been considerable as the seat of a rebel chief, who being subdued, Pias was reduced to a heap of ruins. Scanderoon was found sunk into a poor fishing village. Latakia was now the port of Aleppo; but even this did not secure any extensive trade, in consequence of the low state to which Aleppo itself was fallen. The whole of this country is in a state of complete decay and depopulation, in consequence of the tyranny of the Pachas, and their contests with each other. However, a body of Janissary chiefs, who had obtained possession of Aleppo, had lately been betrayed and massacred, and the place seized by a son of Chapwan Oglu, to the general satisfaction of the inhabitants, who preferred one tyrant to many.

Mr Kinneir afterwards performed a journey through the north of Asia Minor, by a route which European travellers have seldom followed. He came first to Isnikmid, the ancient Nicomedia, under Dioclesian the capital of the Roman empire. It is now a small town with seven hundred families, and presenting even no ruins to attest its former magnificence. He was now in the ancient Bithynia, which he found a beautiful and romantic country, intersected with lofty mountains and fertile valleys, and abounding in vines and forests. He passed through Terekli, now a small place, but which the name and situation point out as the ancient Heraclea. Passing through Tereboli, Modoorly, and Boli, he came to Costamboul, called also Kostamonni, the ancient capital of Paphlagonia, and afterwards the patrimonial estate of the family of the Comneni. It contains about 14,000 inhabitants, and is situated in a rugged and dreary country, surrounded by immense mountains. Its aspect improved, however, when they came to the banks of the great river Kisil Ermak. In general the scenery of this part of Asia Minor is of a grand and picturesque character, the valleys being clothed with luxuriant verdure, and the mountains with trees of every description; so that it often resembled the ornamented park of an English nobleman. Grain, however, was ill cultivated and scarce. They reached Samsoon, the ancient Amisus, capital of Mithridates, a neat little town, composed of white-washed wooden houses. It presents few antiquities, however, though the ancient wall may still be traced, partly covered by the waves. They then passed through Unieh, a small seaport, most beautifully situated, and tolerably thriving, and also Keresoun, surrounded by wooded mountains of stupendous height. From Keresoun, they went partly by water to Trebisond. This is a very ancient city, mentioned by Xenophon in the retreat of the ten thousand. The Romans made it the capital of a province, and under the lower empire it became for some time the seat of an independent Greek monarchy. It now contains about 15,000 inhabitants, is situated in a well cultivated country, and carries on manufactures of silk and cotton. There are several Roman antiquities, particularly one very beautiful church.

Mr Kinneir, indefatigable to explore Asia Minor, crossed it at another time in a north-west direction from Kelendri to Constantinople. Kelendri was a poor town, and the road thence to Caraman might be considered as an immense forest of oak, beech, fir, and juniper, covered with straggling Turkmans and numerous flocks of goats. Caraman, once the capital of a race of Turkish princes, covered still an extensive area of ground, and contained 3000 families, occupied in the cotton manufacture, but was a mean looking place. He now entered the plain of Iconium, where not a tree, nor even a shrub, is perceptible over an expanse of ground as level as the sea. In two days he reached Iconium, now Konieh, considerably declined from what it was when the metropolis of the Sultans of Roum, but still containing 30,000 inhabitants, and presenting a number of antique materials formed into modern edifices. After Konieh the country improved; and having passed through Ladik and Akshehr, he came to Osium-kara-hissar, a city containing 12,000 families, and distinguished for its manufacture of black felt, and extensive culture of opium. Two days then brought him to Kutaiah, the capital of Anatolia, and containing a population of 50 or 60,000 souls. The town is built on the side of a hill, the houses are handsome, and the castle, occupying the position of Cotyœum, appears to have been a place of great strength. To reach Boursa, it was necessary to cross Mount Olympus, covered deep with snow, and over which, by the aid of some guides and companions, he with great difficulty made his way. On the other side was Boursa, one of the most beautiful cities in the Turkish empire, situated in a fertile and finely wooded plain, enclosed within the immense ridges of Olympus. It contains 40,000 inhabitants, 365 mosques, and its baths and mineral springs are celebrated all over the empire. He then proceeded to embark at Modania for Constantinople.

In another excursion through the heart of Asia Minor, our author passed Sivas, the ancient Sebaste, a dirty ill built city, inhabited by a coarse and rude people, and distinguished by the breeding of horses. He proceeded to Tocat, the largest and most commercial city in the interior of Asia Minor, containing 60,000 souls, and situated in a fine valley, watered by the Jekil Irmak. About fifty miles to the south-west stands Amasia, the birth-place of Strabo, and one of the principal cities of Pontus. It is romantically situated in a narrow valley between high and rocky mountains. It contains a population of 35,000 souls, and produces a great quantity of excellent silk.

Few travellers in the East have acted a more meritorious part than Dr Seetzen, who, during a long residence, embraced with ardour every opportunity to extend our knowledge of Syria, Arabia, and Africa. In 1806 he determined to explore the regions of Syria situated to the east of Hermon, the Jordan, and the Dead Sea, where the records, both of sacred and profane history, describe the existence of magnificent cities that are now unknown. The enterprise was attended with hazard, as it carried him beyond even the rude protection afforded by the Turkish government. Undeterred by this consideration, he set out from Damascus, furnished with an order from the Pacha upon the inferior chiefs to supply him with a horse and guide, and to defray his expenses. He then entered the mountainous district of Ladscha, the villages of which, built upon the crumbling sides of rocks of black basalt, had a gloomy and dismal appearance. He traced the Baniass, a beautiful, but not the principal, source of the Jordan. Cæsarea Philippi was found in ruins. Here his guide stopped; but being invited by an Arab to cure an ophthalmy under which he laboured, Dr Seetzen negociated, in return, the means of pursuing his route. Passing the ridge of savage mountains which forms the eastern boundary of Palestine, and separates it from Dschaulan, he came in view of the lake of Tiberias. The town of Tiberiade or Tabaria was now small, though the remains of the ancient city extended for a mile westward to some warm baths erected by Dsjezzar. The fine plain surrounding this lake was almost entirely neglected, and though it abounded in fish, only one paltry fishing bark was found at Tabaria. The whole fishery on the lake is farmed to one man, who uses only the seine.

Dr Seetzen now reached the southern boundary of this sea; and, crossing the Jordan, made his way into the district of El Botthin. Here he found the rocks hollowed into thousands of caverns, which had served as abodes to the ancient inhabitants. Even the present houses are chiefly grottos enclosed with walls; so that the interior is partly rock and partly masonry. There were still also a considerable number of large caves, which received whole families with all their cattle. Dr Seetzen was driven by a storm of rain to seek shelter in one of them for the night. He entered by a long passage, and found part of the family at one end busied in preparing supper. There was then a good deal of vacant space; but when the rest came in, with all their flocks and herds, little elbow room was left. Dr Seetzen describes himself as a good deal *inquieté* at making his first address to these wild inhabitants of the rocks; but he met with much hospitality, and found them quite as courteous and intelligent as those who dwelt in more civilized mansions. Dr Seetzen next proceeded to Mkes, the ancient Gadara. He found considerable remains of marble pillars, edifices, bas reliefs, sarcophagi, &c. Near it were several very extensive caverns, in which five or six families were lodged. He then made his way to Abila, once a city of great fame, now entirely ruined. There was not a single edifice standing; huge fragments and rubbish alone attested its ancient importance. His next visit was to Dscherrasch, the ancient Gerasa; the ruins of which are compared to those of Balbec and Palmyra. He found several palaces, two superb amphitheatres built of marble, and three temples, one of which had a peristyle of twelve large Corinthian columns, eleven of which were still erect. But the finest thing he saw was a long street, bordered on each side with a row of Corinthian columns of marble, and terminating in a semicircular open space, surrounded with sixty Ionic columns. On the whole, he counted nearly two hundred pillars supporting their entablatures, and a much greater number overthrown; yet he saw only half the city, not being able to examine the ruins on the other side of the river. He now passed the Serka into the district of El Belka, the ancient seat of the Amorites; but this country, once so populous and flourishing, was now converted into a vast desert. It contained only one small town called Szalt, situated on the declivity of a hill. Six leagues to the east he found the ruins of Amman, the ancient Philadelphia, one of the principal cities of Decapolis. It contained remains, on a great scale, of all the buildings that usually adorned an ancient city; particularly a very spacious temple, with pillars forming a rotunda, on the top of the mountain on which it was built.

After traversing this district, Dr Seetzen entered that of Karrak, the ancient country of the Moabites. He saw the ruins of its capital Rabbath Moab, the extent of which announced its importance. He remarked only some walls and two marble pillars of the Corinthian order belonging to an ancient temple. The district of Karrak is full of mountains, and the town itself is seated on a very high one, commanded by others still higher, and commanding a very fine view of the Dead Sea and Jerusalem. Dr Seetzen turned the southern side of the Dead Sea, by a track so rugged and difficult, that he could scarcely find a guide to accompany him. He saw here a mountain three leagues in length, composed entirely of *sal gem*, the continual dissolution of which appeared to him the source of the saline character of this great lake. Its western coast is all bristling with lofty and barren rocks. The water is clear and limpid, and as salt as the sea; but the assertions, that iron swims upon it, that light substances sink to the bottom, and that birds flying over it fall down dead, are rejected as fabulous. The inhabitants were not sensible of any thing particularly noxious in its vapours. After making thus the tour of the lake, Dr Seetzen proceeded to Bethlehem and Jerusalem, and from thence to Jaffa.

THE late able and lamented BURCKHARDT, in preparing himself to explore the interior of Africa, performed several journeys, the full narrative of which has not yet been published. In the memoir of his life, however, is inserted a letter containing the sketch of a tour, which in some degree followed the footsteps of Seetzen. He spent some time at Damascus, and confirms the observation of Dr Clarke, that this city, with its Pachalic, were in a much more flourishing condition than either that of Aleppo on one side, or of Acre on the other. This was due to the paternal government of Yusuf Pacha, who had ruled it for four years. That chief was, however, so far avaricious, that he uniformly preferred to retain the revenue in his own treasury, rather than re-mit it to Constantinople. The Porte, finding him inveterate in his attachment to this system, conferred the Pachalic on Soleiman, from whom they expected greater regard to their authority. Yusuf's economy having prevented him from taking any effectual measures to secure adherents, he was driven out almost without a struggle. The new Pacha, who holds also Acre, though bred under Dsjezzar, is said to be by no means a bad man. The Syrian desert is now completely in the power of the Wahabis, who carry their excursions even to the gates of Damascus. Yusuf had set out one year with the caravan in the accustomed military array; but on approaching Mecca, found himself surrounded by a much greater Wahabi force. Their chief, Ibn Saoud, gave notice that he and his attendants might repair to Mecca unarmed and as common pilgrims, but not in any other manner. Yusuf, not chusing either to comply with this offer or to encounter the Wahabi, returned without accomplishing his pilgrimage, which has never since been attempted.

Burckhardt, having left Damascus, proceeded by Saffad to the lake of Tiberias, then ascended the Tabor, and having visited Nazareth, crossed the Jordan to Szalt. He visited the ruins of Amman (Philadelphia); but does not conceive them equal to those of Dscherrasch. He proceeded in two days and a half to Karrak, which he calls Kerek, and describes as the seat of a chief who acts a leading part in the deserts of the south of Syria. He traced the valley of Ghor, fertile though uncultivated, extending from the lake of Tiberias to the southern side of the Dead Sea. Thence, under the name of Araba, it stretches to the eastern branch of the Arabian Gulf, and is probably the track by which Solomon carried on his communication with Eziongeber. At some distance eastward, in a valley called Wady Mousa, he found extensive ruins, which appear to be those of Petra, the great commercial capital of Idumea. There were two hundred and fifty tombs, and one entire amphitheatre, cut in the rock ;—one mausoleum, which had the appearance of an elegant Grecian temple, while other monuments bore an Egyptian character. A place was shewn here as the tomb of Aaron. Burckhardt passed through the valley of Akaba to the head of the Red Sea, and then entered upon the desert of El Ty, which he describes as the most horrid and barren tract he had ever seen. In ten days, during which time only four wells were found, he arrived at Cairo.

# CHAPTER V.

## ARABIA.

*Niebuhr.—Valentia.—Seetzen.—Badhia.*

ARABIA is not a country much resorted to by European travellers. Its interior, composed in a great measure of deserts, presents nothing sufficiently attractive to balance the dangers with which it is beset; while the approach to its holy cities is rigidly barred against every Christian. The travels of Barthema, recounted in the second Book, will give the idea of its interior at an early period; while the adventures of Sir Henry Middleton illustrate the condition of its coasts under the Turkish sway. We shall now, therefore, proceed to NIEBUHR, to whom we are mainly indebted for what we know of this part of the Arabic continent.

NIEBUHR, with several companions, was officially employed upon a scientific mission by the Danish government to explore Arabia. He set out with a caravan from Cairo on the 27th August 1762. On the 30th they arrived at Suez, a city built since the end of the fifteenth century, in the room of Kolzium, formerly the emporium of the Red Sea, which by the Arabic writers was called "the Sea of Kolzium," and the ruins of which are still seen at a little distance. Suez is a thinly inhabited, poorly built place; the chief employment of whose inhabitants is the conveyance of corn and pilgrims to Jidda, the port of Mecca. The soil is a bed of rock, sprinkled with sand; and bad water can be procured only at the distance of two or three leagues.

Niebuhr set out from Suez in search of the Jibbel Mokatteb, or Hill of Inscriptions, reported to exist in some part of the bordering deserts. The Arabs at first professed total ignorance on the subject; but on the offer of a liberal reward, a person was found who offered to conduct him to the hill. He departed first for Sinai, through a country in general stony, but in some places well watered and fertile. On the declivity of Mount Sinai they found still the convent of St Catherine, which the vicinity of the Arabs converts into a species of prison. Both men and provisions are let up and down in a basket; and an excellent garden belonging to the convent is entered by a subterraneous passage. The Arabs often shoot at the monks from the rocks above; and if they can seize any of the straggling brethren, release him only upon payment of a liberal ransom. Niebuhr had seen some inscriptions on the rocks in this journey, but merely names and some rude figures, without any value or beauty. At length he was led to Jibbel Mokatteb; on ascending which he found a number of sepulchral stones covered with hieroglyphics and busts, which were evidently Egyptian. He was proceeding to copy the inscriptions, when the Arabs interposed, intimating their conviction that these, in the hands of Europeans, possessed supernatural powers, and were intended to draw hidden treasures from the bowels of the earth. They insisted that they should either receive immediately a hundred crowns down, or be entitled to a share of all the wealth which the inscriptions should evoke. Why our author should have rejected this latter alternative, does not very precisely appear; but he chose rather to bribe an individual Arab, and privily copy some of the hieroglyphics, which were found to differ little from those of Egypt, except in exhibiting the goat, an animal unknown in that country.

Preparing to sail down the Red Sea, Mr Niebuhr returned to Suez, which, in consequence of the arrival of some great caravans, appeared as populous as Cairo. The ships sailed usually in small fleets, to aid each other in danger, which was imminent, as they sailed close to the shore amid reefs and coral rocks, and guided the vessel in the most unskilful manner. A number of females on board too repeatedly set fire to the linen which they were drying, till the captain caused them to be heartily beaten. They passed by the ancient Tor, but found its port in ruins, though there were in its neighbourhood some considerable villages. They did not thence see any inhabited place till they arrived at Jambo, the port of Medina, where they landed the passengers destined for that sacred place, and sailed into Jidda. They were in much apprehension of ill treatment here, both from general report, and their experience at Jambo; but they were agreeably disappointed to find that they attracted little notice, and were in no degree molested. On learning that they understood astronomy, synonymous in the East with astrology, the governor craved earnestly to know from them the success of a war in which he was about to engage. Niebuhr candidly professed his ignorance of the future; but his companion, Von Haven, gratified the governor by a favourable prediction. Jidda supports itself by transporting pilgrims and provisions to Mecca, and by being the channel of trade between India and Suez. The most violent measures are taken against all vessels which dare to proceed to the latter port without touching at Jidda. Wishing to proceed to Hodeida, they were recommended to a Maskat ship, which, however, when surveyed, appeared more like a hogshead than a ship; the planks thin, without pitch, and navigated by a few naked black slaves. Their friends, however, advised them not to stickle at appearances, as the Maskat Arabs were good sailors. Accordingly, though their accommodation was somewhat defective, they proceeded slowly but safely along a coast as desert as that between Suez and Jidda. On arriving at Loheia, Niebuhr was surprised to find the Arabs becoming always more polished and courteous. The people were here particularly curious and intelligent. Being acquainted only with the Europeans as merchants, the arrival of a physician, botanist, and star-gazer, was an agreeable novelty. The governor invited them to make some stay, and assured them that they might travel in perfect safety through every part of the dominions of the Imam. A country chief, however, being asked to dine with them, replied, "God forbid "that I should eat with infidels that believe not "in God."

The travellers set out along the Tehama, or sea coast of Yemen, where they found journeying as safe as in England; and were only annoyed by the moving sand, which covered some parts of the tract. They found Beit-el-Fakih, a recent city, which had risen to importance through the filling up of the harbour of Ghalefka. This last circumstance had ruined Zebid, once the most commercial city in the Tehama. It was now cruelly oppressed by the large religious establishments formed during its prosperity, and which absorbed three-fifths of its reduced income. Hodeida was at present the port of Beit-el-Fakih, and had a tolerable harbour. Niebuhr now set out on an excursion to Kahhme and Hadie, among the coffee mountains. The rocks here were entirely basaltic, and usually formed into columns, which served as props to the coffee trees, and had often the appearance of artificial supports to the cascades which dashed from their summits. The coffee plantations diffused the most delicious perfume; and some, which were artificially watered, yielded two crops in the year. In the course of a subsequent excursion through another part of the mountainous district, he passed through the small towns of Udden and Dsjoble, but found the country on the whole thinly inhabited. Mr Forskal, the botanist, passed with the natives as searching for plants to be employed in making gold; while Niebuhr's observations on the heavens procured him the fame of a magician.

After these excursions, our party set out for Mokha. They were first mortified by being obliged to dismount from their asses, and walk into this city. They then addressed themselves to a merchant called Salek Ismael, who proved to make it his business to prey upon strangers; and who, not succeeding with them to his wish, did them all the injury in his power. On going to the custom-house, they found all their goods opened out, and very roughly handled. The strongest suspicion was excited by the preserved fishes and serpents, any lawful object for collecting which appeared beyond all comprehension. The spirits in which they were kept formed an article equally profane and odious; while the smell issuing from them, and spreading through the house, gave the most unfavourable impressions. At length it was suggested, that, being doctors, their object must have been to poison the Dola; which appearing highly probable, that officer flew into the most violent rage, caused them to be turned out of the house, and the door to be shut upon them. At the same time they learned, that all their books and effects had been thrown from the windows of their lodgings into the street. They wandered about for a long time, finding every door shut upon them; but at length, through the favour of the Cadi and of an English merchant, got themselves accommodation. Being advised then to wait upon the Dola with a present of fifty ducats, they very unwillingly made up their minds to take the advice. They found then all his wrath evaporated, were kindly received, and had all their effects restored. They were even raised to favour by a wound in the foot which he happened to receive, and for which he solicited their surgical aid. This, however, led to an inconvenient result, as the cure proved tedious, and, till it was completed, the Dola evaded all their solicitations to visit Sana. It afforded much gratification, therefore, when a quack came forward, and undertook, upon receiving the sole charge, to perfect the cure in eight days. They then came to Täas, a large city, surrounded by mountains, said to be the most productive in the world of plants, of which Mr Forskal had only a tantalizing view, as the governor of Täas was in a hostile position as to the ruling Schicchs, and would permit no one to visit their territories. They came next to Jerim, a small town, where they had the misfortune of losing Mr Forskal. Passing then through Damar, Manahhel, and Suradje, they arrived at Sana. At a villa of the Vizier's without the gates they were desired to alight, and fully expected to be introduced to him, but found it was only with a view to the humiliating arrangement of their walking into the town, while their Mussulman servants rode. The Imam, however, sent a present of five sheep, and soon admitted them to a public audience. He was found in a hall, the approach to which was so crowded with courtiers, officers, and horses, that they could with difficulty make their way. He was seated cross-legged on cushions; and allowed them, by peculiar favour, to kiss both the back and palm of his hand, when all present cried aloud, "God preserve the "Imam." The conversation, as it could be carried on only by interpreters, was not very interesting; and they took their departure with the same ceremonies. On returning home they received a present of ninety-nine small coins, the entire value of which was 7s. 6d. neither a very valuable nor genteel donation; however, they were willing to suppose that it was only to obviate the inconvenience of wanting change.

Sana is not a very large city, as it can be walked round in the space of an hour; and within this circuit there are many gardens. The ordinary houses are built of unburnt bricks; but there are several mosques, and many noble palaces, the materials of which are burnt bricks, and sometimes hewn stones. The neighbourhood abounds with gardens, and has been compared to Damascus, but is not nearly so well watered.

From Sana Niebuhr returned to Mocha, whence he sailed for India. The rest of his work is spent in an elaborate description of that extensive part of Asia which he was sent to survey.

The general and almost proverbial character of Arabia is sterility. Although this feature may have been somewhat exaggerated, yet stony mountains and sandy plains form the prominent features in the surface of this vast peninsula. To the north, it shoots out into a very extensive desert, the character of which is entirely Arabian, and which remains interposed between Syria and the countries on the Euphrates. The whole coast of Arabia, from Suez to the head of the Persian Gulf, is formed of a plain called the Tehama, which presents a picture of the most complete desolation. The interior is diversified by extensive ranges of mountains, the declivities of which are covered with trees and shrubs; while the intervening valleys, being watered by copious streams, are capable of advantageous culture. In agriculture, though the implements used by the Arabs be rude, yet a greater degree of industry is displayed than by most of their neighbours. In many parts of Yemen the fields are cultivated like gardens. The supply of water is insufficient for rice, so that barley, millet, and dhourra, are the grains chiefly raised. The Arabian hills are distinguished by some fragrant plants; the coffee, the balm of Mecca, and the tree bearing incense, though this last is produced of much superior quality in the opposite coast of Africa. The coffee of Yemen, so eagerly sought for over t' whole globe, is despised in its native spot. An infusion of its husks is the only form in which it is valued.

The pastoral life is the prevailing one in Arabia; and its pride, as to production, consists in its animals. The horse, the camel, and the ass, seem to be here in their native place, and are in greater perfection than in any other country. Nothing can exceed the care taken in training, and particularly in breeding their horses. Their pedigree is counted as carefully as that of their masters, being often traced as far back as 2000 years. Nor is this so liable as might be supposed to deception, being authenticated by written documents; and though the Arabs are generally addicted to perjury, yet this is a subject of such awful importance, that upon it they have scarcely ever been known to prevaricate. A horse of high birth will sell from 800 to 1000 crowns. Swiftness and lightness are the characteristics of the Arabian steed, while the Turks prefer those of greater strength and bulk. The camel is too well known to require description. The ass of Arabia is a very superior animal to that despised race which we are accustomed to view. It is large, handsome, and spirited. Niebuhr even considers it better fitted for travelling than the horse.

Arabia supports a race of men entirely characteristic of itself, and different from those who inhabit all the other countries of Asia. These peculiarities are best seen among the Bedouins, who inhabit the heart of the desert, and hold little communication with any other people. They live in the most simple manner in tents composed of coarse stuffs, and which have the aspect of tattered huts, with an apartment in front for the men, and one behind for the females. Almost the only furniture consists of the carpet or mat upon which they sit. Their food is composed of dates, millet, and dhourra, with the milk of their camels; and from taste or necessity they are temperate in the extreme. The Schiechs, or chiefs of the Arabians, are distinguished by a pride of birth elsewhere unknown in the East, and resembling what was felt in Europe during the highest pride of the feudal ages. They have regular tables of genealogy, extending backwards for many centuries, and tracing their origin either to Mahomet, or to some earlier Arabian chiefs. Their nobility is the more valued, as it rests upon birth alone, and cannot be conferred by the fiat of any prince. Niebuhr compares them to the heads of clans in the Scotch Highlands. Bedouin honour is still more delicate than that of an European noble. If one says seriously to another, "Thy bonnet is dirty," or "The wrong side "of thy turban is out," nothing but blood can wash away the reproach. The right of private vengeance is fully recognized; and is prosecuted not only against the offender, but against all his family. There is indeed a price fixed for blood; but to accept this is considered much less honourable than to demand blood for blood; and a family feud is thus often transmitted through several generations.

The female sex in Arabia enjoy greater freedom than in other Mahometan countries. The precept allowing polygamy remains a dead letter both with the lower and middling classes, and even some of the most opulent consider one wife as quite sufficient. Neither is it true that the father sells his daughter, and the husband his wife; or that the sex are generally slaves. The jealous guardianship of eunuchs is unknown; and the Arab women have repeatedly shewn themselves to travellers, unveiled, without any displeasure on the part of their husbands.

The vast expanse of Arabia is generally divided among a number of independent tribes, or clans, each governed in an aristocratic manner by its own Schiech. Confederacies are often formed among these for mutual defence; but there seems to be no instance of what can properly be called a republican form. There are three districts however; those of Mecca and its dependencies, of Yemen, and of Ommon, where a denser population gives occasion to form pretty large principalities. These are ruled on an arbitrary, though somewhat unsettled and irregular footing; the first by Sheriffes, and the two last by Imams. The late rise of the Wahabi power, of which more particular notice will presently be taken, has united the whole interior of Arabia under one religious and military head, though it has probably left unaltered the division into clans, and the internal administration.

In the course of Lord Valentia's visit to the Red Sea in 1804, he spent some time at Mocha. That port was somewhat declined, though it still continued to be the great mart for coffee. That trade, within a few years, had taken a new direction, in consequence of the interference of American traders. Instead of being carried up the Red Sea, and distributed by the way of Alexandria, it was now taken off by them and carried round by the maritime route of the Cape. Their competition had raised the price from thirty-six or forty to fifty dollars. The India Company, by this means, was entirely driven out of the market, as they could not import a bale of coffee under L.10, while the Americans brought it to Europe at L.7. The entire quantity exported is estimated at 16,000 bales of 305 lbs. each. Mocha exports also some gum-arabic, myrrh, and frankincense, brought from the opposite coast of Berbera; but Aoben absorbs the greater part of this trade. The present population of Mocha is not estimated at more than 5000. The bordering plain of the Tehama is as barren and dreary as it is possible to conceive. The researches of Mr Pringle tended to confirm the belief of its having formerly been the bed of the sea, as, on digging to a little depth, the strata were found entirely composed of marine productions. The power of the Imam was then visibly on the decline, as the Sheriffe of Abon-arish, who was attached to the new sect of the Wahabi, had obtained possession of Loheia, and was endeavouring to make it a seat of the coffee trade.

The Wahabi were found by Lord Valentia masters of almost all Arabia. This sect originated about forty years before, and is mentioned by Niebuhr; but since that time has been continually gaining new strength. It may be considered as a reform in the Mussulman faith. It recognizes the unity of the Deity, and the genuineness of the Koran, but rejects all the traditions and all the worship paid to the successors of Mahommed. Its military chief, Ibn Saoud, has been the great instrument in its propagation. The most memorable era was in the 27th April 1803, when Saoud entered Mecca, and destroyed eighty splendid tombs, erected in honour of the descendants of Mahommed. In 1804 they took Medina; and the two holy cities have ever since continued in possession of the Wahabis. They do not, however, discourage pilgrimage, unless by prohibiting the approach of any armed body, and the use of certain rites which they regard as superstitious. They are now masters of all the interior of Arabia, and of part of the sea coast; and are supposed able to muster an army of 120,000 men. Although these are inferior in discipline even to the Turkish troops, yet, in the present distracted state of that empire, they cannot fail to be very formidable enemies to it.

Dr Seetzen having assumed the real or feigned character of a Mahometan, conceived himself in a condition to undertake a tour into the interior of Arabia. He took a passage in a vessel at Suez, where there were a number of other pilgrims destined for Mecca. Before reaching Jidda, they came in view of a village called Rabog, when the ceremony took place of putting on the *ehhram*. This is the pilgrim's dress, consisting of two large white cloths, wrapped one round the middle, and the other over the shoulders; previous to which, they shave the head, and wash the whole body with sea-water. Thus transformed into pilgrims, they begin to cry aloud *Lubbaik*, *allahoumme Lubbaik*, an ancient form of prayer, which Dr Seetzen suspects of being appropriated to Bacchus. Arrived at Jidda, he placed himself under the protection of a Moorish merchant, and found the road to Mecca perfectly safe. After having passed the plain of the Tehama, the rest of this way led among mountains chiefly composed of granite. On arriving at Mecca, he hired a *mottaouf* or guide, who soon conducted him to the holy temple. He found it composing a most majestic square, 300 feet by 200, and surrounded with a triple or quadruple row of columns. The houses of the town rose above it, and the surrounding mountains high above them, so that he felt as in the arena of a magnificent theatre. He went through the ceremonies very quietly at that time, but some time after had an opportunity of seeing the Kaaba encircled by more than a thousand pilgrims, Arabs from every province, Moors, Persians, Afghans, and natives of all countries of the East. In their euthusiastic zeal to kiss the black stone, they rushed pell-mell in confused crowds, so that our author was very apprehensive that some of them must have been suffocated. This religious tumult, with the multitude and various aspect of the groupes, presented the most extraordinary spectacle he ever beheld.

From Mecca Dr Seetzen proceeded to Medina, which he found surrounded by a wall and governed by a Wahabite Emir. The country round was entirely composed of a porous lava, whence he inferred that it must have been formerly exposed to the action of volcanic fires. He does not describe the sacred mosque in such glowing terms as Barthema; though he says it is a considerable edifice, with many pillars of marble, jasper, and porphyry, adorned in different places with letters of gold. The Wahabis do not admit pilgrimage unless to Mecca; Dr Seetzen was therefore arraigned before the Emir, who, however, on learning that he was a Frank, dismissed him without farther question.

On returning to Jidda, Dr Seetzen sailed down the Red Sea. Avoiding Comfodah, which was become a resort of Wahabi pirates, he touched at Massuah, and sailed thence to Hodeida. He found all the ports of Yemen subjected by the Sheriff of Abou-Arish, except Mocha, whose walls are considered impregnable by an Arab army. Travelling, however, was still as secure in Yemen as in the streets of London. He penetrated without difficulty to Sana, which he calls Szana. He thought it the prettiest city in the East. Its houses are high, and built of stone; and if the streets were better cleaned and kept, it might rank with some of the best cities in Europe. An ancient Arabic author calls it Asel, whence he suspects it to be the city mentioned under that name in the sacred Scriptures.

Badhia, a Spanish traveller, has published, under the fictitious name of Ali Bey, the narrative of a journey to Mecca, the general correctness of which is confirmed by Burckhardt. He set sail from Suez, and gives a most formidable description of the dangers of navigating down the Red Sea. There are continual rocks either above or under water, so that four men watch constantly at the helm to give the alarm; and if their call be either omitted or mistaken, the ship is dashed to pieces. We know not whether our author's fears did not a little overrate the peril. Being overtaken one night by a storm, when the Captain declaring himself unable to guide the vessel, and burst into tears, Badhia hurried with a few of the passengers into a boat, and by gigantic exertions reached the land. Being thrown, however, on an island of sand, where there was neither food nor habitation, he was in deep perplexity, till the weather clearing up, the ship was seen lying out at sea in perfect safety; and he had only to return to it after this perilous attempt at escape. The port of Jidda was found flourishing, containing 5000 inhabitants. Under the disguise of a pilgrim, he made his way to Mecca, at a period distinguished by the arrival of a part of the Wahabi army to pay their devotions at the holy shrine. They amounted to 5 or 6000, were naked except a bit of cloth round the middle, bore matchlocks on their shoulders, and large knives in their girdle, but had neither flags nor drums. The tumultuary rushing of this crowd of militant devotees to kiss the black stone, presented a spectacle of still wilder confusion than that witnessed by Seetzen. They endeavoured also to procure an effusion of the holy water of Zemzen; but the rush was so terrible, that in a few minutes the ropes, pullies and buckets, were all destroyed. The next observance was the pilgrimage to Mount Arafat, which presented a singular scene at the hour of sunset, the signal for the whole body to return towards Mecca. Yet notwithstanding the immense and confused crowd, no disorder was committed, and though the Wahabis were all armed, only one shot was discharged by accident.

Mecca is described by Badhia to have suffered deeply from the diminution of pilgrimage, which has ensued, partly from the general decay of Mussulman zeal, partly from the dread of the arms of the Wahabi. The greater part of its houses are unoccupied, and instead of 100,000 inhabitants, it is not now supposed to contain above 16 or 18,000. Mecca makes a handsomer appearance than most eastern cities. Its buildings follow the windings of the narrow valley in which it is situated; but they are ranged in regular order, and the streets are sanded, level, and convenient. The houses are very neat, built rather in the Persian and Indian than Turkish style, with stone, and usually three or four stories high; they are externally adorned with paintings and mouldings, and have larger and more open windows than is usual in the East. The inhabitants are careful to preserve this handsome outward appearance, as they derive their subsistence very much from letting apartments to pilgrims. The women are not so rigidly confined as is usual in Mahometan towns, and are supposed not to be altogether inaccessible to amorous devotees. From every pilgrim who is supposed at all opulent, the servants of the temple contrive to extort from seventy to eighty pounds.

Badhia made an attempt also to penetrate to Medina, but was stopped by one of the Wahabi chiefs.

# BOOK V.

## EASTERN ASIA.

## CHAPTER I.

### COUNTRIES BETWEEN INDIA AND CHINA.

*Pegu.—Cæsar Frederick.—Gasparo Balbi.—Symes.—Siam. Missions from France.—Cochin-China.—Borri.—Barrow.*

The region on the east of India, reaching to China and the Eastern Ocean, is occupied by a number of extensive kingdoms, and includes a population of perhaps from fifty to sixty millions. Though thus fertile and populous, however, these countries do not yield any product so valuable and peculiar, or any manufacture carried on to such high perfection, as to become a leading object of European commerce. They do not even present any very prominent or striking forms of social or political existence. For these reasons they have not attracted the notice of European travellers in a degree equal to the place which they occupy on the globe. Although, however, the basis of their institutions be Hindoo and Chinese, and though they nowhere exhibit any forms of civil liberty, their population yet exhibits a more energetic, active, and improving character, than that of the great empires upon which they border; and their social state therefore presents various peculiarities which are worthy of observation.

DURING the sixteenth century Pegu appears to have been the most powerful and formidable of these states, and, by its wealth and splendour, attracted the greatest notice. Soon after the Portuguese had established themselves at Malacca, ANTONIO CORREA, a distinguished naval officer, was despatched with the view of opening a friendly communication with the court of Pegu. He navigated with considerable difficulty in consequence of the violence of the tides upon this coast, but at length entered the river of Pegu, and reached the capital. He found a country composed entirely of rivers, islands, and inundated plains, which were possessed thus of luxuriant fertility. The Portuguese were well received, and obtained permission to establish a factory, but it was soon rendered fruitless by political disasters. The king of the Brammas (Birmans) made war upon Pegu, conquered the whole country, and carried his arms to the gates of Siam. Fernan de Moraes, the Portuguese resident at Pegu, was killed in the sack of the city.

About the middle of the century, Pegu again asserted its independence and greatness. In 1568 it was visited by Cæsar Frederick, when it consisted of two cities, the old and the new, the one destined for the merchants, the other for the court. The houses were "made with canes, and covered with leaves or with straw;" but to avoid the danger of fire incident to "houses made of such stuffe," a large brick building had been erected for containing the merchandise. In the new town the streets were the fairest he had seen, being so broad, that twelve men could ride abreast, and so straight, that you could see from one gate to another. The king's palace resembled a walled castle, gilded all over, and rising into lofty pinnacles. "Truly it may be a king's "house." This monarch calls himself the king of the white elephants, and prizes those animals so highly, that if he knew one to be in the possession of a neighbouring sovereign, he will make war in order to obtain it. He had only four, which were kept in the greatest state, having their meat served in gold and silver dishes, and their feet washed in silver basins. There was also a black elephant, illustrious for its magnitude, being nine cubits high. He relates the mode of taking these animals, which seems to be the same now practised in Ceylon. It is added, "there is not a beast so intellective as these ele-"phants; he lacketh nothing but human speech." The king has four thousand war elephants, who, having wooden castles on their backs, prove the most formidable part of his army. The battle array of this people is, he says, admirable, but their weapons "very naught and weake," the swords being like long knives without points. The infinite number of his troops compensates for any deficiency in their equipments. "There is "not a king on the earth that hath more power "and strength than this King of Pegu." He has twenty-six crowned kings as vassals, and can levy an army of a million and a half. This number, even including all the camp followers, is doubtless exaggerated; but he assures us, that the difficulty of finding subsistence, apparently so formidable, will not weigh much with him "that knoweth the nature of this country and "people." They will eat serpents, scorpions, herbs, grass, and every kind of refuse, "all serv-"eth for their mouthes;" and they require only a few mouthfuls of rice "to serve instead of "comfits."

The commodities chiefly suited to the market of Pegu, were piece goods from the coast of Coromandel, pepper and other spices from the islands. The imported goods are first landed at the port of Casmin, whence they proceed up to Pegu. "God deliver every man that he give "not a wrong entrie, or think to steal custome," for it seems three successive searches are made, and the utmost rigour exercised against those who attempt any evasion. Another danger attends them when "they custome in the great hall of the "king." Then a number of gentlemen are in attendance, with their slaves, whom they regularly employ in pilfering whatever they can lay hold of, without the least shame at being detected, "whether it be cloth, in shewing of it, or "any other thing, they laugh at it." The merchants must therefore act in concert, and watch each other's goods. In trafficking for jewels, however, the most precious and delicate commodity here exposed to sale, they are said to be luckily secure from imposition, even though they do not understand the article. This trade is in the hands of three or four great brokers, who "have always great care that they affoord good "peniworths, especially to those that have no "knowledge." By way of accounting for this miraculous integrity, he states, that every purchaser of jewels is allowed two or three days "to "looke on and peruse them," when if not satisfied, he may annul the bargain, which is considered so great a disgrace, that the brokers are anxious by all means to avoid incurring it. He notices also the silent mode of bargaining mentioned by Tavernier, effected while the hands are covered with a cloth, " by touching of fingers and nipping " of joints. For every joint and every finger " hath his signification."

Our traveller was dazzled by the splendour of the pagodas of Pegu, covered in part, and sometimes entirely, with gold leaf, which must be renewed every ten years. It is remarked, however, that " by this means they make gold dearer in " Pegu than it would be, if they consumed not so " much in this vanitie." He observed several of these gigantic images which are characteristic of the worshippers of Boodh. He saw " a man of " gold very great, with a crowne, and four little " children of gold." There was also " a man of " silver," who surpassed in height the roof of any house, and whose feet were as long as our traveller's whole body. There were besides other " heathenish idols of a very great value."

Gasparo Balbi, who visited Pegu in 1583, found it in nearly the same condition. He had an interview with the King, for the purpose of delivering a present of emeralds. His majesty began inquiring about the King of Venice; and being told there was no king, and that it was a republic, he burst into a fit of laughter so immoderate, as made him for a long time unable to speak. Being engaged in a quarrel with his uncle the King of Ava, who was supposed to aim at dethroning him, and suspecting his nobles to be in the interest of his adversary, he collected them all, with their wives and children, to the number of four thousand, and causing them to be placed on "an eminent and spacious scaffold," ordered his officers to set fire to it. Our author was present, and saw it "with great compassion and "grief, that little children, without any fault, "should suffer such martyrdom." The King then set out with a great force to attack his rival, whom he defeated with immense slaughter, and killed in single combat.

During the two following centuries these countries attracted little attention, till circumstances occurred which brought them again into view. The Birmans, after being a considerable time subject to Pegu, rallying under the auspices of Alompra, not only reasserted their own independence, but conquered that country, to which they added the fertile region of Arracan, bordering on the Bay of Bengal. Some Arracan pirates, who had become obnoxious to the Birman laws, having sought refuge in the British territories, a Birman force, despatched to seize them, entered the eastern frontier of Bengal. This encroachment appearing to call for notice, a British force was immediately marched to the same point. A representation being then made to the Birman commander, he stated the above as the only cause of his having passed the frontier. To this it was replied, that the offenders would be sought out and delivered up, but that he must retire within the limits of his own country. He acquiesced, and the British government acting faithfully its part, the culprits were delivered up, and suffered condign punishment. The Birman empire being thus brought into notice, Sir John Shore, the governor-general, conceived that a commercial intercourse with it might at once afford an opening for British commodities, and a supply of teak timber, the value of which for ship building began to be appreciated. A mission was therefore despatched, composed of Major Symes, Dr Francis Buchanan, and Mr Wood, who set sail from Calcutta, and landed at Rangoon.

Rangoon was found by the embassy a considerable town, containing 5000 houses, and probably about 30,000 inhabitants. It is a sort of general asylum for insolvent debtors, who all find here employment, protection, and some petty trade, that will afford them a subsistence. In the efforts which the government was making to re-establish it after the desolation occasioned by civil wars, the services of intelligent foreigners, even of the lowest rank, were heartily welcomed. The most important offices about the port were held by Baba Sheen, a very intelligent Armenian, and Jaunsee, a Portuguese. The increasing trade and population of the town had extended it considerably beyond the limits originally fixed by Alompra. The streets are narrow, and annoyed with herds of swine, and a set of noisy little dogs; but they are clean, and well paved. The houses of the principal inhabitants are within a fortified space, the defences of which, however, are in a very poor condition.

From Rangoon the embassy proceeded by water to Pegu, through a country bearing marks of former culture and population, but almost reduced to a desert by the wars of which it had been the theatre. This capital, which the early travellers saw in all its glory, had subsequently been plunged into a state of ruin, from which it was just beginning to emerge. The reigning sovereign, impelled, as Dr Buchanan understood, by a superstitious impression from a dream, but Major Symes thinks by a wish to conciliate his Pegu subjects, had determined to restore their ancient seat of empire. A very elegant plan of a town had therefore been formed, covering about half the former site; but it was difficult to find inhabitants, as the princes and chiefs who had composed the former splendour of Pegu were either extinct or dispersed, and the merchants were unwilling to remove from the more convenient situation of Rangoon. Pegu, however, still retained its brightest ornament, the temple of Shoemadoo, or the Golden Supreme, which the piety of Alompra had spared when he razed every other edifice to the ground. It is raised upon two terraces, one side of the exterior one being 1391 feet in length. The body of the edifice is of a pyramidal form, very rapidly diminishing in breadth as it ascends; at the top is an ornamented spire, surmounted by a tee or umbrella fifty-six feet high. The whole structure has much the appearance of a large speaking trumpet. The ornaments are light, showy, and fluttering, but without that dignity and true taste which characterizes classic architecture. The height from the ground is 361 feet; and the whole is entirely solid, without any sort of aperture or excavation. The umbrella is gilded, and the King held out some idea of gilding the whole of the spire.

The embassy were well received both by the Maywoon or viceroy, and by the inhabitants in general. The latter shewed an extreme but courteous and peaceable curiosity. The higher classes came to visit them with very little ceremony, sometimes asking permission at the door, and sometimes not. They merely entered the outer hall, however, and seated themselves on the floor with their legs inverted, without attempting to penetrate into the inner apartments, or touching any thing; and when asked to depart, cheerfully acquiesced. The English found every house open to themselves on the same footing. They happened to arrive on the eve of a great annual festival, which many came from a great distance to attend. The display on the first day consisted of wrestling and pugilism, in the first of which they excelled much more than in the last; on the second, in fire-works, chiefly rockets, enclosed in hollow trunks of trees six or eight feet long, which made a very grand display. The crowd was immense, and the hilarity unbounded; yet there was not the least disorder, nor a single instance of intoxication. Some days after a drama was performed, exhibiting scenes from the Ramayana. Major Symes extols very highly both the dialogue and acting, and conceives that one of the performers could have rivalled any in Britain. Dr Buchanan's criticism is more severe. He admits indeed the unbounded mirth excited in the natives; but states, that the little he was able to understand gave him a very low idea of the sources from which it arose. On the 12th April, being the last day of the Birman year, they were invited to the Maywoon's, to pass through the appropriate ceremony of that day. This consisted in a sort of contest maintained between the sexes, by copiously bedewing each other with cold water. On arriving at the palace, they found standing in the hall three large china jars, duly provided with bowls and ladles. The Maywoon's lady stated her intention to take no part in the proceedings; but in her stead there issued forth about twenty damsels, who surrounded the party, and sprinkled them, to their own infinite amusement, with the most copious libations. The English endeavoured to return the compliment; but the odds was so fearful, that they could make little impression on the numerous band of assailants. In returning home, they found the streets covered with parties engaged in the same amusement, which was practised not indeed upon them, but liberally upon their Birman companions. The whole was conducted with perfect decency, and perfect good humour.

From Pegu the embassy returned to Rangoon; and after a short residence there obtained permission to proceed to the Birman capital of Ummerapoora. They sailed up the great river Irawaddy, the banks of which were in general highly cultivated, and crowded with people, and its stream covered with numerous barks. They passed many villages and towns, of which the principal were Prome, Meeaday, Loonghee, and Pagahm. They took in passing a hasty view of Ava, which had till of late been the splendid capital of the empire.

It presented a complete picture of desolation. On the first order to transfer the seat of empire to Ummerapoora, the inhabitants had taken up their houses of wood and bamboo, and carried them to the new city; and Ava became at once a desert. The walls, the palace, the council-hall, and many of the streets, could still be traced, but all in ruins. They looked into two large buildings, which had been destined for the reception of strangers; bats flew in their faces, and a noisome smell issued from them. Thorns, bamboos, and plantain trees, occupied most of the area of this once great capital. The temples alone, through the reverence invariably paid to them by the Birmans, stood still untouched, but time was working their rapid decay.

After leaving this gloomy scene of departed greatness, the embassy sailed upwards, and had their eyes soon greeted with the magnificent spires and turrets of Ummerapoora, which appeared on the opposite side of an extensive but temporary lake, formed by the overflowing of the river. The King happening to be absent, they were accommodated with lodgings in the village of Tounzemahn, situated on the southern bank of the lake, while the capital was on the northern. The wide watery scene, the furious dashing of the waves, the numerous boats moored to the banks, with the fort and city of Ummerapoora, surrounded by an amphitheatre of lofty mountains, formed altogether a striking and singular landscape. It was hinted that it would be considered neither decorous nor dignified to be seen in public previous to their presentation, but that they might gratify their love of exercise by riding out, as privately as possible, towards the hills. All their wants were liberally supplied, and the King having returned in a short time, fixed a day for their public audience. Some objection was made to the admission of Dr Buchanan, the medical character not being duly estimated here; but as this point was insisted upon, they agreed to admit him, though not to mount him on an elephant.

On the morning of the appointed day, the embassy came down to the lake, where they found three war boats which conveyed them in twenty minutes to the opposite side. Here an elephant was ready to receive Major Symes; but as he had announced his inaptitude, according to the custom of the country, to mount on its neck and take his seat between the ears, a wicker basket had been placed on its back and fastened with iron chains, an apparatus which struck him as not so elegant as could be wished. The two other gentlemen were mounted on little active Birman horses, well caparisoned. They now entered into a broad and handsome street paved with brick, with low wooden houses, which, in honour of the occasion, had been white-washed and decorated with boughs and flowers. The streets and tops of the houses were covered with a vast multitude, who, however, kept the strictest order, leaving room for the procession to move, and whenever it came in sight, squatting on their hams in sign of respect. Thus they proceeded through the city for two miles, when they arrived at the fortress, which enclosed the royal palace, and the abodes of the principal grandees. Being defended by a thick rampart, twenty feet high, it was boasted of by the Birmans as impregnable; and Major Symes did not chuse to mortify their pride by telling them, that half a dozen cannon would in a few hours make it a heap of ruins. Proceeding through several streets, they were ushered into the rhoom or outer saloon, where they were instructed to remain till the princes of the blood had entered. The King's five sons successively passed, the youngest first, and the Engy Teekien, or heir-apparent, last; each attended by large trains becoming always more numerous and splendid according to their birth and dignity. If less magnificence was displayed than in the court of imperial Delhi, there was more dignity and decorum. The embassy, however, was detained two hours, which appeared somewhat tedious, especially as there were some deficiences of respect in the attendance. Being then invited to enter, they passed through an inner court, where bands of tumblers and dancing girls were exhibiting their feats. They were then ushered by a flight of stairs into the lotoo or great hall, where the court was assembled in all the pomp of Birman grandeur. It was supported by seventy-seven gilded pillars, arranged in eleven rows; while at the end a high gilded lattice extended quite across the building. In the centre was a gilded door, which, when opened, displayed the throne. All the princes and grandees of the empire were seated with inverted legs on the floor of this magnificent saloon. A place was reserved for the mission, but they in vain strove to comply with the request to place themselves in the proper Birman posture, and not protrude the soles of their feet towards the seat of majesty. They were seriously disappointed, however, by the King not making his appearance. An officer merely went between them and the royal seat, and put several questions as from his majesty, which when they had answered, a handsome desert was brought in, consisting of about a hundred small dishes, several of which were tasted and proved very palatable. The court then broke up, and the princes departed successively in the same pomp as they had entered.

The ambassador was afterwards invited to wait upon the different princes of the blood. Major

Symes, however, made some stipulations as to a more respectful treatment, which were tolerably complied with. The ceremony and pomp were almost equal at the court of the Engy Teekien, as at that of the monarch. He appeared at a window, and sat for a quarter of an hour erect and motionless, when suddenly the shutters were closed, and he was seen no more. The courts of the younger princes were less ceremonious and more gay. They were led through files of elephants, and entertained with exhibitions of tumblers and dancing girls. They had also an audience of the queen, an old lady of seventy-two, who received them in a very complaisant manner. Hopes were then entertained of a successful termination to the embassy; but there was reason to believe, that French emissaries afterwards arrived, and by a false representation of the state of affairs in Europe, gave an unfavourable bias to the mind of the King. The mission were privately informed that he had determined not to grant them a personal audience at their departure, any more than he had done at their first visit. Major Symes being invited to court to receive the presents which were to be given in return for his, took occasion to put a direct question upon this subject, to which an equivocal answer was returned. Neither the queen nor the princes appeared at the delivery of their presents, and the members of the embassy, who waited on them for the purpose, experienced every neglect short of absolute rudeness. Under these circumstances, Major Symes determined to submit to the government a formal representation. He urged his claim to be considered as the representative of a sovereign power, and in that capacity to be treated with a certain ceremonial, and in particular to be honoured with a personal audience of his majesty, announcing his intention, if these rights were withheld, to depart forthwith, throwing up all the arrangements in contemplation for the mutual benefit of the two countries. This memorial was reported to produce a very strong sensation at the Birman court; but after a long consultation it was understood to be determined to grant every thing demanded, rather than come to an open rupture. Being assured, therefore, of such a reception as they desired, they set out on a second visit to court. They were received, not in the lotoo, but in the royal saloon of ceremony, an apartment equally splendid. In about a quarter of an hour, the folding doors which concealed the throne were opened, and the King was seen walking up the steps which led to it from behind. He appeared to move with difficulty, and to want the free use of his limbs, but this they were assured arose solely from the immense weight of gold upon his person, amounting to upwards of fifty pounds. All the courtiers bent their bodies; but the English were only required to lean a little forward, and turn in their seat, so that the soles of their feet might be in no degree directed towards his Majesty. The King merely remained a few minutes, and uttered some indistinct words, investing some one with an order of nobility; after which he departed, without addressing any words to the embassy. There was nothing particularly flattering in this reception; however, as the stipulated terms were not positively infringed, it was not thought expedient to make any complaint. In fact, on receiving the official reply to his demands, Major Symes found, that he had obtained all the essential objects of his mission. British goods were allowed to be imported at a duty of ten per cent *ad valorem*; while teak timber, by far the most valuable production of the Birman empire, might be exported at five per cent. He soon after took his departure, and, sailing down the river, embarked at Rangoon for India.

According to the information collected by Major Symes and Dr Buchanan, the fertility of the Birman territory appears to be very great. The southern provinces are finely watered, and produce as luxuriant crops of rice as the finest parts of Bengal. The northern districts are partly composed of rude mountains, but with rich plains and valleys, in which wheat is raised of excellent quality. This part of the empire yields some gold and silver, and a considerable quantity of diamonds and precious stones. Besides teak timber, the commercial staple of the empire, it contains various other useful woods. The salubrity of the climate is attested by the health and vigour of the natives. The banks of the river were covered with crowded population; and from all they could learn, the whole number of people in the empire could not fall short of seventeen millions.

The Birmans are entirely different in their disposition from the Hindoos. They are bold, active, fiery, enterprising, full of stir and curiosity. They are also a very merry people, always in search of amusement, and not fastidious in its selection. To the embassy they observed uniform courtesy and hospitality, nor did the excess of their curiosity ever show itself in any offensive form. The fair sex in this country are exempted from that restraint and confinement which they suffer generally over the East. Yet they are not, therefore, treated with the respect due to them, but are subjected to severe labour, and often bought and sold almost as slaves. When a stranger goes to reside in Ava, he is accommodated, even from respectable families, with a temporary female companion, who lives with him as his wife, and proves usually a faithful housekeeper, but whom he is on no account permitted to take along with him. There are other particulars of their treatment, which mark still more clearly the very low idea here entertained of the place held by this fair portion of the species.

In Ava, as in all the countries in the east of India, the religion of Boodh or Buddha is fully established. That person, under the names of Gaudma, Goutama, or Godama, is the universal object of worship. He is supposed, however, to administer the affairs of the world only during a certain period, having had predecessors, and being expected to have successors. He is represented as a young man with a placid expression, Birman features, and usually sitting cross-legged on a throne. The temples are commonly in the form of a pyramid with an umbrella at top. Gilding is the ornament most studiously employed; and many devotees undertake to gild a patch, without any regard to the incongruous appearance it makes. Those entirely covered are called *Shoe*, or Golden. The images are in some cases of the most gigantic magnitude. Dr Buchanan saw in Ava one composed of a single block of pure white alabaster, the magnitude of which may be conjectured, from each finger being equal to the leg and thigh of a large man. Relics of Gaudma, consisting of minute fragments of bone, skin, hair, &c. are reverentially preserved, and are even considered necessary to give sanctity to a temple. Kioums or monasteries, the inmates of which devote themselves to celibacy, and profess abstraction from all worldly concerns, are characteristic of the religion of Gaudma. Those in the neighbourhood of Ummerapoora are very numerous, and though built only of wood, some of them make a truly magnificent appearance, from their magnitude and the immense profusion of gilded columns.

The constitution of the Birman empire does not appear to differ essentially from that of the other monarchies of Asia. In principle it is entirely despotic; the will of the sovereign is the supreme law, and is subject to no check either from the aristocracy or the people. The administration, however, appears to be mild; property is respected; and even those who are employed in maintaining the police, studiously avoid any harsh modes of enforcing it. There are a considerable number of conquered princes, who are allowed to retain the internal government of their own states, upon paying military service and tribute, and residing a certain portion of the year at Ummerapoora. The Birmans are a nation of soldiers, yet no regular army is maintained, with the exception of the royal guards, the number of which, in and round Ummerapoora, was not supposed to exceed 2000 infantry, and the same number of cavalry. When the king wishes to raise an army, he sends an order to all his viceroys and governors, fixing the number of men which each is to furnish. They receive arms and a certain proportion of grain, but no pay; and when the campaign is over, are allowed to return home. Their musketry is bad, and their cavalry drawn chiefly from the northern country of Cassay. Their most imposing military force are the war boats, hollowed out of the solid trunk of the teak tree, some of which are 80 to 100 feet long. They carry from 50 to 60 rowers well armed, besides 30 soldiers. They advance to battle singing warlike songs, draw up in a line, and present their prows to the enemy. They usually endeavour to grapple, in which case a very obstinate conflict ensues. Of these war boats, the king, on a short notice, can command about 500.

The sacred and learned language of the Birman empire is the Pali, which is believed to have been the ancient language of Hindostan, and to bear some affinity to the Sanscrit. The Palis are said, at an early period, to have held high sway in that country, and the name of the celebrated capital of Palibothra to have been derived from them. The finest books are written on thin sheets of ivory, stained black, with the characters enamelled or gilded. The common books are written with an iron pen on Palmyra canes. The more elegant kinds have their boards lacquered and ornamented with gilding, and are wrapt in silk cloth, bound round with a garter, into which the title of the book is woven. They are deposited in large chests lacquered and gilded, the contents of each chest being written in gold letters on the lid. Only a small part of the royal library was seen; but if all the space described to be occupied by it was equally well filled, the library of the Birman king must be very extensive. The greater number related to the mysteries of their religion; but there were also treatises on history, music, medicine, painting, and romance. Their poetry, according to Dr Buchanan, consists chiefly of songs, of which they have great variety, accompanied with very bad music. Their histories, like those of the Hindoos, consist almost altogether of fables and prodigies. Their astronomy is much inferior to that of the Brahmins; and their calendar had become very erroneous, till the present king, under the direction of some learned Brahmins, introduced an intercalary month. The innovation, however, was strenuously resisted by the Rhahaans, and had not been yet introduced in the remote parts of the empire. Their knowledge of medicine is equally low. Dr Buchanan being consulted, found that he was expected to cure diseases by supernatural means, and to give medicines which would render them invulnerable; and on denying every such pretension, his skill was held in very slender account. When a physician in this country is called to a young lady who is seriously ill, it is a very common stipulation, that if he effects a cure he shall receive her as a wife. The doctor could not learn whether, like other husbands, he has a right to sell the wife whom he has thus earned; but the number of handsome damsels whom he saw making part of the household establishment of a physician, seemed to attest the extensive prevalence of the practice.

Of all the countries situated to the east of India, the most opulent and civilized appears to be Siam. In 1516 it was visited by Duarte Coelho, who was well received, and even allowed to erect a wooden cross in a conspicuous part of the capital. It was France alone, however, that made any great effort to establish a communication with this country. In 1685, the King, the Academy of Sciences, and the Jesuits, with a combined view to the interests of politics, astronomy, and religion, joined in sending a mission into this kingdom. It consisted of the Chevalier Chaumont, the ambassador, the Abbe de Choisy, whose dissolute gaiety ill corresponded with his profession, and six Jesuit mathematicians. One of them, Tachard, afterwards wrote the best account of the mission; and two others, Lecomte and Gerbillon, distinguished themselves by their subsequent travels in and around China.

We shall pass over the first part of the narrative, which contains merely the common incidents of an Indian voyage. On arriving in the seas of Malacca, they describe their emotion as being chiefly excited by viewing the scene of the miracles and preaching of St Francis Xavier. Entering the river of Siam, they landed at Bancock, where they were politely received by a Mandarin with a deputation. That officer, anxious to compliment the French, and proceeding on the principles of transmigration, observed to Chaumont, that this country could not be new to him, as it was well known that his soul, though in a different body, had been sent thither on a similar mission about 1000 years ago. The ambassador, however, observed, that he could not now derive any benefit from that voyage, the events of which had entirely escaped from his recollection. They were furnished, however, with handsome *balons* or boats, in which to sail up to the capital. They made their voyage along the river Menam, which presented a magnificent spectacle. The neighbouring grounds being inundated during the rainy season, produced the most luxuriant crops of rice. The stream was entirely covered with barks, many of which resembled houses, in which, as in the Chinese waters, families took up their permanent abode. The villages were numerous; and splendid pagodas, with monasteries attached to them, appeared at every league.

At Siam, the embassy were received by Constantine, the prime minister, who, to their most agreeable surprise, proved to be an European and a Roman Catholic. A Greek by birth, he had gone on board an English vessel, and spent some years in London; thence entering into the service of the Company, he sailed to the Indies. Having made a little fortune at Siam, he equipped a vessel on his own account, but was shipwrecked on the coast of Malabar. He had saved a small sum of money, however, and fancied himself encouraged by the appearance, in a dream, of a majestic figure, which said to him "return." Next day he met on the shore a person, shipwrecked like himself, who proved an ambassador of the king of Siam, in his way from Persia. Constantine could furnish him the means of conveying him home, and thus introduced himself to notice at court, where, by his address and talents, he soon raised himself to the highest place. He had become a protestant in London; but the diligence of the missionaries at Siam brought him within the pale of the Catholic church.

Under auspices so favourable, the ambassador had no difficulty in making early and satisfactory arrangements for their introduction at court. Forty Mandarins came to conduct them, who, on being shewn the King of France's letter enclosed in a gold box, worshipped it three times, with their faces to the ground. The embassy were then embarked in twelve gilded boats, and sailed across the river, which was entirely covered with floating spectators. Having landed, they came to a great square, where were drawn up two long rows of elephants, between which they were led. They now entered a court, round which 2000 soldiers were ranged; and passing two others came to a fourth, where they were surprised to see twenty-four Mandarins lying flat on their faces, without shoes or stockings. The embassy was thence ushered into the presence-hall. Chaumont had made very high terms as to the ceremonial, insisting upon keeping on their shoes contrary to all oriental etiquette, and also upon delivering the letter into the King's own hands, whereas it was customary to transmit it through one of the officers. The ambassador having entered, and found the King seated, made three bows in the course of his advance; then he began a speech, after two or three words of which he put on his hat, sat down, and delivered the rest. He then rose to give the letter; but it appeared to him that the King's position was much higher than had been stipulated, or than would admit of his delivering the letter, without stretching his person in a manner unsuitable to its dignity. In this exigency, he formed at once the high determination not to lift the letter higher than himself. Constantine, who was lying extended on the ground on his hands and feet, implored that he would raise his arm; but the ambassador pretended to hear nothing, and at last the King, laughing, stooped and took the gold box in which the epistle was contained. He then conversed for about an hour with great affability, and made many inquiries about the affairs of France. All the Mandarins who were in the hall remained flat, with their faces on the ground, so long as the King was present.

The Jesuits, during their stay, had several private interviews with the King, in all of which they were courteously entertained. On one occasion he was much amused by seeing through their glasses an eclipse of the moon, and put many questions on the subject. Nothing, however, could shake in him or his learned men the universal conviction of the East, that a huge dragon was then attacking and devouring that luminary. On being asked how, on this theory, it could be possible to predict the period with such precision, they replied, that Europeans knew how to calculate the periodical returns of the monster's appetite, and the moment when his empty stomach would require a new meal. It had been customary with the King to chuse precisely the time when the inundation ceased, to go out in procession and strike the waters, ordering them to retire; of which command the natural diminution appeared to be the fruit. A mistake, however, being sometimes committed as to the period, the waters had proved refractory, and the custom had been given up. The highest pride of the court consisted in its elephants. The French saw the *white* elephant, so celebrated in the annals of eastern India. It made a very sorry appearance, being small, quite worn down, and wrinkled with age. It was kept, however, in the greatest pomp, and had a hundred men to attend it. They were much more gratified by the view of the prince elephant, a very fine and large animal. The least of them was served by twenty men.

A report had been spread that the King of Siam had shewn a disposition to embrace the Christian religion. The Jesuits candidly state, that they had no ground to entertain such an expectation; and that Constantine, though himself a Catholic, had assured them that every idea of the kind was totally out of the question. They went to view the principal pagoda in the city of Siam. It was long and narrow externally, covered all over with a metal called *calin*. On entering, they saw nothing but gold. There was an idol forty-five feet in height, and reaching to the roof, entirely composed of that precious metal. The missionaries, amid their admiration, were deeply grieved to think, that this one idol contained more gold than all the images of Catholic Europe put together.

After some stay, the Jesuits continuing still in high favour, Tachard returned to France, with a petition for twelve new mathematical Jesuits, and also with permission to erect a fort and factory at Bancock. Preparations were made without delay to fulfil these two destinations; the voyage was prosperously performed, and their reception was equally flattering as before. Nothing materially new occurred in this mission; but Tachard had along with him La Loubere, who produced afterwards a general description of Siam, so accurate and intelligent, as to be perhaps the most valuable fruit of the expedition.

Siam exists entirely by the great river of Menam, which traverses its whole extent from north to south. The plain through which it flows is perfectly level and fertile, but at a little distance on each side the ground rises into mountains, forests, and uncultivated grounds, overrun with wild beasts. There are some mines of gold and silver, which the King is said to have expected to equal those of Peru, from the consideration of Siam being the precise antipode of that part of

America; but this analogy seems the only ground for such an expectation. A more curious mineral production consisted in a mine of loadstone, which the Jesuits visited. It attracted the pieces of iron with extraordinary force; but the needle in its vicinity became quite irregular. So far as could be judged from the direction of the iron instruments, the poles of the mine were from north to south.

Siam appears to be a complete despotism, there being no popular assembly, and no individual dignity, except what is derived from office, and expires with it. The Siamese are all held bound to military service. A register is kept of the whole free male population, every one of whom, when called upon, must join the army for six months in the year. The dignities, as in the Mogul empire, are according to the number of men placed under the command of each. No salary is attached to them: the emoluments are derived from land, slaves, or edifices assigned for the support of the office, and remaining attached to it. But the mode of enriching themselves, to which the officers chiefly trust, is exaction, which is winked at by the sovereign, and carried to a vast extent in every department.

In the Siamese tribunals, though composed of several members, the power of decision rests entirely with the president; the others are there only to aid with their counsel. They have an authoritative book of law, in three volumes. In all intricate cases, however, their main dependence is placed upon ordeal. This is administered in various forms, such as walking over red hot iron, which is not, perhaps, excessively perilous to those who can summon courage sufficient, as their feet being always naked, the soles become hard like horn. Another proof is by putting the hands into boiling oil. A Frenchman being robbed by a native, felt such imprudent confidence in the justice of his cause, as to accede to this test; but drew out his hand burned in the most cruel manner, and was covered at once with shame and agony, while the thief triumphantly exhibited his, perfectly uninjured. Others are thrown to tigers, who, it is supposed, will spare the innocent.

The religion of Siam, though the missionaries do not seem aware of it, is evidently that of Boodh, or Buddha, called also Gaudma, or Godama, which is also established in Ava, Thibet, Tartary, and so many other countries of Asia. Their chief object of worship is called Somono-Codom, which last part of the name differs probably from Gaudma only by a variation in European pronunciation. Their sacred books are in the Bali language, doubtless the same in Ava called Pali. The monks of the order denominated Talapoins, like all the others, reside in spacious convents, and profess rigid celibacy. They appear to preach with a diligence unknown in any other country where the same system prevails. A Talapoin will harangue the people from six in the morning till the hour of dinner, and will begin afresh in the afternoon. The people, if satisfied, not only express their feelings by murmurs of approbation, but by solid gifts; so that a Talapoin preacher, if popular, soon becomes rich.

Poetry is much relished, and extensively cultivated among the Siamese, though both their versification and sentiments are very different from those which are relished in Europe. As there are no public assemblies, and no pleadings in their courts of judicature, no scope is afforded to eloquence. They shew some knowledge of mathematics and astronomy, though not nearly equal to that of the Brahmins. Medicine is in a very low state. It is not founded on the least idea of anatomy, nor any thing but a few ancient receipts, which are blindly followed. The rudeness of their practice may be inferred from one of their favourite cures, which consists in laying the patient flat, and trampling him under foot. This gentle process is used even in the case of pregnant females, to facilitate the accouchement. Should these powerful remedies not produce the intended effect, witchcraft alone, it is supposed, can account for the failure. The guilty persons are therefore inquired after, and proceeded against with the utmost severity.

The Siamese do not distinguish themselves as artisans, for this very sufficient reason, that whoever rises to any eminence in them is immediately sent for by the King, and obliged, during the rest of his life, to work for his sole behoof. They make little cloth, silk and woollen not at all, and cotton not to a great extent. They embroider well, understand working in gold and silver, and are skilful founders, for which occupations ample scope is found in the embellishment of temples and manufacture of deities. In general, the Siamese character appears to be such as despotism usually forms. They are mild, polite, courteous, but artful, deceitful, timid, avaricious, incurious, proud to such as they think in their power, and cringing to those who treat them with haughtiness. They are said, however, to be honest in their dealings, and so kind to their relations, that beggary and pauperism are scarcely known.

Cochinchina, with its bordering territories of Cambodia and Tonquin, bear nearly the same relation to China that the Birman empire and Siam bear to Hindostan. From it they borrowed the basis of their laws and institutions, which exist however in a ruder, looser, and freer form than in the parent empire.

Cochinchina, eclipsed by the superior splendour of its neighbour, and possessing no great characteristic staple of trade, has not attracted any large share of European notice. Its first explorers, as in other countries of the East, were the Portuguese missionaries. A curious account of their proceedings is given by CHRISTOPHER BORRI, one of the most active of their number. The first Catholic priests were brought thither from Manilla by the Portuguese merchants, merely to say mass and administer the sacraments. These persons did not hesitate to transmit accounts to Europe of their having converted many great ladies, and among others the Infanta of Cochinchina; whereas it was afterwards found that, besides there being no such person as the Infanta, there was no one about court who had given any "token of "being a Christian, or so much as knowing what "a Christian is." Thus encouraged, however, the superiors at Macao sent an eminent father, Francis Buzome, with several companions, to cultivate these favourable prospects. On his arrival, the chaplains boasted of the number of those whom they had brought to the profession of Christianity; but Buzome, on sifting the matter, soon found that their converts had not even an idea of what the word Christian meant. The question put had imported, if they would enter into the bosom of the church; but the word *church* they had understood to mean Portuguese, and had merely supposed themselves to be changing their country. This was manifest from a play which he saw acted in the public market, where a man whose body, by a peculiar arrangement of dress, was swelled to a most enormous size, addressed the usual question of the chaplains to a boy, who, assenting, entered into his huge body, to the infinite amusement of the spectators. Buzome lost no time in changing the formula, and in endeavouring to convey to the converts some idea of what they were asked to become. He met with considerable success, and even prevailed on a number of natives to join in building a very handsome church. The observation of this excited the envy of the *omsaiis* or priests, who took advantage of a drought with which the kingdom was afflicted, and represented, that it was no wonder if the Gods denied rain, when a body of strangers were allowed to preach a doctrine by which these deities were so deeply dishonoured. At the same time the chief omsaii proceeded to the top of a mountain, where he "began to "call upon his devils," and thrice struck the earth with his feet, when a shower came, which was quite inadequate indeed to the relief of the country, yet the multitude declared that none of the foreign priests had done so much. They therefore loudly demanded from the king their banishment, and the prince, though reluctant, was driven by the fear of rebellion into compliance. Unfortunately, the wind blew in such a direction that no vessel could leave the port; so that being thrust out of the city, they were thrown unsheltered into an intermediate state between land and sea, and exposed to the most doleful sufferings; at the same time that their eyes were greeted by the flames of the church ascending. The congregation at Macao learning this distressed state of their brother, sent a merchant vessel to afford what relief it could; and in it went Borri, our narrator, under the disguise of a slave. Being observed, however, composing a dispute between two Portuguese, the people cried out, that only a priest could have such influence, and ran to carry the tidings to the governor. Hereupon, "believing I "was certainly a dead man, I resolved to die as "what I was;" he, therefore, put on his surplice and stole, and began to preach. Presently after, a torrent of rain came on, which sunk in oblivion all the enmity with which the friars were viewed. A person of distinction happening to come to the place, saw Father Buzome reduced to the most extenuated state, and hearing that it was on a charge of having withheld rain from Cochinchina, was seized with equal mirth, amazement, and pity. He carried him home, therefore, and procured the best medical aid. Through his friendship a new church was erected, and their affairs appeared in a prosperous state, when his death threw them back into difficulty and neglect. While the missionary was sitting in a somewhat solitary and disconsolate state, he heard a noise, and looking out saw with surprise a long train of elephants, on which a number of ladies, richly dressed, were seated. In their rear rode one whom the peculiar splendour of her attire, and a blaze of jewels with which she was covered, announced as their mistress. She stated the information she had received as to the unblemished life he led, and the doctrine he taught, which last appeared to her the only true one. She, therefore, besought to be bathed in his holy water, so as to insure to herself a passage into paradise. The father hesitated a good deal, as he wanted both time and sufficient knowledge of the language to instruct her duly in the doctrines of the faith. This delay much afflicted the lady, who was in daily fear of dying in her heathen state, and seems to have considered her salvation as solely depending upon this rite. To shew her humility, she laid aside her elephants, and repeatedly walked a mile barefooted through the mire to solicit it. The Father at last could not resist her importunity; but a greater difficulty arose in regard to her women, who stood all in the capacity of secondary wives to her husband, who was ambassador to the King of Cambodia. On learning, however, that this would prevent him from opening to them the gate of paradise, they all protested that they would rather leave him and each look out for a husband to herself, in which search the lady charitably pledged herself to assist. On these conditions they received baptism, whereupon they broke in pieces their idols, and received in their stead Catholic images; then taking from their neck the gold chains and strings of pearls that were round them, put on Agnus Deis, crosses, medals and relics. The ambassador arriving home soon after, was not a little surprised at seeing them thus bedecked; however, upon their earnest representations, and the exhortation of the friar, he soon showed favourable dispositions for becoming a convert. Till these appeared tolerably confirmed, it was thought best to say nothing of his wives, who were twenty-five in number; but when he began to press for the ceremony, the missionary judged it needful to state their dismissal as a requisite preliminary. Hereupon, "like fire with water "thrown upon it, the ambassador presently cool-"ed." He demanded at least time to consider, and next day sent a learned omsaii to argue the matter. The missionaries however reasoned so well, that the ambassador became sensible they had right on their side. He came however asking, " is there no remedy or dispensation from the " Pope, or any other means, though never so dif- " ficult, to have this point remitted ?—We told him " it was in vain to seek any redress whatsoever in " this case." The ambassador hereupon piously resolved to obey, and gave orders that the whole should be dismissed that very night. The ladies, however, who, after obtaining the boon, seem to have thought very little of their engagements, only laughed, evidently thinking the house as much theirs as his; and even the principal wife rushed in, declaring these were persons who had been brought up with her from her infancy, whom she loved as her children, and whose services she could not do without. All that could be agreed to was, that they should no longer officiate as wives, but simply as her attendants. The ambassador, however, confidentially stated to the friars, that situated as he was thus to be, with all his *quondam* wives in the same house, he could by no means consider his virtue as fully secured.

Another circumstance from which the missionaries drew some important benefits, was their knowledge of astronomy, and consequent power of predicting eclipses. These were truly important phenomena; for as it is universally understood in the East, that a huge dragon is then endeavouring to devour the sun, it becomes incumbent that the King march out with his whole army, that all the artillery be fired, every drum, trumpet, and bell throughout the empire sounded, and that even the kitchen-maids should rattle their pans and kettles, in order to frighten the monster from this mischievous attempt. It was therefore a pretty serious dilemma, when the astrologers having predicted an eclipse of the moon, the friars fixed a different hour and day for it. The governor declared, that " if our doctrine " was so certain and infallible in these hidden " and heavenly things, and their's so erroneous," their religious doctrines were likely also to possess an equal pre-eminence. Accordingly, when their prophecy proved true, he declared " there were " no such men as the fathers ;" and their skill even attracted notice at court. The astrologers there some time after were able to predict an eclipse, but not to know that it would be invisible ; disregarding which, the king led out his army in full array to frighten the dragon ; but was much disappointed, and his esteem for the fathers greatly raised, by no eclipse appearing. They had therefore liberty to preach ; and the chief obstacle arose from the unfortunate and so often lamented resemblance between their own worship and that of the natives. The latter had processions, crosses, strings of beads, begging friars, and convents of every kind, exactly as in Catholic Europe. Our author protests, in despair, that there is not a dress, office, or ceremony in the church of Rome, to which the devil has not here provided some counterpart. Even when he began inveighing against their idols, he was answered, that these were the images of departed great men, whom they worshipped exactly in the same principle and manner as the Catholics did the images of the apostles and martyrs.

Our author vaunts in an extraordinary manner the fertility of Cochinchina, occasioned by the *lut* or inundation which takes place in September, and is so complete, that their sea and land "seem to be all of a piece." It often comes on so suddenly, that the natives are imprisoned in their houses, and cattle are drowned, when they are considered the property of the first that can take them. There is thus produced the greatest abundance of grain, fruits, and cattle, though they have no dairy, "looking on it as a sin to "milk the cows." He mentions as peculiar to this country the edible birds' nests, so much valued in China; not aware that they are produced through all the Indian Archipelago. The pride of animal nature is here the elephant, which is stated to be larger than any where else in the world, and double that of India; a fact partly, at least, confirmed by Mr Barrow. They carry habitually on their backs a coach containing thirteen persons, with which they often cross broad rivers; and our author could not see without wonder "such a vast lump of flesh swimming "under such a weight." He has seen them launch a vessel, and pull up large trees as we would do a cabbage or a lettuce. Their docility and intelligence are also wonderful, the *nayre* or driver laying before them the whole plan of their journey, when the elephant performs what he expects from him "as regularly as any man of good "sense could do."

Scarcely any country in the world is so happy in harbours as Cochinchina, which has sixty excellent ones in a coast of little more than a hundred leagues; the two best in the bay of Turon. The trade is chiefly carried on by vessels from China and Japan, resorting to a fair which lasts for four months in the year. The Cochinchinese manufacture little themselves, and are curious of foreign commodities. Till lately this country had been a province of Tonquin, but had been rendered independent by the grandfather of the present King. This prince could levy an army of 80,000 men, whom he had trained so thoroughly to the use of fire-arms, that Europeans could not equal them in firing at a mark.

The Cochinchinese have the same outward forms of manners and behaviour as the Chinese, "always punctually observing all niceties;" but they are at bottom a very different people. He describes them as "the most courteous and affable "of all the Eastern nations;" and Europeans, whom the others "naturally abhor," are treated by them with the greatest kindness. There is also much love and concord among themselves; and "it would be looked upon as a most vile ac-"tion, if one man eating any thing, though ever so "little, should not share with all about him, giv-"ing every one a bit." They make it a rule, indeed, to give whatever any one asks; in return for which, they expect to receive whatever they ask themselves, and hold the refuser ever after in utter contempt; "so that a man must either "hide or be ready to give what he shews." They give very large dinner parties, thirty or forty being considered very small ones; and our author has seen two thousand. A person of very moderate fortune is expected to give at least a hundred dishes, piled over the table in frames of cane, and containing every variety of meat, fish, fruit, and fowl, which the country affords: "If "but one were wanting, they would not count it "a feast." Our author, however, had but little enjoyment at these feasts, "nature finding a very "great want of bread and wine." The former is supplied by rice, the latter by a spirit distilled from it; while between meals they drink hot water, with the *root* of the tea tree infused in it. At last our author became so far reconciled to this diet, that when he returned to France he "coveted nothing but the rice of Cochinchina, which "I thought satisfied me more than any other "thing."

Without touching on some other incidental narratives, we shall proceed to the account of Cochinchina given by one of the most eminent of modern travellers, who has done so much to extend European knowledge of Eastern Asia. Mr Barrow enjoyed opportunities of making observations upon this country, while proceeding to China as secretary to Lord Macartney's embassy. Sickness having spread through the ship which conveyed its members, they were induced to touch at the bay of Turon for supplies and refreshment. On their arrival, however, Manuel Duome, the captain of a Portuguese vessel, assured them that the country was in such a distracted state, as to be altogether incapable of affording them the wished-for supplies. This report seemed confirmed by the aspect of the first native whom they met, a fisherman, whose aspect was so haggard and meagre, and his dress patched of so many different rags, as suggested nothing but the most extreme misery. However, the case being very urgent, they determined to wait the result of a few days' observation. The natives at first presented provisions very scantily and timidly, but as soon as they understood that good prices were to be had for as much as they chose to bring, the supply increased most rapidly, till in a few days a plentiful market was established. Their friend Manuel, it appeared, to serve his own commercial jealousy, had made an entirely false report. The natives even erected on the shore a large shed, in which they prepared daily for the English a dinner, consisting of several hundred small bowls piled in rows over each other. These were filled with various preparations of meat, fish, and vegetables, eaten with chop sticks, without either table linen, knives, forks, or plates. After dinner they usually repaired to the theatre, where the actors performed the whole day without intermission, with or without an audience. The spectators paid no fee at admission, but were expected to testify their approbation by throwing upon the stage a due number of small copper coins. The dialogue, unlike the Chinese, was light and comic, and interspersed with much music, some of which was soft and plaintive, reminding them of the Scotch; but in general the main object was the production of a noise altogether stunning and tremendous, compared to which the gentle airs played by the English were judged wholly unworthy of notice. This part of Cochinchina was then in possession of a rebel chief, who resided at Hué, about forty miles in the interior. They received an invitation to visit him, which, from several considerations, they did not judge it prudent to accept, and confined themselves to an exchange of presents. The only discourtesy experienced was when they attempted measurements of different points on the coast; a step at which the most marked displeasure was expressed. An English gentleman having attempted to penetrate up the river, was taken and put in close confinement, the commanding officer at the place amusing himself with brandishing a naked scimitar over his head, and with loading his legs with enormous wooden and iron chains. However, every thing else being done to forward their views, they were enabled, in less than a month, to accomplish all their views, and resume the prosecution of their voyage to China.

Mr Barrow learned, in the course of his stay, that extensive revolutions had taken place in this part of Asia. In 1774 Caung-shung, the reigning King, became the victim of a conspiracy formed by four of his principal subjects. He was dethroned, and supposed to be put to death; while the rebels not only divided Cochinchina among themselves, but conquered the extensive neighbouring kingdom of Tonquin. Meantime the young Prince, on the presumption of his father's death, was crowned King by a few followers; and passed through a series of adventures, which might figure in the pages of romance. After some vain attempts to make head against the usurper, he repaired to the court of Siam, where he distinguished himself in a war which was waging against the Birmans. Incurring the jealousy of the King, he escaped from Siam, and in concert with a Jesuit missionary of the name of Adran, came over to France. He was well received there; and in 1787 a very remarkable treaty was concluded, by which, in return for being restored to his native dominions, the prince agreed not only to grant to the French ample commercial privileges, but to cede the bay of Turon and the neighbouring islands, and to allow them to levy and discipline troops within his territories. The execution of this treaty, which might have changed the aspect of the Indian world, was first retarded by accidental circumstances, and finally prevented by the breaking out of the French revolution. The Prince, however, with the few adherents whom he could collect, determined to try his fortune in Cochinchina. He came at a most auspicious moment. The old King was found on the solitary island of Palowai, where, with a handful of his people, he had subsisted for two years on herbs and roots. The usurpers were worn out by struggles among themselves, and the people ready to flock to the standard of their lawful sovereign. Accordingly he soon assembled an army; and at the time of Mr Barrow's visit was master of all Cambodia and Cochinchina, except the territory upon the bay of Turon. It is understood that he has since included it within his acquisitions, and that he has even extended them to Tonquin.

The reigning monarch of Cochinchina is described as almost a second Peter. In the course of ten years, he has raised his navy from a single vessel to twelve hundred of various descriptions. He purchased a Portuguese vessel for the sole purpose of taking it to pieces, plank by plank, with his own hands, and fitting in every piece afresh, till a new one was constructed on the same model. He has been equally active in improving his army, which amounts now to 113,000, of which upwards of 40,000 are disciplined after the European system. He is said to prefer the name of general to that of sovereign. He knows the greater part of his army by name, talks to the soldiers of their adventures and exploits, and inquires particularly about their wives and children. He is the main-spring of every movement which takes place within his kingdom; not a nail is driven in, nor a gun mounted, without consulting him. Nor has he overlooked other concerns connected with the more solid interests of his kingdom. He restored the culture of areca and betel, the plantations of which had been destroyed by the usurping government; he encouraged that of silk, sugar, and other commodities for the production of which his territories are well fitted. He has done much also in building bridges, and facilitating all kinds of commercial intercourse.

All the names by which the countries on this coast are designated by Europeans, are unknown to the natives, except that of Tonquin. The appellation of Anan or Anian is generally applied to them. Cambodia is called Donnai, and different parts of Cochinchina receive the appellations of Chang and Hué. All these territories were once included in the Chinese empire, from which they were severed towards the end of the fourteenth century. The external forms are still Chinese; while the general spirit and character of the nation exhibits rather a striking contrast. The people of Cochinchina have thrown off the thick shoes, quilted stockings, and stuffed petticoats, with which the Chinese motions are encumbered. They are open, familiar, always gay and talking, while the Chinese are reserved, always grave, and wearing the appearance of thought. The former pay little regard, either in words or practice, to those precepts of morality which the Chinese ostentatiously display in golden letters on all their streets and public places. Women are not confined, and are entirely exempted from that artificial diminution of the feet which in China forms an effectual bar against their gadding abroad. They are as gay and unrestrained as the men; but are ungenerously treated, in being doomed to perform all those labours which require the greatest bodily strength. Besides the usual domestic tasks, all the occupations of tillage, carrying the goods to market, the steering of boats, and even the repairing of the cottages, falls to their lot. So excessive, indeed, is the toil they undergo, that the natives usually remark of them, as we do of cats, that they have nine lives, and bear a great deal of killing. What is worse, their virtue is openly set up to sale, both by themselves and their friends; and overtures of the most shameless kind were repeatedly made, even by persons of distinction, to the members of the embassy. Hopes were, however, entertained, that in the parts of the country less visited by strangers, more decency might be observed. Mr Barrow was much struck with that promptitude in asking whatever appeared agreeable to them, which was remarked by the missionaries; nor docs he notice, like them, the readiness to give what is asked. In failure of begging, stealing was usually employed with very little hesitation; even officers of government required a good deal of attention to prevent them from employing this mode of gratifying their wishes.

The religion of Cochinchina appears to be a modification of the widely extended system of Buddha or Fo, though its ceremonies are carried on with less pomp and formality than in China. The figures of Fo were often placed in cages fastened to the branches of the banyan tree, to which the priest ascended by a ladder, and presented the offerings. Other figures are kept in little caskets, which may be carried even in the pocket. Christianity is allowed and even favoured by the present King, who has derived benefit from the services of the French missionaries. All other religions are tolerated. The principle of government appears to be the same as China; but it is exercised in a much milder manner, the successive pretenders to the crown having continual occasion to court the favour of the people. Instead of the cries with which a Chinese village continually echoed, executed by the application of the cangue or bamboo, the English did not witness here a single instance of legal infliction.

Mr Barrow is strongly of opinion, that a commercial establishment on the coast of Cochinchina would be attended with considerable advantage. This people, who have not the same inveterate attachment to old customs as the Chinese, might take a considerable quantity of our manufactures; in return for which they would give rice, sugar, pepper, sea-slug, and other gelatinous substances, which are in constant demand at the markets of Canton. The effect would be the same as if we sent our commodities directly thither. In fact, Mr Hastings, in 1778, made arrangements with a mercantile house to send two vessels to Cochin-china, investing a member of the firm with a demi-official character. The Orientals, however, pay little regard to the character of merchant, especially as connected with diplomatic functions. The expedition called at several ports, and even penetrated to Faifo, the capital, but without being able to find confidence anywhere, and at last, being drawn into actual hostilities with the ruling power at Hué, narrowly escaped with their lives and part of their goods. In 1804, the directors caused another mission to be sent; but the person employed knew nothing of the language, and was obliged to communicate through the medium of the French missionaries, who doubtless caused every thing to appear in the most unfavourable light for the English. The consequence was, that the King received them in a very cool manner, and allowed it plainly to appear, that the shorter their stay was made it would be the more acceptable. Mr Barrow, however, is of opinion that this monarch would show himself by no means ill inclined to the English, provided a royal mission were sent, composed of duly informed and qualified persons.

## CHAPTER II.

### CHINA—PORTUGUESE AND SPANISH DISCOVERIES.

*First Discovery.—The Andradas.—Thomé Pires.—Venetian report.—Notices from Mexico.—The Augustines.—The Franciscans.—Ignatius.—Ricio.—Navarate.—Expulsion of the Missionaries.*

CHINA is not a name new to the reader of the present work. This celebrated empire, at once the most civilized and most distant of any in Asia, was early viewed by the traveller of that continent as the grand terminating object of his career. Under the name of Serica, it seems to have formed the main and ultimate point of those Greek and Roman caravans which traversed anciently the entire breadth of central Asia. To the early modern travellers, we have seen it, under the name of Cathay, forming an object equally conspicuous. The Portuguese navigators, who reached it across the Indian seas, recognized it under the name of China, by which alone it is there known; but some time elapsed ere Europeans became fully aware that this China was the same country with the Cathay of Marco Polo and the early travellers.

The Portuguese at Malacca were not long of receiving tidings respecting the existence and greatness of this empire. In August 1516, Albuquerque caused Rafael Perestrello to proceed to Canton, in the junk of a native merchant, and collect all the intelligence in his power. Perestrello accomplished his voyage, and returned to Malacca in the following June, at the moment when Fernando Perez d'Andrada, with a squadron of eight vessels, was hesitating whether to set out for Bengal or China. The tidings given by Perestrello made him prefer the latter, and departing immediately, he found himself, on the 15th August 1517, in the road of Canton. A large Chinese flotilla made its appearance, hovered closely round the Portuguese, and even discharged some shots over their heads. Andrada, however, continued the whole day beating his trumpets, and making signals of peace. The Chinese did not come to any parley; but he sailed forward without opposition to the island of Beniaga (called by us Bankshall), and anchored off the port of Tamou, which we have greatly changed to Whampoa. Here he found Duarte Coelho, who, in coming out of the river of Siam, had engaged a large fleet of Chinese pirates, and being roughly handled, took shelter in this harbour. He stated, that the fleet which had placed itself in so jealous and menacing an attitude, had no absolutely hostile design, but was merely sent out by way of guard and precaution. By his advice, Andrada sent a messenger to the governor of Canton, stating that he came from the King of Portugal, with the most peaceable intentions, and wishing to send an ambassador to the Chinese emperor. The governor replied, that he was welcome, and would be supplied with every thing he wanted, but that he could not be permitted to proceed farther, without the permission of the Pio of Nanto (Nanciam), who was instructed to watch and report respecting all vessels that entered the bay. A messenger was then despatched to the Pio, who replied in the most polite terms, but at the same time could do nothing without communicating with the governor of Canton. The Portuguese commander was thus tossed between these two officers, and after repeated messages, saw no prospect of the affair coming to any positive issue. At length, losing patience, he put his flotilla in motion, determined to sail into the harbour of Canton, with or without permission. His purpose was frustrated by a violent storm, which suddenly arose and drove him back, with his vessels considerably damaged. The Chinese were supposed to view this incident with no little satisfaction, and even to anticipate with pleasure the Portuguese being obliged to remain through the winter, when they hoped to be able to treat with them on their own terms. For this reason, boards, planks, and every thing which could serve for the repair of the vessels, were carefully withheld. Fernando, however, by actively and skilfully using the superfluities of his own vessels, succeeded in putting the squadron soon into sailing condition. He then proceeded with his two best vessels to Nanto, where, after a long discussion with the Pio, he wrung out from him permission to enter the harbour of Canton, and pilots to conduct him thither. His arrival there somewhat startled the Canton authorities; however, upon proper explanation, it was tolerably acquiesced in. He was told, however, that the three governors, who, according to the gradation of their rank, were called Tutam, Cantam, and Chumpim, being then absent, no audience could take place till their return. It was afterwards understood that this absence was a mere manœuvre, to dazzle the Portuguese by the pomp of their entry. This took place on three successive days, each rising above the other by the dignity of the person, and the splendour of the ceremony. The river could not be seen for the multitude of boats waving with silken flags of various colours. The walls of the city also, and lofty masts erected within it, streamed with ensigns of silk so large, that they might have served as sails to ships of war. Andrada was then invited on shore to an audience, but chose rather to send Joannes Empole his factor, with as splendid a retinue as possible. The factor then stated, that they came from the King of Portugal, and more immediately from Albuquerque his general, who learning that the King of China was the greatest sovereign in all the East, and his people the wisest and most prudent, was desirous to open a communication with him, and had therefore brought an ambassador, with letters and a present. The governors expressed pleasure at their coming, and requested that the ambassador might come on shore, where he would be supplied with every thing, and might wait till the pleasure of the King was known as to his proceeding to the capital. This ambassador was Thomé Pires, who exercised the somewhat humble occupation of an apothecary, but who is said to have possessed an intelligence, application, and address, which admirably suited him for the high office with which he was to be invested. The commander found here three vessels from the Lequio (Loochoo) Islands, and would have proceeded thither; but the lateness of the season rendering this impossible, he returned to Malacca.

Fernando d'Andrada left a favourable impression, and no opposition was made to Portuguese merchants coming to the port of Tamou, and discharging their cargoes. In 1518, his brother,

Simon d'Andrada, was sent with another squadron. Simon, it is admitted, "was pompous and "glorious, and did all things with great majesty." He began with erecting a fortification on the island, contrary to every Chinese regulation; and in front of it he raised a prison, which was announced as destined for all those Chinese who should do any injury to the Portuguese. Several ships having come in from Siam and Cambodia, Andrada took strong measures to prevent them from receiving any cargo till his vessel was first supplied. There existed, it seems, such a right in the East in favour of the first comer; but the Chinese disapproved entirely of the manner in which it was here enforced. But the wrong which they considered most deadly, was the number of children, belonging even to persons of distinction, whom he bought as slaves. There is a regular formula in China for selling children. The father and mother go to the judge, whose secretary writes down on a paper their names, and the obligation under which they come to deliver up the child as the property of the purchaser. The father then puts a coarse colouring matter on the palm of his hand, and impresses it on the paper, and does the same with the sole of his right foot, after which the child is delivered up, and the money received. The Portuguese were not aware, that in consequence of the ready market, as well as concealment which they afforded, a number of the slaves brought to them were stolen, and were the offspring of wealthy parents; besides, that the poorest viewed in a very different light their children being held in a gentle slavery at home, and being sold to a strange and foreign people, by whom, it was currently reported, they were immediately roasted and eaten. These discontents grew always stronger and stronger, and were farther heightened on seeing the Portuguese fleet reinforced, by the arrival first of one, and then of two additional vessels. At length the Chinese governor determined to proceed to the last extremity. He fitted out a fleet of fifty vessels, which surrounded and attacked the Portuguese. By the advantage of skill and situation they stood out for some time, but found at length that they could not long maintain their ground against such fearful odds. Collecting, therefore, themselves and their most valuable effects into the three best ships, they made a vigorous effort, cut their way through, and returned to Malacca. The result was, that the Portuguese were completely excluded from all the ports and seas of China.

We have now to trace the career of the ambassador Pires. He was long detained at Canton, in consequence of the excessive caution of the Chinese government, which sent three successive messages, making the most minute inquiry into his character and intentions. Before he obtained permission to proceed, Simon d'Andrada was already arrived, though he had not yet become extremely odious. At length Pires sailed for the capital in a splendid bark, with silken flags, and an awning also of silk to screen him from the weather. He passed the range of mountains which separate northern from southern China, and in four months arrived at Nanquin, where he was ordered to attend his majesty at Pekin. A considerable time then elapsed before he obtained any notice, the King being employed in investigating and punishing a conspiracy set on foot by one of his relations. At length he sent for the letters, which were three, from the King of Portugal, from Andrada, and from the governor of Canton. The two first were couched in the usual terms of address to sovereign princes; but the translators, not accounting these duly respectful, framed other letters entirely different, better calculated, as they thought, for the perusal of their imperial master. They stated, that the King of the Frangi had now sent this ambassador to the Son of Heaven and Lord of the World, for the purpose of acknowledging himself his vassal, and soliciting his seal, which is affixed in sign of subjection to every writing of the kings tributary to China. The letter of the governor of Canton was then read, which was not absolutely hostile to the Portuguese, the grand causes of dissension not having yet arisen. It stated, that they sought permission to establish a factory at Canton; that they had taken Malacca, and were very powerful in the Indian seas; and finally, described them as persons of very lofty pretensions, and exceedingly difficult to satisfy. The tenor of these letters, so strangely different, threw the imperial court into the greatest perplexity; and they began to suspect that the whole was a pretext, and Pires merely a spy. About the same time came other letters, representing the Portuguese in a much more unfavourable light; stating, that they had driven out the King of Bintam, in the Malayan peninsula, who was a vassal of the Emperor, and had received his seal; that they were behaving at Canton in the most imperious manner, and were sending ships to survey the coast. Hereupon Pires was refused an interview; but farther proceedings were suspended by the Emperor's illness and death. His successor, having inquired into the affair, rejected the advice given by his council of putting to death Pires as a spy, but remanded him to Canton, to be there treated as farther experience and inquiry might make him appear to deserve. When Pires arrived at Canton, open war had ensued, and every thing Portuguese was considered as hostile. He was therefore thrown into prison, where he soon after died.

After this catastrophe, rigorous orders were issued that not a Portuguese vessel should be allowed to enter the harbours of China, or even to approach its coasts. A number of years elapsed ere the mutual wants of commerce led to an agreement, by which they were allowed to land and erect tents on the island of Sanciam. About the end of the sixteenth century, they obtained a much more important concession. The coast of China being ravaged, and Canton itself blockaded by a very formidable pirate, they were applied to for aid, when they defeated and killed the pirate, and took Macao, where his head-quarters had been established. In gratitude for so important a service, the Emperor granted them the valuable privilege of forming an establishment upon this island, though cooped up within very narrow limits.

The discovery of this vast and opulent empire could not fail to excite a strong sensation in Europe, and to give rise to various and extravagant rumours. The Venetian senate felt always a peculiar interest relating to the affairs of the East. I have seen a manuscript report of considerable length, but without name or date, made to them on the subject of China. The writer begins with long details from Marco Polo, Haiton, and a "Cavaliere Inglese," whom I presume to be Mandeville. He then assures their excellencies, that a person of the greatest integrity, who had been many years in all parts of India, never heard of such a city as Quinsai in China. The capital of that empire was Pacyn (Pekin), which differed from Quinsai in situation and many other particulars. About 260 leagues south from Pacyn, however, was Lanchi, (the Portuguese name for Nankin), not like Quinsai unless in its lake, but greater and more stupendous. It was described as seated upon four great rivers, along the principal of which it extended for three days' journey; as containing 1,800,000 houses of moderate height, but built of stone; as surrounded by many most delightful enclosed gardens; as having the surrounding hills cut so as to serve for a wall. All goods from China to other countries, and other countries to it, pass through Lanchi. The whole empire is represented so fertile and populous as to be properly one great city, having for its walls the ocean on the east, the mountains on the north, and the rivers on the west.

Another somewhat curious account is contained in an English pamphlet of a few pages, translated from a Spanish original, and entitled, "The "strange and marvellous newes lately come from

" the great kingdom of Chyna, which adjoineth " unto the East India." The notice is mentioned as having come by the way of Mexico, and as not generally known, but " remaineth among " worshipful personages." He says " a credyble " person dooth declare," that the Spaniards, from certain islands (the Philippines), had sailed 40 leagues along the coast of China, had landed and engaged in some conflicts with the natives. Their ambassadors soon penetrated to a large city, 40 leagues inland, surrounded by a double wall, and governed by a viceroy. They found here " many doctors and lawiers, which weare four " cornered caps made of hair; other licentiats " who use round bonetts like unto Portugall " priests; also many religious persons who go " with shaven heads, having one locke of haire " hanging over eche eare." During their whole stay they did not see fifty women, and remarked the defective feet of these fair ones, oddly asserting, that " when they are borne they use to wrest " one of their legs, whereof they ever remain " lame, because they should continually kepe " their houses." He mentions also the long nails used by the men, but misses probably the real cause, when he describes it as " a profitable thing " for the warres." Specimens of Chinese dress were brought to Mexico, consisting of many rich pieces of cloth of gold, silk, and purple, "which is a thing marvailous to beholde." The viceroy of Mexico was so much moved by these descriptions and specimens, that he was preparing an expedition of a thousand men, with which he expected to conquer all China; and it is added, that "the citizens are moved with desire to go "thither for love of the great quantity of gold."

We have had repeated occasion to observe the ardent, though not always enlightened zeal, with which the Roman Catholic orders sought to propagate their faith throughout the East. With this disposition it was not likely that the vast and populous empire of China should escape their notice. St François Xavier, indeed, the great apostle of the Indies, merely touched at Canton on his way to Japan, which appeared to offer a fairer promise. But it was not long before repeated attempts were made, from the side of the Philippines, to overcome the barrier which opposed the entrance into this great empire of every stranger, more especially of those who had any innovation to introduce.

The coast of China was then infested by a pirate of the name of Limahon, who spread devastation through all the neighbouring seas. Having ventured, however, on the coast of the Philippines, he encountered a Spanish squadron, by which he was defeated, driven up a river, and so closely blockaded, that his escape was considered impossible. In this crisis a Chinese squadron arrived in chase of the pirate, whose commanders, Omoncon and Sinsai, were so highly gratified by finding the extremity to which the Spaniards had reduced him, that they assured the governor he might depend upon obtaining almost any favour from the monarch of China which he chose to ask. It was determined to improve this for the attainment of their favourite object; and the Chinese officers readily agreed to convey into China two friars of the order of St Augustin, who had lately arrived from Mexico, with hopes of their being permitted to remain and to teach their religious system. Taking with them two soldiers, they departed from Manilla in June 1575, and soon arrived at the port of Tansuso in the province of Fokien. They found the shore covered with a great body of men drawn up in military array, which they understood to be in honour of them. They were not, however, permitted to land without a written order from the governor; but they were then handsomely accommodated and supplied with every thing at the expense of the Chinese government. The Insuanto, or provincial governor at Chincheu, was understood to have sent a list of directions, in which every accommodation to be afforded, and even every dish to be put on their tables, was minutely specified. After three days they set out for Chincheu. In this journey they saw with surprise not a foot of land uncultivated, and town following town so closely, that it appeared all one town. When they asked the name of places containing 10 or 12,000 people, they were told that these were not worth naming, and that they should wait till they came to towns of some consequence. In entering Chincheu, they passed over one of the finest bridges in the world, 800 paces in length, and composed of stones 22 feet long by 5 broad. The river was so covered with vessels and barks, that the water could not be seen, and the streets, though three times as broad as usual in Spain, could not contain the multitudes that flocked to see the *Castilians* pass. They were still more delighted next day in going through the most splendid of the streets to the governor's palace. The edifices and triumphal arches were so superb, the shops filled with such precious commodities, and the multitude of people so incredible, that they remained astonished, and as it were out of themselves. Force was required to effect their entrance through the crowd into the palace, and they were then ushered into a most magnificent hall. Here they received the unwelcome notice, that an audience of the governor was not to be obtained, unless they should place themselves on their knees, and remain fixed in that attitude during the whole interview. Hereupon a pretty warm discussion arose, the soldiers insisting that this was altogether a base and unworthy submission; but they were overruled by the friars, unwilling that any scruple of this kind should frustrate their mission. On these terms the interview passed in the most amicable manner, and mutual presents were exchanged. The Insuanto afterwards sent for the two soldiers by themselves, and put many questions respecting the affair of Limahon, in the course of which it transpired that the Chinese officer had given the most false and vain-glorious account of the transaction, claiming for himself the merit of all that had been done by the Spaniards. The Insuanto, however, seemed rather disposed to believe them than him, and he soon after invited the whole party to a magnificent dinner. Before each of the friars were placed seven tables, and before each of the soldiers five, respect being shewn by the number of tables. One was covered with gilt cannisters, in which sugar and confectionary were formed into the shapes of castles, dogs, bulls, elephants, and various other objects. The other tables contained dishes of fowl, eggs, bacon, beef, and meat of every kind, with fruits and confections, so that, upon the whole, each person had upwards of fifty dishes. The services were arranged in a circle, in the interior of which plays, music, and games of various kinds were performing during the whole time of dinner, which lasted four hours. At the close of the entertainment the Insuanto sent for them, and advised them to go to the viceroy at Auchieo, (Outcheon), who could alone give a definitive answer to their demands. The friars readily consented, and lost no time in setting out. In a few days they arrived at Auchieo, and had travelled through the suburbs for about half a league, when a message came from the viceroy, advising them to delay their entrance till next morning. The advice was equivalent to a command; and he accompanied it with a supper so plentiful, that it might have sufficed a hundred men, not only for that night's supper, but for next day's dinner. Next morning they travelled an hour and a half through the suburbs; and had they not been told, they would never have doubted them to be the city. They passed a great river by three bridges, so lofty that large ships could pass under them. At length they reached the entrance of Auchieo, where a large body of nobles were drawn up to receive them, with a crowd of spectators so immense, that it seemed to them as if the whole world was assembled. They were soon after introduced in great pomp to the viceroy, in whose presence they kneeled without hesitation. He asked them if they had any mission from the King; and on being answered in the negative, dismissed them very abruptly, saying that he would consider the subject, but that, from the distance of the emperor, it would be some time before his pleasure could be known. He gave them a dinner, however, in the same style as that at Chincheu, but more splendid, and at which a regular comedy was performed. A considerable time elapsed without any decisive answer; during which the missionaries employed themselves in going about Auchieo, observing the city and people, and purchasing books. These proceedings, however, roused the jealousy of the viceroy, who directed that they should remain in their own house, and ordered every one to be beaten who carried any thing to them to sell. They learned also that Omoncon and Sinsai had quarrelled, and were giving reports of the affairs of Limahon in which each contradicted the other, and both the missionaries, so that the viceroy was beginning to doubt if there was any truth at all in the matter. In short, a meeting of the provincial council was held, in which it was determined that the friars should quit China without delay. This was announced to them in a manner which admitted of no dispute, but at the same time with great courtesy. They received an entertainment more splendid than any former one, and were escorted back to the coast with great state and attention. They arrived at Manilla on the 28th October 1577.

The event of this mission afforded little hope of any license being ever obtained to reside or preach in China. Yet two years after, a body of Franciscans determined, at every hazard, to find their way into an empire, where they understood that there were such an infinite number of souls in the chains of Satan. They fitted out a small vessel, in which four friars embarked, with three soldiers and one native Chinese, whose services they had engaged at Manilla. On approaching the coast of China, they met three vessels, whom they begged to assist in their design; but when those on board heard that they were attempting to enter China without license, they hoisted all their sails, declaring it was as much as any one's life was worth to be seen in their company. They found their way into the Bay of Canton, where they saw, as it were, a city of ships, all of which, however, fled from them as from a pestilence. They therefore moved their vessel into the middle of the river; and by taking down the sails, and every thing which could render them conspicuous, succeeded miraculously, as they conceived, in reaching the shore without attracting notice. They even landed, and began to walk upon the pier; but their very extraordinary costume at length drew the attention of the multitude. A crowd collected round them, confounded with which they entered the city, without being observed by the guards, who, however, being informed of this oversight, which made them liable to severe punishment, hurried after them, and rudely pushed them out. A Chinese Christian, who happened to be in the crowd, then came up, and told them they must return to the bark in the first instance, but he soon came to them with an order to land, and to appear before a magistrate. They found this person seated in such pomp, and so richly dressed, that had they not been told, they would have believed him to be the governor of Canton. A body of men attended, with large canes, ready to execute prompt sentence upon all culprits. Being then required to state their motive for landing, they replied, they had braved every danger in order to reach China, on a mission fraught with the most important benefits to that country, the nature of which they fully explained, and trusted he would not obstruct them in the fulfilment of it. Their Chinese friend, who acted as interpreter, judged this a very inexpedient reply, and preferred to deliver one wholly of his own invention. He stated, that they were holy men like the Bonzes; that they had not the remotest intention of entering China, but in sailing from the island of Luzon to that of Hilocos, had been shipwrecked, and had saved themselves in this little bark, when they were obliged to commit it to the guidance of the waves, which had driven them into the Bay of Canton. The friars did not learn till long after the metamorphosis through which their speech had passed; and they had reason to believe, that but for it they would have been either thrown into prison, or put immediately on shipboard, with private instructions to the captain to throw them overboard. The magistrate, however, was mollified by the answer, and having examined over and over the contents of the bark, found them to correspond with the statement. The view of the relics, the images, and particularly of a black polished stone, shining like glass, which they used as an altar, pleased him and put him in good humour. The decision of the case was delayed, and they underwent repeated examinations, without any final resolution being formed. In the mean time, they were obliged to obtain their subsistence by begging, which being contrary to the law of China, increased the jealousy of the authorities. However, the Viceroy at Auchieo hearing that strangers in a strange garb were arrived at Canton, was moved with curiosity to see them, and they set out for that city. They were equally struck as their brethren by the vast population upon the road, so that they thought it should be called, not the kingdom, but the city of China. They were surprised by a singular mode of ploughing, with one buffalo, and the ploughman riding upon it. On their arrival at Auchieo, the fathers were conducted to the palace, and ushered in at the gate, amid a tremendous report of artillery, drums, trumpets, and various musical instruments. They found the viceroy in the seat of justice, composed of ivory and gold, while on the opposite wall was painted the figure of a huge dragon, vomiting fire. A guard of two thousand soldiers attended, which they were surprised to find all Tartars, without one native Chinese. While they were in waiting the viceroy passed sentence upon fifty culprits, who were punished on the spot, by being cruelly beat with bamboos. The friars were then admitted to an audience, and the viceroy viewed with admiration their books, images, and above all, their black stone. The principal father, seeing his kind and courteous humour, began a speech, stating their most anxious wish to be allowed to settle in China, to build a monastery, and to teach their religion; and assuring him of their conducting themselves in the most inoffensive manner. This oration was committed to the interpreter, who deemed it expedient to give it quite a different turn. He gave a doleful account of their shipwreck, and being cast by hard necessity upon the coast of China, stated their most anxious wish to leave it, but lamented, that for two or three months the season would not admit of their sailing with safety. He besought, therefore, that they might be allowed protection and a house during that interval. The viceroy replied most graciously, that their demand was perfectly reasonable, and should be granted in its fullest extent. This being reported, and understood as applied to their own request, filled the friars with the most joyful surprise; since whatever hopes they might entertain of ultimate success, they never dreamt of so prompt and full a consent. They considered themselves now at the summit of their wishes, and were only annoyed by the vehement desire with which an officer of high influence at court was seized to become possessed of their black stone. The black stone was the pride of the mission; and they produced in its stead a Mary Magdalene, made of feathers, of which they solicited his acceptance. This new object excited admiration, without prejudice to the first; so that they were at last obliged to part both with the black stone and the feathered penitent. Luckily the officer was seized with a dread of discovery, and returned both.

The missionaries now found that arrangements had been made for their proceeding to Canton; a measure which they did not fully understand, but they were as willing to preach there as elsewhere. The governor of Canton received them with the most smiling courtesy, said that they appeared indeed to be favourites of the viceroy, and that it should be his care to fulfil all their wishes. They were shewn to a handsome house, and all their wants supplied; but were surprised when they found themselves not allowed to go out, and when day after day elapsed without any opportunity being afforded of carrying their views into execution. They were thus led to make inquiries, in the course of which they learned, with the deepest consternation, what was the real nature of the promise made by the viceroy. They now overwhelmed the interpreter with the bitterest reproaches. The interpreter, however, protested that he had acted a most meritorious part, and had saved their lives, since had he delivered the petition they were so rash as to confide to him, they would have been ordered to sea immediately, and at such a season must have certainly perished. They at first thought of denouncing him, and making a new attempt to obtain their object; but no one would undertake to deliver such a message, and all agreed that it would be equally fruitless and dangerous; so that at last they found they had nothing left but to accept the ample provision made by the Chinese government for their return to Luzon.

A still more unfavourable result awaited the next mission, composed of St IGNATIUS, with six other friars, who set out in like manner without any provision or arrangement. On their arrival off the coast of China, they were surrounded by a number of barks, which began and continued a heavy fire, without any regard to their quiet and submissive deportment. At length the Chinese came on board, and presented their naked swords to their breasts. The fathers remaining entirely passive, were put under a guard, and carried to the nearest port. They underwent repeated examinations, both in the ship and in the courts of justice, when they were treated with such violence and harshness, and such furious menaces thrown out, that they fully expected every visitation to be the last. In the courts of justice they saw constantly the unhappy culprits beat furiously with bamboos, and heard their shrieks; only an earnest, they thought, of what was to befal themselves. Two of the friars, who had been the loudest in professing their desire to suffer in the cause of religion, were seized with such a panic, that one of them was some days delirious, and the other died at Canton of fear. A soldier, who had amassed a considerable sum, threw it all into the sea, that he might die in the order of St Francis, which requires complete poverty. They were conveyed to Sauchieofou, and then to Uchieofu

(Outcheou); but no ray of hope ever shone on this unfortunate mission. They were treated every-where with equal severity, and at length conveyed to Canton, where they fully expected the final catastrophe. The influence of the governor of Macao, however, was there so powerfully exerted, that he obtained their lives, and permission to leave China, to which they never seem to have attempted a return.

THESE successive disappointments did not quench the zeal of the Catholic fathers. The task was now undertaken by RICIO and TRIGANTIO, of the order of the Jesuits, a body possessed of greater experience and address in such enterprises. Establishing themselves at Macao, they began to solicit, not permission to preach a new religion, the granting of which they knew would be foreign to every Chinese maxim, but merely a small spot on which to erect, for their own worship, a small house to "the Lord of Heaven." They had not much promise of success, however, till they promulgated the promise of a considerable sum to any one who should obtain this favour for them. Then a common soldier, by some means not stated, or easily to be conjectured, procured from the governor of Sciauquin (Chaotcheou) the boon solicited. They were a good deal puzzled to raise the sum offered rather in desperation than with any idea of success; however, by begging and borrowing, they at last paid it. They set out, therefore, in September 1583, under the guidance of the soldier, whom they found really in a condition to perform his engagement. The governor received them courteously, and allowed them the choice of any spot which they might find convenient. They chose one in the suburbs, by the river side, where they began to erect a tower, and to fill it with their images and ornaments. These the people flocked in crowds to view, and were much struck with admiration, both of their novelty and beauty. There was particularly an image of the Virgin, to which the Chinese testified their respect in their national mode, by prostrating themselves three times, and beating their foreheads against the ground. A scandal having arisen, however, that they should "worship a woman," the missionaries were obliged to provide another image, not liable to that objection. The governor, an intelligent man, was caught by Ricio's skill in the mathematical sciences. His geography, above all, astonished the Chinese, whose maps China alone almost entirely filled up, while all the other countries of which they had heard scarcely equalled one of its provinces. They were much amazed to see the extent of the globe, and "themselves streightened "in an eastern corner of it;" but Ricio found it requisite to place China at least in the centre. He presented the governor with a clock, but it was soon brought back, no one knowing how to keep it in order. When the missionary also began to construct globes and sun-dials, he was universally pronounced to be the greatest astrologer in the universe. The governor then having obtained some considerable promotion, conceived that it could be owing solely to their incantations. He treated them now with the highest respect, calling them "the flower of divine men," and "the holy nation of the West."

Notwithstanding these favourable dispositions, as soon as the novelty was over, the national aversion against strangers began to operate. They were accused as spies, as decoying away children, and as guilty of various malversations. A false convert represented them as possessing the art of making silver, on the promise of his disclosing which, the Chinese supplied him with funds to purchase a wife; and the disappointment of this expectation, with the loss of their money, heightened their irritation against the friars. At length the governor was so harassed with complaints and law-suits, that, sensible of their innocence, he assured them of a residence in any other place, but intreated they would leave their present one. They were at the same time assured, that to have a full view of Chinese splendour and polity, they ought to pierce into "the very "pith and marrow of the kingdom." After touching at several cities, they at length reached Nanquin, which appeared to answer this description better than any other, and where they formed an establishment, which subsisted for a number of years. They had now experienced the impolicy of passing for Bonzes, or holy men, a character held in very low estimation among the Chinese. They put on the habit of the learned class, the character which in China leads alone to high consideration, and which they were here well qualified to support. At Nanquin they drew the notice of the President of the Temples, who was so much pleased with their information, that he often visited, and allowed them to walk about at full liberty. They now applied themselves to make "the mathematics baits to the "Gospel." The Chinese seem to have felt very particular interest and curiosity with regard to European science. The Mandarins of Nanquin now learned, for the first time, that the earth was round, which they had always supposed to be square, and that there were men beneath their feet. The fixed positions of the stars, the wandering of the planets, the elevation and depression of the pole, and consequent change of seasons; the construction of spheres and sundials, were all new to them. They never till then accounted the air an element, believing it to be nothing, because they did not see it. In short, a great doctor declared himself ashamed, and said, "You may think of us as we do of Tartars "and barbarians, for you begin where we end." The Chinese were quite astonished to see that the world contained other books than their own, and even handsomer ones as to outward appearance. In short, the missionaries observe, that though their own knowledge was very inferior to what was possessed in Europe, it was sufficient to render them almost miracles in the eyes of the Chinese.

Although the Jesuits were thus well received and entertained in China, they admit, that beyond a general admiration excited by the image of the Virgin, their progress in conversion was very small. It is true, the Bonzes, or priests, instead of being held in the same veneration as the Bramins of India, are, "in the common con-"ceit of all men, most base and contempti-"ble." Indeed they seem to merit this character, since, instead of giving any useful instruction, the constant tenor of their exhortations is to "give them somewhat." Although the people too had numerous idols, they did not testify any deep veneration for them; and being of a reasonable and judicious turn of mind, "we easily "make them say that they are naught." Even when the zeal of the fathers impelled them to seize these idols and dash them to pieces, they were easily pacified. This indifference, however, was unfavourable to them in another point of view. All the other oriental nations had deep religious impressions of some kind or other; but here the Chinese differed from them all, "not "knowing nor worshipping neither false nor true "God, nor never thinking what shall follow after "this life." The learned, in particular, from whom better might have been expected, valued themselves on their indifference to every thing connected with this subject. Their respect was exclusively devoted to the works of their ancient sages, "whom they reverence little less than if "they were their God;" and the missionaries being found unacquainted with their writings, were held exceedingly unlearned persons. To this being added the limitation in the number of wives, the consequence was, that all the Mandarins and literati shewed an uniform hostility to the introduction of this new faith. There was one, indeed, whom they considered as already a convert, and in the height of their confidence exhibited to him an image of the crucifixion. The Mandarin, however, was moved with the deepest indignation, declaring that all the rumours against them, to which he had hitherto lent a deaf ear, were now fully confirmed. This frightful image, he conceived, could only be a charm to kill the King. The missionaries laboured in vain to give him sounder views; he still declared, that till "that crucified man" was committed to the flames, they had no favour to expect from him.

The Jesuits having thus gradually insinuated themselves into the kingdom, were enabled to maintain themselves for a considerable time. They were even allowed to build churches, and to make the limited number of converts whom their preaching could influence. Four of them, the principal of whom was Adam Schaal, called sometimes Scaliger, were entrusted with the management of the observatory at Peking, and of the imperial calendar. An essential function of this body was, to determine, upon astronomical *data*, the lucky or unlucky days for holding all the great court ceremonies. A son of the Emperor having died, it was referred to Schaal to decide the day on which the funeral should take place. He fixed upon one; but not long after, the Emperor's mother, and then the Emperor himself, died. No cause could be suspected, except that an unfortunate day must have been named by Schaal for the ceremony; and the discontents which had been brooding against the Jesuits rose now to a violent height. The question being referred to the tribunal of Rites, they decided that they should be summoned from all parts of the kingdom to Peking, for the purpose of being put to death. NAVARETE, to whom we are indebted for the history of this disastrous period, happened to be at Fonganhyen, in the province of Fokien, when the order arrived. He was immediately arrested, and conveyed to Hang-chou-fou, whence he was conveyed up the great canal to the capital. He found here twenty-five friars, brought in from the provinces, besides four resident in Peking. They were kept for a considerable time in uncertainty as to their fate; and indeed there appears to have been considerable vacillation in the imperial councils. At length the sentence of death was remitted, and it was determined only to banish them into a desolate region of Tartary. The Emperor softened even this, and merely directed that they should be sent to Canton, to be forwarded thence to the Portuguese settlement of Macao. The four who were at Peking were detained, in consideration of having eaten the King's bread and salt, but were thrown into prison, where Schaal soon after died. Navarete, with the others, had a most hard journey of six months, during which, the winter being severe, they suffered the most intense cold, from which no means of shelter were afforded. Their first reception at Canton was very inhospitable; but soon after a despatch arrived from the Emperor, announcing that his views had taken a more favourable turn. The missionaries were then well treated, and Navarete found his way in safety to Macao.

## CHAPTER III.

### CHINA—EMBASSIES AND MISSIONS.

*The Dutch.—Nieuhoff.—The French.—Lecomte, &c.—Their favour at court.—Expulsion.—Russian Embassies.—Isbrand Ides.—Lange and Bell.*

CHINA, so closely shut against travellers attracted by curiosity and commerce, has been accessible only by embassy. Jealous as the court is of the entrance of foreigners, yet when it can announce to its subjects, that the representatives of a great potentate are coming from afar, bearing tribute and homage to the Son of Heaven, and the Ruler of Mankind, they do not usually deny this gratification to their own vanity. They even, according to the custom which the early travellers found established among the successors of Zingis, defray all the expenses of each mission, from the moment that it sets foot in the Chinese territory. This is done, too, not in the scanty manner deplored by Carpini, but with the greatest pomp and plenty, so that the expense incurred probably exceeds in all cases the value of the presents, even without deducting those which his Chinese majesty gives in return. The ambassadors, on their way to court, proceed by a regular and established route, which includes, indeed, the richest cities in the empire. It is probably wished that they should be dazzled with the splendour of these objects; but they are carefully watched, cut off from all communication with the people, and studiously prevented from seeing more than the mere surface of things. They usually, therefore, behold a grand and splendid, but little varied scene. He, says Du Halde, who has seen one Chinese city, may form an idea of all. Little occurred to vary the different parts of the same journey, and still less to diversify one journey from another. The chief details of this grand route will be introduced under the head of Lord Macartney's embassy. In regard to the others, we shall content ourselves with exhibiting a general view of their destination and fortune.

The Dutch, who succeeded the Portuguese in the dominion of the eastern seas, were still more bent upon every thing which could lead to gain. They were not long of attempting to open a trade with China; but whenever any of their vessels approached the shore, they were surrounded with clouds of junks, who prevented them from landing, trading, or speaking with any one. If they asked leave to trade, there was an express order from the Emperor against it; and if they asked that a request to that effect should be preferred to the governor or sovereign, it would cost any one his life, or at least his place, to convey such a message. At length some conferences took place with the Mandarins, of whom the Dutch remark, "These are the gravest gen-"try in the world; they always appear with a "more composed air than the ancient Stoics." A meeting, however, was arranged between an officer of distinction and Coen, the Dutch commander. The Mandarin sat the whole day immoveable in a large hall, without saying one word on the subject of the meeting. His object was understood to be, to make the opposite party speak first, that he might sound his intentions. However, Dutch patience and gravity were his match. Coen was equally silent; and the interview broke up, without a word of business on either side. These conferences not promising to bring the affair to a speedy termination, the Dutch determined to proceed to action. They took possession of the Piscadores, some small islands near the coast of Fokien, and having begun a fort, seized a number of Chinese junks, whose crews they compelled to labour at its construction. Hostilities now began, when the Chinese were so inveterate, that they refused all exchange of prisoners, though the Dutch once offered eighteen for one; but they declared that they would not accept a thousand for one. However, finding it difficult to make any impression on the Dutch naval force, they endeavoured by negociation to induce them to remove to Formosa; and when this proved ineffectual, collected at length such an immense host of junks, that the Dutch, after considerable loss, were obliged to accept the proposed terms. They then erected a fort at Taywan, in Formosa, whence, however, they could only effect an occasional and precarious trade with the Chinese coast, and from whence they were driven in 1661.

This commencement of the intercourse between the two nations was far from conciliatory; and the Dutch, desirous to send an embassy to the Chinese court, for some time in vain solicited permission to do so; but on the conquest of China by the Montchew Tartars, obtained the consent of the first prince of that dynasty. They made not a very happy choice of Goyer and Keyser, two merchants; a profession little reverenced in the oriental courts. These were accompanied by twelve subordinate individuals, one of whom, NIEUHOFF, has written a good account of the embassy. They proceeded by the same route that the embassy of Lord Amherst returned. Travelling by water to Nanyong-fou, on the frontier of Quangtung, they crossed that ridge of mountains, the loftiest in all China, which here runs across the empire. They were astonished at the vast height of many of the peaks, and the rugged and precipitous rocks into which the sides were broken. They then descended the Kan-kiang, viewed the romantic scenery of the Poyang lake, and the majestic cities with which it is bordered; then proceeding along the great river Yang-tse-kiang, arrived at Nankin. Being admitted to wait upon the three governors, they had a full opportunity of viewing the most splendid of the Chinese cities. Its temples, towers, triumphal arches, and other edifices, surpass those of any other in the empire. The ordinary houses are very mean, having only one storey, and one room to eat and sleep in, and a small square hole covered with reeds for a window. They had an opportunity of observing and delineating the porcelain tower, the pride of Chinese architecture; a huge pagoda, nine stories high, glazed all over, and painted with various colours, having at the top a large pine apple of solid gold. All its galleries are hung with bells, which sound as they are moved by the wind.

From Nankin the embassy proceeded along the great canal, and on the 17th July 1656 arrived at Peking. They were soon waited upon by several Mandarins, who, after welcoming them, and learning the nature of the presents, began a train of very strict inquiry, what sort of people and nation they were. They had considered the Dutch, it appears, as having no home or possession but in the sea, nor could they, without much difficulty, vindicate themselves as really having an abode upon *Terra Firma*. Then the Chinese could not form the least idea what a commonwealth was; so that it became necessary to state that their mission was from the Prince of Orange. They were desired to say what relation they bore to that prince, it being usual in the East to send members of the royal family as ambassadors. They were then asked, what office they held under him? how many men they commanded? with other questions tending to throw light on their personal dignity, the result of which, in an eastern court, could not be very satisfactory. After all, they underwent a long examination before the council, at which Scaliger or Schaal, the Jesuit, was present. This person it seems asserted, that their country belonged properly to Spain, which was still the rightful possessor; however, the chancellor did not choose to insert this in his report. After putting all imaginable questions, and examining the presents, they dismissed the ambassadors. The emperor then issued a rescript in their favour, and, after a delay occasioned by the death of his youngest brother, they were admitted to an audience. There were introduced at the same time the Kalmuk ambassador, dressed in a coat of sheep skin dyed crimson, his arms naked, a horse's tail rising from the crown of his head, and on his legs such enormous boots that he could scarcely walk; one from the Mogul, in a blue coat embroidered all over with gold; and one from the Lama, resembling a Roman Catholic, with a hat like a cardinal's, and a string of beads at his side. The Emperor appearing, all did obeisance according to the grand ceremonial, striking the ground nine times with their foreheads. The Dutch never hesitated, having been doubtless instructed to scruple at nothing from which profit was likely to accrue. No words were addressed to them by the emperor, and they were even so far in the back ground, that they did not distinctly see him. A feast was then spread before them, and they were invited to carry off what was left; of which the Tartars gladly availed themselves, stuffing their pockets and drawers with roast meat, the juice of which was seen dripping as they went along.

In a few days the ambassadors received the Emperor's answer, which was to the following tenor. He expressed his high esteem for the Dutch, and his gratitude to Messrs Goyer and Keyser for coming ten thousand miles to visit him. His heart, therefore, greatly inclined unto them; and he hoped the greatest benefit might arise to his subjects from the trade which they proposed to open. Being impressed, however, with the most tender anxiety for their safety in navigating these boisterous seas, he desired that they might not come oftener than once in eight years, nor with more than a hundred men.—This most unfavourable answer being final, they were obliged to depart with this sole result of so distant a voyage, and of ten thousand pounds, which they calculate to have been expended in the journey and presents.

The issue of this embassy, prepared with such cost and diligence, appeared so discouraging, that the Dutch government did not for many years renew any similar attempt. About ten years after, however, their hopes of finding favour with the Chinese court revived, in consequence of their vessels having assisted in the reduction of Koringa, a great pirate, who had set at defiance the power of the Chinese empire. They sent first a mission to the viceroy of Fokien; but that officer replied, that he would do all in his power to favour them, but that he could not allow a vessel to enter his port without express permission from the Emperor. In 1667, therefore, another splendid and costly embassy was fitted out under "the Lord Van Hoorn." This ambassador landed in Fokien, and proceeded by Hang-chou-fou to Peking. Here he went through the usual routine of audience and presentation, at the end of which he received merely a sealed letter, the contents of which could not be known till it was opened by his masters at Batavia. Its tenor is not stated in the narrative; but we believe that though it put an end to all commercial dealings with Fokien, it allowed trade with Canton, in the terms which have since been attached to all European intercourse with China.

The religious, political, and scientific embassy which Louis XIV sent into Siam in 1684, had instructions to penetrate if possible into China, a still more splendid, though more arduous theatre. In the course of a year's residence at the court of Siam, they formed some connexions with Verbiest, the Portuguese missionary at Peking; and when, at the end of that period, Tachard departed for France, Fontaney, Gerbillon, de Visdelon, and Bouvet, set sail for Macao. A leak in the vessel induced them to disembark on the coast of Cambodia, where they set out with the view of penetrating by land to Canton. They soon lost their way, and were entangled in trackless woods, where there was not to be found a particle of food, nor any living thing, except tigers, serpents, and musquitoes. After wandering for a fortnight, and being reduced to the most miserable condition, they happily lighted upon a small village, the inhabitants of which charitably reconducted them, more dead than alive, to their vessel. They were too happy to find their way back to Siam, where some time was necessary to refit their bodies, before they ventured on a second voyage. They now persuaded Lecomte to accompany them, and all five, in June 1687, set out in a Chinese junk for Ning-po. Here they suffered much from the superstitious habits of the Chinese sailors. As no savoury food was allowed to be eaten till it had first been offered to a little black idol, they were thus virtually interdicted from every thing better than plain boiled rice. They saw the sailors worshipping the very compass by which they steered, and even offering meat to it. When the sea was rough, they threw in little paper boats, hoping thus to amuse the waves, and prevent them from seriously attacking the vessel. Once a large one was constructed, wherein were traced, not only every part of the ship, but even the figures of all the passengers. When the storm became violent, they burned feathers, hoping by the noisome stench to drive away the demon by whom the storm was raised. Our friars suffered continual fear, in sailing amid the perilous rocks and desert islands which border every part of the coast of China. On approaching Ning-po, they were thrust into the hold, which was shut down upon them, lest they should be espied by any jealous observer. They were thus almost suffocated with the heat and close air, till the captain procured from a Mandarin an order to bring them before him. They found him seated, with a grave and severe countenance, his executioners attending with rods, like Roman lictors, to chastise all who were given into their hands. The friars endeavoured to propitiate him, by stating their connexion with Father Verbiest, who was then in favour at court. In the course of two or three interviews, the display of their images and mathematical instruments put the Mandarin in good humour, and induced him to grant them lodgings in the suburbs. The viceroy, however, on receiving information of the affair, sent down a sharp rebuke to the Mandarin for such indulgence, at the same time transmitting to Peking a most unfavourable report, with a recommendation of the prompt expulsion of those strangers from the empire. This report was highly approved by the Lipu tribunal, who drew out an order to that effect for the emperor's signature. Had this been affixed, they anticipated the most doleful consequences, as they would have then been thrust back on shipboard, and the captain, thus put into the very worst humour, would probably have vented it by throwing them overboard. Verbiest, however, seeing this distress of brother Jesuits, though of a different nation, repaired to the Emperor, and pleaded strongly in their favour. He urged, in particular, the benefits which mathematics and astronomy might derive from their skill; and these being objects for which the Emperor was inspired with a species of passion, the argument prevailed, and orders were sent, that the missionaries should not only be allowed to remain in China, but should be immediately sent forward to Peking.

The fathers departed from Ningpo on the 27th November, and passing through Hangtcheoufou, Soutcheoufou, and along the great canal, arrived at Peking in February 1688. To their grief, they found their friend Verbiest dead; but they were received by Father Grimaldi, and found easy access to court; a great change in which had taken place since the accession of the Emperor Kanghi. We have already noticed the general expulsion of the Portuguese missionaries, when the few who were allowed to remain at Peking were thrown into close confinement. The new Emperor, however, then very young, was of a penetrating judgment, and particularly attached to scientific inquiries. One of the most important parts of Chinese state policy, consists in the composition of the imperial calendar, prepared by the tribunal of astronomy, and exhibiting for every day the places of all the planets, and that of the sun in the zodiac. It is presented with great pomp to all the members of the royal family, and to the officers of state, who receive it on their knees. This work, indeed, is of indispensable use to every Chinese, affording the materials from which he calculates the lucky hour and minute for sowing, planting, shearing his sheep, cutting his hair, and all the necessary functions of life. The Chinese and Arabian astronomers having waited upon Kang-hi with the calendar which they had prepared, that prince had the sagacity to see that there was something wrong, without being able to discover what. After some perplexity, he bethought himself of the European priests, and ordered that the nine chains with which they were loaded should be taken off, and that they should be brought to the palace. On being shewn the calendar, they declared that it was erroneous, and committed no less a blunder than that of throwing thirteen months into the following year. The Emperor hereupon ordered a meeting of the Mandarins of the first class, and the members of the high tribunals, to deliberate on the subject. An assemblage took place, such as had never been held on any astronomical question; and one would rather have supposed, that the very existence of the empire had been at stake. Most of the members professing total ignorance of astronomy, it was referred to a few who were supposed to possess the requisite skill. The Jesuits then exhibited their processes, which satisfied all the impartial examiners; though a few still exclaimed, that the empire was ruined if this important concern of state was placed in the hands of foreigners. A great majority, however, gave a decided verdict in favour of the Jesuits. Yet it appeared still shocking to the imperial council to acknowledge so gross an error as that of a month in a calendar already completed and circulated through the empire. They entreated Verbiest to contrive, if possible, some means of throwing a veil over this one blunder. Verbiest replied, that he could not alter the heavens; and a proclamation was issued, directing all loyal subjects not to use this intercalary month; to the great perplexity of the whole empire, who could not conceive what had become of so large a portion of time, thus arbitrarily lopt off.

The missionaries were now placed at the head of the tribunal of astronomy, and had the sole direction of the calendar. The French, being even superior in scientific knowledge, experienced at court a still more cordial welcome. Bouvet and Gerbillon were attached to the person of the monarch, and accompanied him wherever he went. Among the results of this arrangement, were the journies of the latter into Western Tartary, in which we have had occasion to follow him. The Emperor, eager in the acquisition of every kind of knowledge, and not satisfied with that which China afforded, sought to be instructed in the European sciences of geometry, algebra, natural philosophy, astronomy, physic, and anatomy. The fathers spent several years in composing lectures upon these subjects in the Tartarian language, which they delivered twice a-day at the palace. Peking became now a kind of home for the Jesuits, who resorted thither successively in considerable bodies. The profession of Christianity, however, was not legally permitted throughout the empire, and severe persecutions were even carried on in several of the provinces, till 1692, when an edict was obtained from Kanghi, allowing its free exercise. He even granted, within the extensive inclosure of the palace, a considerable spot of ground for a house and church, and supplied money to build the edifice, which was completed in four years.

It cannot be denied, that the Jesuits, during this period of their favour, made very considerable exertions to convey to Europe information respecting this vast empire. A body of them was employed to survey the different provinces, and to fix the leading positions by astronomical observations: so that our maps of China are now constructed on more accurate data than those of almost any other country out of Europe. To them we are indebted for almost all we know of the vast regions comprehended under the appellation of Chinese Tartary. The history of China by Duhalde, the *Memoires sur les Chinois*, by Amiot and others, and the treatises by Parennin, Premare, &c. in the *Lettres Edifiantes*, include a vast mass of valuable materials. The translation of the History of China, by Mailla, is also a work of great labour and merit. The Jesuits, indeed, have been accused of flattering the *Chinomania*, which raged in France during that period. Although, however, there prevail in their narratives a tone of vague exaggeration, I am not aware of the facts being in many cases actually misrepresented. They err chiefly in want of comprehensive views, and in the injudicious selection of the subjects to which their long treatises are devoted. The recent delineations given by our countrymen, though derived from much less extended means of observation, are drawn up in a strain more enlightened and judicious; and the Protestant missionaries have even penetrated farther into the secrets of Chinese language and literature. From them, therefore, we shall form a better idea of the real character and present state of this great empire.

After the Jesuits had basked for thirty years in this sunshine of imperial favour, the storm burst upon them. The Mandarins had made repeated complaints, and had obtained several restrictions upon the Catholic efforts at conversion, but these being found ineffectual, the Tsingtou or viceroy of Fokien drew up a long memorial, representing all the fatal consequences which ensued from the diffusion of this foreign sect. The reasons assigned are curious, from the view they afford of Chinese manners and ideas. He states, that the new converts are taught to pay no honours to their deceased father and mother, and to consider themselves as a stream without a source; that they are equally instructed to disregard the doctrine of the ancient sages, and even of Confucius, and to reserve all their respect for a foreigner, named Jesus. He complains of the vast sums spent in building churches, drawn out of the very entrails of the people, who, however avaricious in other points, are taught to spare nothing in this. He brands the conduct of the women and girls, who went publicly to church along with the men, contrary to all propriety; and at other times went alone into a dark chamber, to speak secret words to the Europeans, (confession). But the disorder in the new sect, from which he anticipates the most fatal effects, is the want of zeal for the raising of progeny. Though this be the first duty of every Chinese, and though it be the deadliest of sins to leave no posterity, he complains, that with them celibacy is considered as the most meritorious state; that many females are trained to it even from their infancy; that mothers, on their daughters coming of age, do not consider themselves bound to provide them immediately with a husband; and that men who lose their wives, instead of presently looking out for another, judge it more laudable to remain for some time single. Unless a stop were instantly put to these enormities, he insists that all the good laws and customs of the empire must be entirely ruined. This remonstrance, being transmitted to Yongtching, the new emperor, who had recently succeeded Kanghi, was referred by him to the tribunal of Rites. The decisions of that body had been always of one tenor. They drew up a decree for the imperial signature, which announced, that the missionaries at Peking, being of use for the construction of the calendar, should be allowed to remain; but that all others should quit the empire, for which the ample period of a year and a half was allowed. The exercise of the new faith was entirely prohibited. Notwithstanding all the interest which the Jesuits could make, this decree was signed and promulgated, and the Mandarins lost not a moment in acting upon its provisions. Scarcely had it passed, when the fathers learned with dismay, that the church in the nearest town to Peking was converted into a granary. Others were formed into public schools or colleges, or into halls established in honour of their ancestors.

After this burst was over, the persecution appears to have sensibly slackened, and a considerable number of Jesuits again insinuated themselves into the empire. In 1746, however, under the government of Kienlong, a new and warm remonstrance was made by the Mandarins, in consequence of which the persecution began afresh. Many were tortured; five preachers and a catechist were condemned to death, the first instance of capital punishment for the sake of religion. Chanseaume, the missionary who gives the account, consoles himself with the thought, that though the fire kindles easily, it is soon extinguished; and that they will find an opportunity of making their way back. The next great persecution was in 1771. Cibot, the narrator, observes, that the emperor was quite in their favour, but was unable to stem the torrent. He laments indeed the praises with which this monarch continually loaded them, declaring they were the only astronomers and painters in the kingdom; which, with a jealous people, added continually new fuel to their enmity. All the prince could do was to prevent the punishment of death from being inflicted; and one convert who went to demand martyrdom for himself, his wife, and infant son, was dismissed as a madman.

The Mandarins, however, still exercised the power of whipping the converts, laying them naked on ice, or hanging their feet in the air; and it is lamented, that though their first word was usually good, they wanted firmness to persevere. The persecution, after declining, was renewed in 1772, 1773, and 1778; and there is reason to believe that it has ever since been renewed at occasional intervals, without the Christian faith being entirely rooted out.

CATHAY, the Tartar name of China, which sounded so great in the ears of the early western travellers, was not likely to escape the notice of Russia, after that power began to stretch its domain into the east of Asia. Even before she had penetrated beyond the Obi, or come in contact with the Chinese Tartar frontier, she sought to open a communication across the vast deserts by which she was separated from this celebrated empire. In 1619 EVASHKO PETTLIN, a Cossack, was despatched from Tomo (Tomsk) by an officer bearing five names so uncouth that I shall not attempt to recite them. He bore an embassy in the first instance to a Tartar prince called the Altine Char, or the Golden King, and was then instructed to endeavour to search out his way to Catay. From Tomo he went in ten days to Kirgis (the Kirghises). He only passed through a corner of their country, and came to Mutalla, called elsewhere Mugalla (Mongolia). This, it seems, was the country governed by Altine Char, who is therefore the Khan of the Mongols. The country of Mugalla is described as "great and "large," and "there groweth all manner of "graine," and "fruit they have of all sorts. "The men are not faire, but the women are very "faire." The churches were filled with numerous idols, some gilt, and of very large dimensions, with candles burning before them. The ceremonies have a great resemblance to those of the Greek church; and the priests assured him, that "their religion and ours was all one, only the "Russe monks wear blacke, and theirs white." After five weeks travelling through Mugalla, they came to the realm of the Duchess of Manchika. We should not suppose a female reign to be very usual in this part of Asia; but the name Manchika plainly suggests the Mantchou Tartars. At the end of the Duchess's territory, they came to the great wall of Catay. It is reported to be built of brick, fifteen fathoms high; and they counted a hundred towers in view at one moment. There were only five gates, and those so low and narrow that a man could not pass through on horseback. Being admitted through this gate, they came to Shirokalga (Kalgan), the first town within the wall, which they found strongly fortified with artillery, "after the manner of Mosco castle;" and the governor's attendants walked before him with rods, "as before our Emperor at Mosco." Passing then through Yara to Tayth (Taitongfou), they found a city much larger and more splendid than any of the former, two days' journey in circuit, the shops and warehouses richly furnished. He saw there all the fruits known in Russia, and many others there unknown; so that "they want nothing whatsoever groweth in the world." After passing through several other places, he came to the greatest city of all Cataya, called Catay; for the name of Peking seems to have been unknown to him. He describes it as a very great city, four days' journey in circuit, and surrounded with "very fine towers high built and white." In the midst, at half a day's journey from each side, is the imperial castle or fortification, which he strangely imagines to be composed of *magnet*. Within this magnetic wall is the palace, the roof of which is said to be all gilded over. Four days after their arrival a secretary arrived with two hundred men mounted on asses, who presented drinks of various kinds, and asked the motive of their visit to Catay. On stating this, and expressing a wish to be introduced to the King, they were told, that for this purpose a present was indispensable; and the secretary lamented much the total absence of this requisite. He said if their "white emperor" had sent something even of trifling value, the Chinese monarch, considering it as a first visit, would have gladly received him; but that there must be something. The messenger, however, having absolutely nothing, was obliged to depart with a letter only. He returned to Tobolsk; but unfortunately that city did not contain any one of learning sufficient to decypher a single syllable. What, therefore, might be the scope of his imperial Majesty's communication, remained for ever a secret.

In 1656 a mission was sent under an ambassador of the name of Boicof; but as he refused to perform the ceremony of the Kotou, he was dismissed without obtaining an audience.

The Russian empire continually extending itself through Siberia, came, in 1680, in contact with the Chinese near the banks of the Amoor. This collision led, in the first instance, to some hostile encounters, till a treaty was concluded at Nertsthinish, fixing the limits of the two empires, and allowing the subjects of each to trade, with passports, in the territory of the other. Considerable profits being found to arise from this intercourse, Peter the Great conceived the design of improving and enlarging it.

In 1693 he despatched Everard Isbrand Ides, who spent three years in going and returning between Moscow and Peking. We shall take other authorities for the part of his journey which lay through Siberia, and shall join him at the great wall, which he considers one of the wonders of the world. He then proceeded to Galka (Kalgan), where the governor entertained him with a feast prepared in the usual Chinese style—the meat cut into mouthfuls, served in bowls piled over each other upon small tables, and eaten with chopsticks only—tea and brandy for liquor—music and plays performing during the meal. He was particularly pleased with the soups, composed of an herb found in rocks, without leaves, and which some reported to be birds' nests; a just statement, this substance being in fact eagerly sought for by the Chinese through all the Indian archipelago. He assures us that no German cook could have mended them.

In a few days the embassy reached Tongchou, which carries on a considerable trade with Japan and Corea, and bears all the Chinese marks of commercial prosperity. The river was covered with junks, having masts of bamboo, with sails of rush, and cemented, instead of pitch, with a species of glutinous earth. The ambassador was much dazzled by the display of beautiful porcelain in the market. He then proceeded through a fertile country, diversified with fine gardens, to Peking, and was carried through the usual immense crowd to his apartments in the hotel of ambassadors. Three days after, he received the imperial feast of welcome, when the Emperor's uncle and four other lords seated themselves on the floor with him to a cold collation of seventy dishes. A few days after he received instructions to appear next morning at the castle with the credentials of his czarish majesty. He was escorted by three Mandarins, and was led to the imperial hall, where a vast number of officers, richly dressed, were in waiting. Soon after the Emperor appeared, and the ambassador delivered his credentials with the usual ceremonial, which, I presume, must have included the Kotou, though it is not expressly specified. They were afterwards invited to a grand dinner, at which the Emperor was present. This was of course more splendid than any of the former ones, though served in the same style, and all the dishes were cold. The ambassador was seated near the monarch, who directed him to be brought still nearer, and sent him several dishes from his own table. Having then asked what European languages he understood, the Emperor caused the missionaries Gerbillon, and Thomas, a Portuguese, to be called in. Gerbillon put a number of questions in Italian concerning his journey, and the country through which he had passed, reporting the answers to the Emperor. The monarch concluded by giving him a draught of the Tartar liquor koumiss, when the ambassador took his leave.

During his stay Isbrand Ides witnessed the festival of the new year, which is celebrated with universal and enthusiastic festivity. The discharge of rockets and other fire-works, the sounding of the large idolatrous drums, the blowing of trumpets, and the acclamations of the people, produced a noise as great as if there had been a pitched battle between two armies of a hundred thousand men. During the day the streets were crowded with processions of images, attended by lamas, bearing pots of incense, and strings of beads. Many Tartar ladies were seen riding on asses, with their servant-maids behind. All the usual plays and juggling tricks were carefully exhibited. He was particularly amused by the elephant stable, the inmates of which had not only been trained to place themselves in every imaginable position at the command of their keeper, but had even been instructed to imitate the sounds of different animals; the roar of the tiger, the low of the ox, and even the note of the canary bird. The Romish missionaries, at present in high favour, shewed him the large convent which they had built, and enclosed with a high wall. The church was capable of containing two or three thousand people, and was richly adorned with altars and images. For the amusement of the Emperor, they kept a museum of rarities, and a pair of globes six feet in diameter. They drank in rich wines the healths of the monarchs of Europe.

The audience of leave took place in a different hall from that of introduction, but with ceremonies nearly similar, and with every mark of amity. During this embassy arrangements were made for the passing of regular caravans to Peking. These were understood to belong to the Russian government, and had all their expenses within the empire defrayed by the Chinese court. The Russians, however, soon gave considerable umbrage by their habits of intoxication, which produced disorders altogether shocking to this sober and orderly people. The complaints became so numerous, that Kanghi began to threaten their entire expulsion. To obviate this danger, the Czar, in 1715, sent Leoff Vassilovih Ismayloff as envoy to the court of China. A narrative of the journey was afterwards written by Laurence Lange, the caravan agent; and a still more valuable one by our countryman Bell, to whose fidelity ample testimony is borne by Mr Barrow.

The embassy stopped at Selinginsk till notice was sent to the court of Peking, and permission obtained to proceed. This caused a delay of about two months. At length, on the 8th of September, they took their departure. On viewing the vast extent of rich land lying here uncultivated, and covered with wood, Bell could not help comparing it to the American colonies, and figuring to himself the cultivated fields, villages, and farm-houses, with which it would one day be covered. There is good land here, he says, enough to feed two or three great European nations. On the 20th they passed a rivulet called the Saritzyn, or New Moon, which forms the boundary between the Russian and Chinese empires. The plains here are covered with rank and thick grass, so dry that it would make excellent hay. The Mongols, however, merely set fire to it, and cause a wide conflagration, that it may be manure to the next crop. From this time all their expenses were defrayed by the Chinese government; but some females whom they were bringing in their train were imperatively stopped. They passed over fine plains and valleys, covered with rank grass, and producing rhubarb abundantly, but without inhabitants. By degrees the aspect of the country altered for the worse; and at length they arrived on the borders of the desert of Shamo. On the 4th October, at Tola, they filled their bottles for the last time with pure and wholesome water, and entered on what the Mongols called the Hungry Desert. Although, however, the grass is short and thin, it appeared to be very nourishing, from the good condition of a considerable number of cattle. This arises perhaps from the saline character of the soil. The ground was strewed with numberless pebbles, some of very considerable beauty and value. On the 11th they came to a spring of pure running water, which appeared to them as delicious as Burgundy or Champaigne. Numerous springs and lakes of brackish water here occur, which, notwithstanding their bad quality, render the country habitable. Their heaviest toil was in crossing a tract of moving sand, formed into shifting waves twenty feet high, and sinking beneath their feet. So laborious was this road, that though it was only twenty miles broad, they spent three days in passing it. At length, on the 4th November, one of the party cried out *Land!* and the rest, on looking, beheld, at forty miles' distance, the wall of China majestically stretching along the tops of the mountains. As they approached nearer, it became always the more majestic, running from one high rock to another, with square towers in the intervals. They found the gate guarded by a thousand men, and commanded by two officers, one Tartar and the other Chinese. They were entertained in the guard-room with fruits, confections, and tea; and four miles beyond arrived at Kalgan.

The embassy proceeded to Peking by the same route as the former mission. They entered amid the usual crowd, and were received with the usual ceremonies. A very warm discussion took place on the subject of the Kotou, or nine prostrations, which were most strenuously resisted by the embassy; however the Chinese remained inflexible, intimating that without it there could be no audience. At length the Russians yielded, endeavouring to save their honour by the stipulation, that since they in China had followed the Chinese ceremonial, the Chinese in Russia should follow the Russian one. This was readily granted; yet the operation of prostrating themselves nine times in the dust proved still very ungrateful, and even when the crisis came they made repeated attempts to abridge the process; but the unrelenting Mandarins called out continually *morgu-boss*, in a tone which admitted of no contradiction. After the ceremony, the King addressed them in a very courteous manner, admitted them to several interviews, and took them out to hunt with him. During a stay of several months at Peking, our author had a pretty full view of the genius and character of the Chinese. He places them in rather a more favourable light than most travellers. The Chinese, he says, are a civilized and hospitable people, complaisant to strangers, and to one another; their regard for their parents, and decent treatment of their women of all ranks, deserve great praise. He says they observe the strictest honour and justice in their dealings; yet immediately after adds, not very consistently, that not a few of them are much addicted to knavery. He praises them also for their great patience in finishing every thing they undertake; and instances the street of Peking, which appeared to him the finest in the world, and the canals, lined with freestone, by which water is conveyed into the city.

In this embassy the negociators obtained the consent of the Chinese government to continue the trade on the same terms as before. The Russians, however, still indulging in the same excesses, were at length, in 1722, entirely banished from the empire. A new treaty was made in 1727, by which the crown was allowed to send a caravan once in three years, and a frontier station was fixed for carrying on the general trade between the empires. In 1755 the caravans were dropped; and the whole intercourse has since been confined to the two contiguous towns of Kiachta on the Russian side, and Maimatshin on the Chinese. With the latter also it is confined to a certain number of merchants, licensed and regulated by the government.

Mr Barrow, in his valuable account of China communicated to the Encyclopædia Britannica, has given the substance of a most curious document, being the secret instructions given by the Chinese to their Board of Merchants, of which the Russians by some means had obtained possession. It instructs them to proceed on the most complete system of concealment and deception. Every letter received by any one merchant must be opened in a public assembly, "that they may "act in concert against the Russians." False information is to be given on the prices of all goods in the interior of China; and if any one article is particularly in demand, the merchants must all join in decrying it, while no one on any account shall outbid the other. Whoever betrays to the Russians any secrets of the interior trade, is to be sent to the galleys for three years. They are to carry on all transactions in the language of the Russians, so that the latter may be under no necessity of learning Chinese. Every effort is to be made to discover the secrets of the Russian government; but the punishment of death is pronounced on all who betray to the Russians the secrets of the Chinese government. The extent and value of the trade carried on in this extraordinary manner is very imperfectly known.

# CHAPTER IV.

## BRITISH EMBASSIES.

*Lord Macartney.—Lord Amherst.—Captain Hall.—Present State.*

CHINA had hitherto been traversed only by merchants and missionaries, who had viewed it only in a limited and partial manner, and wanted skill and judgment to arrange the copious materials which they had been enabled to collect. Britain had first the honour of sending out a mission, which, with the usual political objects, combined arrangements for acquiring an accurate knowledge what sort of country China, under every point of view, really was. For this purpose, it was composed not only of diplomatic characters of the highest distinction, but of men of science and intelligence in every department, well qualified to appreciate all the objects which nature or society should present to their view. Accordingly the narrative of Sir George Staunton, and the still more valuable and judicious one of Mr Barrow, has afforded us very ample means to estimate the place which this great empire holds in the scale of social existence.

Lord MACARTNEY, already distinguished in the annals of diplomacy, was selected, at once in consideration of his approved skill, and of his rank, so well calculated to dazzle a people among whom titles are viewed as an object of the first importance. The subordinate situations were filled by Sir George Staunton, Mr Barrow, and Dr Dinwiddie. Instead of landing at Canton, they determined to sail round and disembark in the Yellow Sea, whereby they would avoid the delay and obstacles of a long land journey, and would view an extent of coast not hitherto visited by Europeans. In navigating the eastern coast, they came to the great archipelago of Tchusan, consisting of not less than four hundred islands. Boats came out in crowds to view a vessel, the construction of which was so new to them. Besides boats, there were a number of larger vessels conveying wood, which was piled on them to such a height as apparently to involve the greatest danger of their being overturned. The larger vessels were of the most cumbrous construction; the hull presenting the form of the new moon, while the ends rose on each side to an enormous height, and the bow was of the same square form with the stern. The mast, however large, is composed of a single piece; and to each mast is attached a single sail, composed of the fibres of the bamboo, which often furls and unfurls like a fan.

It seemed inconceivable how, in such clumsy vessels, they could perform long voyages, especially amid seas where they are exposed to the tafang or tuffoon, a blast so tremendous, that at its height, as an experienced commander assured Mr Barrow, if ten thousand drums and as many trumpets were blowing at the same moment, they would not be heard. Accordingly ten or twelve thousand persons are said to perish annually in this navigation.

The mission landed at Tchusan, where they were received with courtesy. They observed on the tables a singular ornament, consisting of pines, oaks, and other forest trees, none above two feet high, yet some bearing marks of age, and surrounded with rocks, earth, and mosses, so as to give the appearance of a real forest. The Chinese, by a peculiar art, have been enabled to effect this miniature imitation of nature. Their object was here to procure a pilot into the Yellow Sea, whereupon all the inhabitants who had ever been at sea were put in requisition, and came dropping on their knees before the governor. Two poor men were obliged to leave their trades, and accompany the English, but proved so ignorant, that the latter were solely indebted to their own skill and vigilance for a safe navigation through these dangerous seas. They succeeded, however, in entering that great gulf, and after anchoring in the bay of Ten-choo-foo, came to the mouth of the Peiho. Provisions and fruits were sent out in vast quantities; and at the mouth of the river there were found from thirty to forty vessels of two hundred tons each, for their conveyance upwards. These vessels were entirely rigged with bamboo, but were exceedingly convenient, rising high above the water, and being divided into thirteen distinct compartments. The flags bore in black characters the following inscription: *The English ambassador carrying tribute to the Emperor of China.*

The embassy were disappointed in the first approach to this great capital of China. The country was low and swampy, cultivated only in parts; the villages, though numerous, were small, and every thing had a poor appearance. The banks were crowded with spectators, among whom they observed many females; but among those fair ornaments of the creation, none had ever been seen whose charms were embellished with so little judgment as on the banks of the Peiho. Large bunches of artificial flowers were stuck in their hair, but without the least taste; their faces and necks were daubed with white paint, their eyes blackened, and their chin decked with two bright vermillion spots. Ancles enormously thick protruded over feet which had been reduced by unnatural compression to the length of four or five inches, while the diminutive shoe was tawdrily ornamented with fringe and tassels. As the English penetrated into the more crowded districts, females no longer appeared in public.

On approaching Tiensing, the embassy saw the first object calculated to give them an idea of the vast population of China. This consisted in the piles of salt here accumulated for the use of the neighbouring provinces, which were judged sufficient for the annual consumption of thirty millions of people. On entering the city, the multitude of large vessels lying close together, the throng of small craft, through which it was scarcely possible to make their way, the numberless spectators standing in rows behind each other, presented a complete scene of crowd and business. The countenances of the people were extremely prepossessing, their behaviour courteous and accommodating, and their features bore the stamp of innocence and simplicity. After leaving Tiensing, the country again ceased to present a crowded population; but the deficiency on land was made up on the water. In the course of ninety miles, they counted, besides numberless small craft, a thousand vessels fitted up as houses, and each containing ten or twelve apartments, sufficient to hold a family. At length they landed, and proceeded in about twelve miles to the capital of China. The first aspect did not correspond with the ideas formed of the greatest city in the world. Although the walls were only twenty-five feet high, neither house, tower, spire, nor dome appeared above them. This wall, like all others in China, is merely composed of the earth dug out of the ditch, faced on each side with masonry. On entering, however, the streets were found straight and broad, and the houses, though only one storey high, were painted with various colours, and adorned with flags, so that the whole had the air of a large encampment. The crowd of moveable workshops, the tents and booths for selling provisions, the processions of men in office, with their numerous retinues and strange insignia, mourners, marriage parties, pedlars, jugglers, conjurors, mountebanks, musicians, composed so numerous and confused a crowd, that the Tartar soldiers could scarcely with their whips enforce a passage. This multitude, amid the varied noises raised by bawling their wares, wrangling, talking, and laughing with each other, cast a curious glance at the passing embassy, but without intermitting any of their own occupations. The English were conveyed at first to apartments eight miles beyond Peking, but found them so wretched, that they solicited a return to the capital. The Emperor, however, was then at his hunting palace of Gehol, within the frontier of Tartary; and they were requested to repair thither, for the purpose of being introduced to him on the anniversary of his birth-day. Mr Barrow and Dr Dinwiddie, however, continued at Peking, and were accommodated in the palace of Yuen-mien.

Twenty miles after leaving Peking, the embassy found the level of the country beginning to rise. The mountains, forming the approach to a table land, were steep towards the sea, but declined gently on the Tartarian side. The party were accommodated in palaces built at regular stages for the accommodation of the Emperor in his summer excursions into Tartary. On the fourth day they saw, as it were, a line stretching over the whole extent of the mountain horizon; it was the great wall. On approaching, their astonishment was still increased at seeing this immense erection carried over so rugged a barrier, ascending the highest mountains, and descending into the deepest valleys, with towers at the distance of every hundred steps. The transport of such massive materials to the height often of five thousand feet; the space of fifteen hundred miles through which it is continued; and its perfect preservation after the lapse of two thousand years, afforded all new subjects of wonder. In proceeding into Tartary, the level of the ground became always higher, the climate more severe, the mountains more rugged and naked. The elevation was further indicated by the prevalence of *goitres* among the inhabitants; and some of the peaks were supposed to be 15,000 feet high. An opening among these rugged mountains disclosed the valley in which Gehol was situated. This imperial village contained only the palaces of the Prince and grandees, mixed with a few miserable Tartar huts—no medium between the extremes of grandeur and wretchedness. Pretty warm discussions now took place with the Colao, or first minister, concerning the performance of the Kotou; and it was at last conceded, that Lord Macartney should merely perform the obeisance usually paid to his own sovereign, by bending one knee to the ground. This decision was supposed greatly due to the Emperor himself, a man of liberal mind, and no lover of ceremony. When announced at Peking, however, Mr Barrow found the courtiers and tribunals struck with the deepest consternation, and considering it almost of evil omen to the empire.

The hour fixed for the audience was the dawn of day, which, however singular it appears to Europeans, suited well a hunting court, where every thing was arranged with a view to that favourite amusement. It was given, not in the palace, but in a spacious tent within the precincts of the gardens; a remnant of Tartar manners. When they had waited for some time, the approach of the Emperor was announced, by many instruments playing, and by a number of persons celebrating aloud his virtues and his power. He was carried in a chair by sixteen men, wearing a robe of dark coloured silk, and a velvet head-dress, resembling a Highland bonnet. The ambassador was brought to the left side of the throne, which is the Chinese place of honour, and held above his head the rich gold box, adorned with diamonds, which contained the King's letter. The Emperor received it very graciously, and took it into his own hand, which is considered as a favour even contrary to usage. The interview was closed by an imperial feast in the usual style.

During Lord Macartney's stay at Gehol, he had an opportunity of viewing the imperial gardens; an object which, besides displaying the wealth and pomp of China, exhibits even its taste in a favourable point of view. The English entered first through magnificent woods and lawns, resembling an English park; after travelling through which for three miles, they came to a lake so formed as to appear to lose itself in the distance. Entering a magnificent barge, they sailed along this fine piece of water, which presented at every turn such varied features of shore, bay, rock, and wood, and the art which embellished all so carefully concealed, that it appeared the grandest specimen of ornamented nature anywhere existing. They landed at numerous pavilions, filled with vases, porcelain, spheres, orreries, clocks, and other instruments, of such exquisite workmanship, and in such profusion, that the presents, which they had hoped would at least have the charm of novelty, sunk into insignificance. Yet they were assured that these were greatly surpassed by what were preserved in the apartments of the ladies, to which they were not allowed to approach.

The Emperor's birth-day formed a festival which, according to a Tartar custom, of which we have seen examples, was distinguished by the assemblage of great lords and officers of state from every extremity of the empire. Twelve thousand Mandarins are said to have been present at the great review, the troops at which amounted to eighty thousand. For several days after, games of various kinds, pantomimes, dances, fire-works, in which the Chinese excel, continued to be exhibited.

The embassy now returned to Peking, and were soon followed by the Emperor, whom they went out in procession to meet. They were sensible that their stay ought to be drawing to a period, especially as the entertainment afforded to them was so sumptuous as must press heavily on the Chinese finances. They soon found that the ideas of the imperial ministry had anticipated their own upon this subject. The Colao began to warn them of the danger of being overtaken by the ice; and when they hinted a desire to see the festival of the new-year, he assured them that it would exhibit nothing beyond what they had witnessed at the birth-day. At length a day was positively named for their audience of leave, which is considered as the immediate signal of departure. The interview took place in the audience-hall of Yuen-mien, a spacious apartment, 110 feet in length, 42 in breadth, and 20 in height. It is built of wood, and has as little excellence in point of architecture as materials, but possesses every splendour which gilding and colouring can give it. The answer, contained in a roll of paper covered with silk, was placed on a chair in the middle of the hall, for the purpose of being conveyed to the ambassador's apartments. Lord Macartney was now solely occupied with preparations for his departure, and Suntagin, an officer of high rank, as well as a very courteous and well informed person, was appointed to conduct him and his suite to Canton.

In sailing along the banks of the Peiho, the embassy were struck with the dead level of the country through which it flowed. The tide comes up 110 miles, and often causes the river to overflow. The enormous quantity of mud washed down by the Yellow River, calculated at 2,000,000 solid feet in an hour, has reduced the greatest depth of the Gulf of Pechelee to twelve fathoms, and caused the formation in it of a number of sandy islands. After passing through the crowd of shipping at Tiensing, they entered the great canal, here 100 feet wide. The country is described as in only a tolerable state of cultivation. An incident occurred which gave no very high idea of Chinese humanity. A crowd of vessels being collected to view them, one was overset, and several on board drowned; an event which passed without the surrounding barks taking the least notice, or making any effort to save them. After passing Tiensing, they came to an extensive morass, which being below the level of the canal, could be used as a drain for its superfluous waters. It contained numerous lakes, covered with fishing vessels, very busily employed. One truly unique instrument in this trade was a species of bird called *leutze*, about the size of a duck, which dived and brought up fishes sometimes almost as large as itself. After passing these swamps, they entered on a most delightful country, every spot of which was cultivated, except a few for ornamental trees and gardens. The canal, as they approached the Yellow River, presented a grand spectacle, being nearly 1000 feet broad, bordered with quays of marble and granite, with a continued range of houses; while both itself, and the various minor canals branching out from it, were covered with crowds of shipping. Some oblation was deemed needful, to propitiate the genius of the Yellow River, before launching into its rapid stream. Fowls, pigs, wine, oil, tea, flour, rice, and salt, were the chief component parts, and were carried to the forecastle, whence the liquids were poured into the river, while the meat was reserved for the table of the captain and crew. This river, though there had not been a drop of rain for several months, flowed at the rate of seven or eight miles an hour, and as thick and muddy as if torrents had just fallen. A voyage of about a hundred miles brought them to the Yang-tse-kiang; but this grand and beautiful stream flowed so gently, that no propitiatory offering was judged requisite. The appearance of the country was now superior to all that they had yet seen. The fleets of vessels of every description moving to and fro, the continued succession of cities, towns, and villages, the varied aspect and high cultivation of the lands, produced a truly striking combination. At Soutcheoufou, they sailed three hours through the suburbs before arriving at the city. Here, and in the surrounding places, the inhabitants appeared more opulent and cheerful than in the northern provinces, and were usually well dressed in silk.

The ladies were handsomer, and shewed themselves with much less reserve; which, however, was somewhat discreditably accounted for, by the statement that the concubines of the Mandarins and great men throughout China were chiefly drawn from that neighbourhood, and were there trained to fulfil that destination.

The next great town at which the embassy arrived, was Hang-tchoofou, the celebrated Quinsai of Marco Polo. Even in its decline it struck them with high admiration. In magnitude it appeared almost to rival Peking. They describe, in terms almost as glowing as his, the magic beauties of its lake, the numerous pleasure parties which covered it, the gilded barges with floating streamers sailing to and fro, with the aerial pavillions with which its margin was studded. At Hang-tchoofou the canal terminates; and they now ascended a river, through whose pebbly stream the barges were dragged almost by main force. They crossed a small neck of land, in order to reach another river which fell into the Poyang lake. Having thus reached the Kan-kiang, they were conveyed up its stream to that ridge of lofty mountains which forms the boundary of Quangtong, and all the southern provinces. Another short land journey over a high portion of this chain, called Melin, brought them to the

Peikiangho, which flows to Canton. The stream was at first so shallow, that it could be navigated only by small barges; and the country round was in an extraordinary degree wild, mountainous, and barren. The summits of the cliffs were often seen almost touching each other above the river, so that they sailed as through immense caverns. Extensive mines of coal were working in this defile. On entering Quangtong, the embassy experienced a mortifying change from that respectful courtesy with which they had elsewhere been treated, to an extremely rude and insolent behaviour. The very peasantry bawled out of their houses, *Imps, foreign devils*. This contempt of strangers, which always increased as they approached nearer to Canton, was considered as clearly emanating from that city, and as the fruit of the habits there prevalent. In this city, the lowest Chinese who hires himself to an European in the most menial capacity, makes a faithful servant, but still considers his master as many degrees beneath him in the scale of existence. Their official conductors, however, were uniformly respectful and attentive, and seemed in the end to become extremely attached to them. One of them calculated that the embassy had cost the Emperor L.173,000, while the whole expense to England had been L.80,000.

The embassy of Lord Macartney having failed in its object, no farther official intercourse took place till the recent embassy of Lord Amherst. Some differences had taken place with the Canton provincial government, in which the latter indeed were obliged to yield, but which inspired the Company with a wish to open a direct communication with the court, and to obtain thus an appeal from the caprices of the local government. With this view, they proposed to the British Government that an embassy should be sent from the Prince Regent to the Emperor, of which they undertook to defray the expense. This proposal was readily acceded to; an embassy was prepared, at the head of which was placed Lord Amherst. Mr Elphinston and Sir George Staunton, who held the highest situations in the factory at Canton, were to occupy the second and third places in the commission; but in case either of these gentlemen should happen to be absent, Mr Ellis went out to fill the station thus left unoccupied. On reaching Canton, they were joined only by Sir George Staunton, who took the second place, and Mr Ellis the third. They were accompanied also by several members of the factory, and among others by Mr Morrison, a gentleman well skilled in the Chinese language, and who acted as interpreter. The viceroy and the Portuguese at Macao shewed an unfriendly disposition, and spread unfavourable rumours; but, before leaving Canton, the embassy received a communication from the Emperor, expressing the most cordial welcome, and assurances of a favourable reception. In the end of July they arrived at the mouth of the Peiho. They were soon waited upon by three Mandarins, two of whom, Chang and Yin, had the one a blue and the other a red button, which indicated high rank. The third, Kwang, had only a crystal button, but as Chinchae or Imperial Commissioner, he took precedence of the other two. Indications of Chinese haughtiness were occasionally manifested; but, upon the whole, theybehaved with tolerable politeness, and arrangements were made for the disembarkation and voyage up the river. An early opportunity, however, was taken of introducing the subject of the Kotou. The question as to the performance of this ceremony had come under the consideration of the Government at home; and the instructions given to the ambassadors seem to have been very judicious. They were to adhere, if possible, to the precedent of Lord Macartney, who had obtained access to the imperial presence without the performance of a ceremony so revolting to European ideas. At the same time Lord Amherst was left at liberty to act as circumstances at the moment might seem to dictate; in short, should it seem advisable, the Kotou was to be performed. On the other hand, Sir George Staunton, and the other members of the Canton factory, objected to it in the most decided manner, as likely to produce injurious effects, by lowering the English character in the eyes of the Chinese. The first questions were prudently evaded by Lord Amherst, who merely said, that every thing proper and respectful would be done. The embassy and suite were therefore embarked on the Peiho; and it was soon intimated, that at Tiensing an imperial banquet awaited them. The pleasure afforded by this testimony of respect was damped by the intimation, that they were expected to perform the grand ceremony in presence of the dinner, in the same manner as if his Imperial Majesty had presided, which he was judged to do, having given the entertainment. This proposition was rejected by Lord Amherst in the most decided terms; he refused even to kneel before the majesty of the table; and, after long discussion, the Chinese compounded for nine bows, to correspond with the nine prostrations, which they themselves made. The dinner was handsome, after the Chinese manner; and they continued their voyage up the river to Tong-chow, the port of Peking. During the voyage and the residence there, the Kotou was almost a perpetual subject of discussion; and the Mandarins spared no urgency which could induce Lord Amherst to agree to it. They even made the most solemn and repeated asseverations that it had been performed by Lord Macartney; and they had the unparalleled effrontery to appeal to Sir George Staunton, who had been then present, for the truth of their statement. Finally, they brought forward an imperial edict, in which the same assertion was made. The ambassadors extricated themselves as politely as possible from the embarrassing situation in which they were placed by these scandalous falsehoods. Sir George evaded the references made to him; and Lord Amherst steadily referred to the archives of the former embassy, which bore that no such ceremony had been performed. To the first band of solicitors was now added *Hoo,* whom Mr Ellis terms a duke, though the expression, we think, cannot be properly applied in China, where there exists no high hereditary rank corresponding to the idea which we attach to it. This duke, as he is called, began by endeavouring to carry his point by roughness and blustering; but finding that these produced no effect, he assumed a more conciliatory tone, and held out high prospects, almost assurances, of solid marks of imperial favour, which would follow upon this point being conceded. Lord Amherst and Mr Ellis were inclined to yield; but Sir George Staunton having held a formal consultation with the Canton members of the mission, gave it as his and their decided opinion, that compliance would prove more injurious to the interests of the Company in China than any concession which could be hoped for. The resolution of refusing it was, therefore, irrevocably fixed. The Chinese officers did all in their power to induce the ambassador to change his resolution; but when it appeared immoveable, they seemed to yield the point, and said that the Emperor would receive them on their own terms, by which kneeling upon one knee was to be substituted for the Kotou.

The object was now to hasten their departure, which, through the exertions of the Chinese, took place on the afternoon of the 28th of August. They travelled that evening and the whole night round the walls of Peking, not being admitted into the city. Soon after day-break they arrived at the palace of Yuen-mien, where the Emperor then was. They were ushered into a small apartment, filled with Princes of the blood, Mandarins of all buttons, and other spectators. Chang, one of their ordinary attendants, then came and announced the Emperor's wish to admit them to an immediate audience. Lord Amherst objected, on the ground of his exhausted state, and want of all proper equipments. Chang finding all argument ineffectual, reluctantly carried the information to Hoo, who sent repeated messages, and at last came himself, and exhausted every form of argument or entreaty to induce Lord Amherst to enter. At length, with a shew of friendly violence, he made a movement to draw him in, which was very properly resisted. The ambassador then repaired to the apartments provided for him.

The principle of the Chinese government is to make every officer responsible for the success of the affairs intrusted to him, with very little inquiry whether they have failed through his own fault, or from unavoidable causes. This had led to the eagerness of the Mandarins for the performance of the ceremony, and it now made them dread being punished for the disrespect shewn to their imperial master. Their usual system of deception was resorted to. The Emperor was told that the ambassador had been seized with a sudden illness, which rendered it impossible for him to appear in his Majesty's presence. This passed off well. The Emperor delayed the interview, and permitted the British to retire into a neighbouring house, where ample accommodation was provided. Unfortunately, he added the farther kindness of sending his own chief physician to assist in their cure. That person found Lord Amherst in the most perfect health, and with no visible impediment to have prevented him from appearing at Court; which being reported to the Emperor, sealed the fate of the embassy. In two hours an order arrived to set out for Canton without a moment's delay; and no plea of fatigue being listened to, the party were obliged to set out by four of the same day. On their arrival at Tong-chow, they found the triumphal arch which had been raised to celebrate their arrival thrown down, and the house provided for their reception shut up. Their fallen state fully appeared, when a beggar, who had risen up as Lord Amherst passed, was ordered to resume his seat. Yet, in the course of their voyage down the canal, an edict arrived, in which the Emperor complained of having been deceived, and directed that the English should be treated more favourably. On their arrival at Canton, however, they found a new edict, in which they were bitterly reproached for the disrespect shewn by refusing the offered audience. The viceroy was instructed to treat them with marked coldness, and even to give them a sharp reprimand.

In China, where nothing changes, a new traveller can see little that has not been seen before. It was impossible that the present embassy should add much to the copious details of the missionaries and Sir George Staunton, and the living picture drawn by Mr Barrow. Indeed Mr Ellis, though his remarks are correct and sensible, does not appear to us to have been smitten with the true exploratory spirit. He sailed, however, down the great river Yang-tse-kiang, which he describes as truly majestic, and decidedly superior to the better known stream of the Hoangho, or Yellow River. This entirely agrees with the account long ago given by Marco Polo, who represents it as the greatest then known in the world. The embassy had also an opportunity of viewing the noble scenery of the Poyang Lake. An extensive sheet of water, surrounded with mountains, is a feature not unknown to ourselves. But these mountains, covered to the summit with woods and varied vegetation, crowned with pagodas, and with vast cities stretching along their feet, must have formed a combination of grandeur, which scarcely, perhaps, any other part of the globe can equal.

We now hasten to that part of the expedition which presents by much the most interesting results in the view of discovery. This was the return of the Alceste and Lyra to Canton, which they performed by a route hitherto unknown to European navigators. A very pleasing account is given of it by Lieutenant Macleod of the Alceste; and a more elaborate, scientific, and truly interesting one by Captain Hall of the Lyra, son to Sir James Hall, President of the Royal Society of Edinburgh, a gentleman to whom science is deeply indebted. The vessels began by making the circuit of the Gulf of Pechelee, which brought them upon the coast of Corea. They discovered a group of islands, to which Captain Hall gave his father's name. They landed; but the only intercourse which they could obtain with the inhabitants consisted in signs made by the latter, expressive of the most eager wish that they should go away; one of which consisted in blowing a piece of paper in the same direction with the wind, and pointing to the ships. The English were at length obliged to comply, and landed on another part of the coast, where they could obtain no courtesy till they turned their backs to regain the ships, when the natives shewed the utmost alacrity in helping them over every impediment. They now came to a very populous part of the coast, and resolved to make another attempt to attain a footing on land. As soon as they put out their boats, a number came rowing from the shore to meet them; and they soon distinguished one personage, whose dress and deportment announced him as a chief. He was an old man of venerable appearance, with a beard reaching below his middle,—a robe of immense size flowing round him, and a hat of enormous brim, reaching more than three feet across. He received them graciously, but, on their proposing to go on shore, intimated the most decided preference in favour of proceeding towards the ship. The British complied; and he was, with great difficulty, hauled up with his bulky appendages, and placed upon deck. He then shewed extreme satisfaction, and endeavoured to enter into conversation; but it soon proved that signs were the only possible mode of communication. He behaved, however, with great courtesy and gaiety; eat and drank after the English fashion; and searched every corner of the ship with eager curiosity, though to explore some of them he was obliged, with great reluctance, to lay aside his hat of state. After several interviews, the English pressed so earnestly the proposition of returning his visit on shore, that he found himself obliged to comply. No sooner, however, had the landing taken place, than his countenance changed, and he was soon seen melting into tears. The party proceeded towards a village in sight; but the old man soon began crying violently, and at length sobbed, and even bellowed aloud. The English, entreating to know the cause of such direful affliction, he made a long speech, in which nothing was intelligible except the sign of passing his hand frequently across his neck, which was understood to intimate that his head was in danger. Every attempt to abate his agony having proved unavailing, there remained no choice but to return to the ship. He appeared then ashamed of his conduct, but made no attempt to repair it by inviting them again on shore.

The expedition proceeded southwards; but they were soon surprised to find, that what had been supposed to be the coast of Corea, was in fact a numerous collection of small islands, the existence of which had been hitherto unknown. The number of these islands baffled all calculation. From a high point which they reached in one of the group, they could count a hundred and twenty in sight, and, during a course of upwards of a hundred miles, the sea continued as closely studded with them. There does not, perhaps, exist in the world such an archipelago of islets. Wherever they landed, the same eager anxiety was shewn for their re-embarkation; so that there seems no doubt that the Corean government is as rigidly adverse to the admission of strangers as those of China and Japan.

The vessels now left the shore, and, after a considerable run, passed a volcanic island, called Sulphur Island; but the surf prevented them from landing. They soon after came in sight of the great island of Lieu Kieu, or, as Captain Hall calls it, Loo Choo. The very first view of it inspired a pleasing sentiment, as it resembled, according to Mr Macleod's description, rather the environs of the finest country-seats in England, than the shores of a remote and unknown island.

The deportment of the people soon confirmed every favourable impression. Several canoes came up, which handed water, provisions, and fish, without asking, or seeming to expect any return. Their manners were at once gentle, and ceremoniously respectful: they uncovered their heads in presence of the English, and bowed whenever they spoke. The shore was soon covered with spectators; and the ships were visited by several chiefs, who behaved in the frankest and kindest manner. When, however, the English began to make overtures for returning these visits on shore, every mode of polite evasion was studiously employed. They pretended to consider themselves so much inferior to their new acquaintances, as to have no claim to such a return, which would even, they said, have degraded the English. Captain Maxwell having complained of illness, they offered to send a physician on board; and when he said that his physician had recommended a ride on shore, they merely laughed, and changed the subject. After several visits, however, the Captain pushed the offer so home, that they could not reject it without an open breach. Five of the officers accordingly landed, and were received with much ceremony, being led by the chiefs through two files of people, ranged on each side for the purpose of viewing them. They soon reached a temple, where they found a large japanned table spread, and were regaled with a dinner, consisting of hard boiled eggs, fish fried in butter, smoked pork, pig's liver sliced, several kinds of cakes, and other dishes, most of which were found palatable. The entertainment was conducted with much gaiety and good humour. It was still in vain that they solicited permission to land their stores, and to take up their quarters on shore, for the benefit of health and exercise. This, however, was at length brought about. The natives had at first recommended a harbour ten miles to the southward; but their new visitors, when better known, becoming daily more agreeable, they shewed no wish to part, and always shunned furnishing the promised guide to this new station. One morning, however, the Lyra disappeared, and they found, on inquiry, that it had gone to reconnoitre the harbour in question. The dread of losing the English altogether made all their demands be at once agreed to. They were received on shore, and commodiously lodged in a large temple. Their range, however, was always confined within the narrowest possible limits. They saw at a distance a large building, which they had reason to believe was the King's palace; but all positive information on the subject was steadily withheld. At the same time, the intimacy and cordiality of the English with the natives daily augmented. They had a

Chinese interpreter, so that they could communicate from the first by words; and both parties soon made great progress in each other's language. The most interesting personage was a young man of the name of Madera, who appeared first as a common native, and associated with the sailors, but gradually rose in consequence, till he proved to be a man of very high rank, who had assumed this disguise for the sake of observing the strangers more intimately. He appears to have been remarkably distinguished by intelligence, as well as by a good-humoured, gay, and friendly disposition. Before leaving Loo Choo, they were visited by a prince of the blood, a very polite personage, but who had nothing striking in his manners or appearance. On their expressing a wish to be introduced to the king, he stated, that the custom of the country forbade this, unless they came on an express mission from their own sovereign. The English soon after took their departure, which drew forth deep demonstrations of grief from Madera and their other friends.

The inhabitants of Loo Choo appear, indeed, to be a very interesting people. In their manners and political state, they seem to hold a middle place between the people of China and those of the South Sea islands, and, by a rare good fortune, to have united the good qualities of both, without the faults of either: They combine the civilization of the one race with the simplicity of the other. There was every reason to believe that they were unacquainted both with arms and with money. Their honesty was quite unimpeachable. Although they had free access to every part of the ship, and of the temple in which the stores were afterwards placed, no instance of pilfering was ever observed; and when any thing was missing, no one ever suspected that it could have been carried off by the natives. They are a gay and social people, carry about their dinner in boxes, and have frequent *pic-nic* parties among themselves. They appeared to enjoy much the hospitality of the ship, and did not always confine themselves within the most rigid rules of temperance. The population could not be conjectured. The part of the island immediately under observation was highly fertile and cultivated, but the opposite side was understood to be much less improved.

THERE may be now room for some general remarks on the Chinese empire.

The population of China has been always a subject of much wonder and speculation. The number of 333,000,000, which was given by a Mandarin to Lord Macartney, as founded on official *data*, seems given up on all hands as an empty vaunt. It is by much the largest ever given. Mendoza, who collected the reports of the Spanish friars, and stands accused of great exaggeration, reports the persons paying taxes only at 40,500,000, which, taking the perhaps high average of five to a family, would not give more than 200,000,000. It is certain, that with a view to taxation, the census is very frequently taken; but besides being liable to inaccuracies, it is studiously concealed, and often misstated. Some enumerations have reduced the population to between 50 and 60,000,000; but, upon the whole, the accounts deserving of greatest credit seem to place it somewhere about 150,000,000. This amount, compared with the dimensions of China, does not exceed the proportion of 100 to the square mile—no very extraordinary density, when compared to districts, and even kingdoms of Europe; yet probably no other continuous extent of land throughout the globe contains so great a population. Certainly no number nearly so great is anywhere united under one government.

In comparing the Hindoos and Chinese, the two most numerous and polished nations of Asia, we are struck at first with a certain general resemblance. They both exhibit the same smooth and polished surface of character. Both are distinguished by quietude, courtesy, domesticity; and more unfavourably by meanness, cowardice, deceit, and dishonesty. On the other hand, there are other points in which they appear even as strikingly contrasted. The literary and speculative pursuits in particular of the two nations have taken an entirely different direction. Perhaps the fundamental distinction consists in religion, or rather superstition, forming in the one the basis of literature and of political society, while in the other it is excluded from both. The mind of the Hindoo soars continually in the clouds, and amid objects beyond the limits of earth; while that of the Chinese is always absorbed in the objects of common life, and directed towards purposes of plain practical utility. The literature of the Hindoo consists entirely of wild romances and mythological poetry; while the Chinese have a history extending back for two thousand years, and their lighter compositions consist of domestic tales and didactic poetry. The ideas of the one lose themselves in vague and hyperbolical grandeur; those of the other are cramped within a narrow and confined sphere. In the abstract sciences, the Chinese seem to fall short even of that limited measure of excellence which the Hindoos have attained. Their *swanpan*, formed of balls strung on wires, is far behind the arithmetical digits; and the astronomical observations for the imperial calendar have been long made by foreigners. Their scale of mechanical arts is different, but on the whole not inferior. Their silks and satins indeed, though excellent, can scarcely bear a comparison with the splendour of the cotton fabrics of Indostan; but their porcelain surpasses, in the excellence of its material, and the brightness of its colours, all the imitations which Europeans have laboured to make. Their paintings are distinguished by colouring and close imitation of nature, though the design is poor, and they have not the least idea of perspective. Mr Barrow enumerates, as minor articles in which they excel, their transparent horn lanterns, their cutting of ivory into fans, baskets, and toys, their silver fillagree, their lacquered wares, only inferior to those of Japan, their ornamented furniture, their ink, which is an object of export to Europe, and their paper used in printing, which may challenge ours. Their agricultural implements are as poor as those of Indostan; but they carry the process of irrigation to a still greater extent, and they collect manure with almost ludicrous diligence. Tea, the most characteristic produce of China, is cultivated to a great extent only in a few of the mountainous provinces. It undergoes the process of roasting in iron pans; the greater or less extent of which process gives rise to the difference between the black and the green teas.

The most prominent feature in Chinese policy, and which appears at first to exalt it above that of Europe, is the high place assigned to learning. Proficiency in study is the essential qualification for high office; the candidates for which undergo a course of examinations, much more extensive and severe than await an European entering upon any of the learned professions. It is not said that these examinations are carried on with any very gross partiality. Such a system, it might be supposed, would lead to great progress in the arts and sciences; but the real effect appears to be directly contrary. This official learning is necessarily connected with the formation of standards, which it would be contrary to every maxim of state to alter. These have continued the same for two thousand years, and may probably continue so for two thousand years more; during all which time science, so far as political influence is concerned, remains completely stationary. The Chinese, however, impelled by such strong motives, learn with great diligence the science, such as it is, which leads to these high honours. A taste for letters is universally diffused; there are schools in every village; and education may be obtained at a very cheap rate. The press is even free, at least as to the first publication, though the severest chastisement doubtless awaits those who use this privilege in any manner hostile to government; indeed any thing so daring scarcely ever enters the mind of a Chinese.

It is probably the cause now stated which has arrested the Chinese language in the present singular stage of its progress from hieroglyphics to the use of an alphabetic writing. Every word, instead of being expressed by the varied combinations of a few letters, has a distinct character of its own. It is not wonderful that the view of this crowd of varied symbols should have struck the early missionaries with consternation, and have made them represent this acquisition as a task equal to the duration of human life. The labours of several of our learned countrymen have untied in a great measure this Gordian knot. They have shewn that all these characters may be reduced to 214 simple marks, one of which must enter into the composition of every single word. In the Dictionary constructed by Mr Morrison these marks are used like letters, as heads under which the different words may be arranged. A more elegant, though less precise analysis, has been formed into 417 characters, which represent natural objects and simple ideas, by the often fanciful combination of which, all those of a complex nature may be expressed. In this view Chinese writing approximates to a natural, and what might become an universal language; as in fact the Japanese, Coreans, and other neighbouring nations, whose speech is entirely different, use the same written language.

The Chinese government encouraging and supporting no state religion, the people must look abroad to satisfy this imperious want of the human soul. The system introduced, and almost exclusively professed, is that of Fo, a modification of the almost universal religion of Boodh, or Buddha, distinguished here, as elsewhere, by numerous images of departed worthies, some of gigantic size; by processions, bells, beads, tapers, and other external marks, which have given to it the strong and often observed resemblance to the Catholic rites. The Christian religion, when its teachers could find access, usually made considerable impression upon the people; and the Jesuits boast at one time of 300,000 converts. Their career, however, was always stopped by that hostility to change which is so deeply fixed in the ruling powers. Perhaps if a Protestant mission could find entrance, their practices might not give such deadly offence. Neither confession, nor the high honours paid to celibacy, would here shock the Chinese; and if they could grant indulgence to a little amiable superstition in the honours paid to deceased parents, they might introduce their faith without any very decided opposition to those habits, the observance of which is here considered indispensable.

Among the most prevalent Chinese customs we may number the culpable one of exposing children, which seems to be carried on almost under public sanction. Every morning persons are employed to go through the streets of Peking to collect the infants thus abandoned by their parents. Those exposed in the streets of that city alone have been said to amount annually to 30,000; and Mr Barrow cannot reduce them lower than 9000. In the provinces the practice is less extensively prevalent. The children exposed are chiefly female; nor is this the only particular in which disrespect is shewn to the fair sex. They are treated in every respect as inferior beings, are subjected to the hardest labour, and have sometimes even been seen yoked in the plough. The Chinese proverbs dwell much on the disturbance which they occasion in a household, complaining that what has been taken from their feet has been added to their tongue. In regard, however, to this artificial reduction of the lower extremities, effected by painful compression from their earliest years, it may be questioned whether it be intended as auxiliary to the system of confinement, or be not rather, like the small waists till lately so prevalent in Europe, the offspring of fantastic ideas of beauty attached to extreme exility. It certainly, however, diminishes much the locomotive power of the fair sex in China.

In summing up the general character of the Chinese, Mr Barrow begins by stating its dark side, on which he observes, that "the boasted "morality of the Chinese is built on no principle "of feeling or propriety of action between man "and man; and where public decorum is not "offended, there is no breach of moral duty. "Great crimes are not common, but little vices "pervade all ranks of society. A Chinese is cold, "cunning, and distrustful; always ready to take "advantage of those he has to deal with; ex-"tremely covetous and deceitful; quarrelsome, "vindictive, but timid and dastardly." In opposition to these bad qualities, he sets "his sober "and industrious habits—submissive disposition "—a mild and affable manner—an exactness and "punctuality in all which he undertakes to per-"form. He has at least the merit of believing "in the God of his fathers—of obeying the com-"mands of his superiors—and of honouring his "father and mother."—Some very positive moral and political advantages, says Sir George Staunton, are attributable to the system of early and universal marriage; to the sacred regard that is habitually paid to the ties of kindred; to the sobriety, industry, and even intelligence of the lower classes; to the almost total absence of feudal rights and privileges; to the equitable distribution of landed property; to the natural incapacity and indisposition of the government and people to an indulgence in ambitious projects and foreign conquests; and, lastly, to a system of penal laws, if not the most just and equitable, at least the most comprehensive, uniform, and suited to the genius of the people for whom it is designed, perhaps of any that ever existed.

# CHAPTER V.

## JAPAN.

*Portuguese Missionaries.—Kaempfer.—Thunberg. Kruzenstern.—Golownin.*

The stormy sea which dashes along the eastern shores of Asia, is traversed from north to south by three large islands, which, united, constitute one of its most civilized and flourishing empires. The people, in whom the external forms of manners and society, and even their bodily aspect, indicate a Chinese origin, display, however, a superior character of energy and intelligence to that of almost any other Asiatic nation. Our interest with respect to them can be only partially gratified; for amid the eager curiosity with which foreigners are regarded by individuals, they are excluded by the government with a jealousy more than Chinese. It was not always so, however; and till the Portuguese missionaries, by their imprudent measures, excited the alarm of the ruling power, they obtained much fuller access into Japan, than into any other country of the East. To them, therefore, we are indebted for the most copious, though not the most judicious narratives, on the subject of this extremity of the continent.

Guzman, the leading historian of the Japanese missions, begins with some general views of that country and its people. The Japanese, he says, do all things in a manner opposite to Europeans. When we take off our hats, they take off their shoes; we rise up to receive a visitor, they sit down; we dislike to see a man's head bald, they are at the greatest pains to extirpate the hair, leaving only a small tuft on the crown. They set the greatest value upon things which we esteem as of none. An instance is given of certain cups or vessels (porcelain), in which they receive the juice of an herb called *cha* (tea). For one of these, if old or of fine quality, they will give from four to six thousand ducats. Being asked why they gave so much money for things of no value, they urged the universal admiration of diamonds and precious stones, which were of no use whatever, while these were of some. The properties of this *cha* are stated in very lofty and exaggerated terms. By drinking it, a man, it is said, may spend the whole night without sleep, yet be as fresh in the morning as if he had enjoyed the most undisturbed repose. A drunk man, by taking a draught, feels his head as clear as if he had not tasted a drop. The Japanese, however, have no strong liquor, except a species made of rice, and even this is used in very limited quantities. They eat on the ground, upon mats of palm leaves, without either cloth, towel, knife or fork. They eat with two pieces of wood or ivory, which they use so skilfully, that not a crumb falls to the ground. They avoid milk as if it were warm blood, and cows' flesh as if it were that of horses. Their diet consists of rice, fish, and fowl. Only the principal houses are built of stone; the rest of wood, the inside cedar and cypress, the floor and walls covered with mats.

Of all the eastern nations the Japanese are said to be the most elevated, both as to character and intellect. Their conversion could be effected only by arguing with them, and by resolving their doubts. They entertain a high sense of honour, and observe towards each other the most ceremonious politeness. Their courtesies and ceremonies are infinite; they have many books teaching how to take a draught of water, how to give and receive presents, and all the other minutiæ of behaviour. Their chiefs are said not so much to resemble our Counts and Dukes, as tributary sovereigns like those of Arragon and Castile. They are supposed the entire proprietors of the land, part of which they keep for the support of themselves and families, and divide the rest among their nobles, who have vassals under them. These princes have little revenue, but they easily collect great armies and numerous attendants.

In regard to religion, the historian grieves to say, that though the devil obtains high reverence over all the East, it is in Japan that he reigns with supreme and almost unrivalled sway. After this it is somewhat wonderful that he should immediately proceed to lament, with more than usual emphasis, the almost total impossibility of distinguishing between his ceremonies and those of the Catholic church. The clergy wear the same dress; they have monasteries, male and female; and the rosary is continually in their hands. They preach from a raised place like a pulpit, proving that no one can be saved out of their sect. They have three sects, one called Xenxus (Sintos), chiefly followed by kings and great lords. These do not believe in a future life, and erect temples to deities who are supposed to be distinguished by their prowess in war. The other two are the adorers of Amida and of Fo, which, however, are only two different forms and names of the widely diffused religion of Boodh. The latter, he says, are obstinate in regarding the book of Fo with the same entire reverence as the Mahometans do their Alcoran. In order to save themselves, they think they need only repeat five words, *Namu, Mio, Foren, Qui, Quio,* which no one can comprehend or explain the meaning of. The missionaries suspect this to be expressly contrived by the great enemy, so as to render it impossible to say any thing in their refutation. Both these sects distribute to their votaries bits of paper covered with figures of idols and mystic words, as sure passports into paradise.

Japan had the honour of being the great theatre of the labours of St Francis Xavier, the great apostle of the East, and in fact an exceedingly worthy and pious man. The favourable accounts from Firando, where the Portuguese had established a factory, induced him to set sail for that place in a Japanese vessel. Here, however, his eye was grievously offended by the view of a little deformed idol, to which the most profound reverence was paid; and he was struck with still deeper dismay on learning, that it was to be the arbiter as to the nature and extent of the voyage. The first reference made was, whether they would arrive in safety at Firando? to which the answer was favourable. It was then asked, whether they would return in safety? which question, through the artifices of the devil, received a negative. To the despair then of Xavier, the captain determined to proceed no farther than Canton. On reaching that port, however, they learned that there were enemies' vessels in the harbour, and found the wind so prosperous that they were carried on almost involuntarily. Thus Xavier saw with triumph the deep laid plot which the devil had laid to prevent his reaching Japan entirely frustrated. His first letters do not indicate any strong motive which that personage could have to oppose so strongly his arrival. He states himself to find in this situation only two advantages; first, that whereas in every other place there was some social enjoyment or outward comfort, here nothing of that nature occurred to distract the exclusive attention due to his spiritual functions. The next comfort was, that the religion which he taught appeared to be the object of an enmity so deadly, as to afford full assurance of severe suffering, and even a distant hope of the crown of martyrdom. It appears in fact, that the strangeness and poverty of his aspect and attire made him become the object of public derision; he was considered as a madman, and the boys amused themselves by pelting him with stones. He himself became at last sensible, that in his present uncouth and humble garb he could never make any impression upon a people who receive such powerful impressions from the senses. He applied in this extremity to the merchants at Firando, whose zeal impelled them to clothe him in somewhat more seemly attire. They even furnished him with a clock and harpsichord, as introductory presents to some great man. Considering the extent, however, to which the Firandese had committed themselves against him, it appeared advisable to change the scene. He repaired to Amanguchi, where he obtained an introduction to the King or Governor, who was so greatly delighted with these new objects, that he granted him favour, and full liberty to preach. A brilliant career now opened to the missionaries; they found free access to all the neighbouring districts of Bungo, Arima, Satzuma, &c. Several of the governors, or tributary kings, openly professed Christianity. The King of Bungo sent four lords in embassy to Europe, who visited Lisbon, Madrid, Toledo, Florence, Rome, and other great cities, carefully viewing all the images and relics preserved in the chapels. They brought over from Philip II. rich presents, consisting chiefly of crosses and medals. In a district called Cochinozu the Jesuits appear to have obtained not only the full establishment of their own religion, but the entire prohibition of every other. The author of the *Oriente Conquistado* relates the following exploit with peculiar triumph. There was a rock in the sea, separated from the continent by a narrow channel, containing an excavated shrine, which was an object of deep veneration and frequent pilgrimage from this part of Japan. Hither the Bonzes, in their distress, had conveyed the most sacred of their images, to be reserved until happier times. The Jesuits, however, determined to storm this unhallowed repository. The Bonzes had destroyed the bridge, thrown by a difficult operation over the gulf, which alone communicated with it, and had done every thing possible to render the approach inaccessible. A large body of Japanese Christians, however, armed with proper instruments, repaired the bridge, and cut a way to the cavern, whose black and horrible aspect resembled the mouth of hell. They entered fearless, and found within it a hundred huge and horrible statues, with an altar, and various other superstitious symbols. The Jesuits instantly applied hammers to the marble, and fire to the altar, and in a few hours, instead of this pompous display of idolatrous worship, there remained nothing but stones and ashes.

Notwithstanding these prosperous beginnings, the zeal of the grandees who had embraced the Catholic faith began quickly to cool. The first point of discussion arose here, as elsewhere, from the conscientious urgency of the missionaries for the dismissal of the vast train of wives which each of them thought fit to maintain. They were very willing, it is said, to believe well, provided this particular point of practice were not dwelt upon;

they wished to be Christians in their creed, but heathens in their life. The missionaries, adhering to this point with their usual determination, were reproached with refusing baptism, and giving up many valuable souls to perdition on so slender a ground. At the same time, furious internal wars began to rage in this part of Japan, and the missionaries found themselves in danger of being crushed between the contending parties. At length a military chief of the name of Combacundono subdued all his competitors, and became complete master of the empire. The Jesuits, therefore, applied themselves to obtain his favour and protection, and for some time they supposed themselves successful. On a sudden, however, without any cause stated, he issued an order that every missionary should within three weeks depart from the empire. The Jesuits having humbly solicited to know the motive of such unheard of rigour, a rescript was delivered to them, in which it was stated, "that they terrified the people "out of their old customs and modes of worship, "and introduced the service of the devil in their "stead; that moreover, they eat horses and cows, "a proceeding altogether contrary to reason, those "animals being exceedingly useful to the state." The missionaries replied, "that they had come "from a distant region of the globe, with no possi-"ble motive but the good of the Japanese; that

" they had no means, even if they had the inclina- " tion, to do any thing which could justly give um- " brage to the ruling power." The eating of horse-flesh they denied *in toto*, and even that of cows, unless in a very limited degree, when it appeared at the tables of the Portuguese merchants. They allege, that the real source of enmity arose from the inclinations of the Emperor towards the fair sex, the most beautiful of whom his agents were diligently instructed to collect from every corner of the empire. The Bonzes, who scrupled not to act as assistants in this capacity, had even made overtures to some Christian ladies, whose indignant rejection was supposed to have greatly sharpened his displeasure. He refused, therefore, to recal his order; but as they represented that no ship would sail for six months, he consented that they should be collected at Firando, and await that period. A consultation being then held, it was determined that they should remain at all hazards, but as quietly as possible. Accordingly, at the end of the period, Combacundono seems to have forgot the affair; hearing no more of them, he took no steps to enforce his order, and they continued silently spreading their doctrine.

Combacundono was at this time deeply immersed in other concerns. Having set out on an expedition against China, he left the command of the army at home to his nephew Taycosama, a popular and distinguished officer. During his absence, Taycosama had so ingratiated himself with the troops, that his power was little inferior to that of the sovereign. Combacundono, unable to crush this unexpected rival, was obliged to conciliate him by courtesy and negociation, in the course of which he invited him to a feast, the splendour of which dazzled extremely the eyes of the Portuguese. There were spread 13,000 tables, of those small dimensions, indeed, which are used in the East, one-half for the male, and the other for the female guests. Nothing, however, could equal the splendour of the procession made by the attendants and nobles who followed Taycosama, and by his hundred and fifty wives, each of whom had borne before them several boxes covered with silk and gold, containing the dresses which they were to wear at the festival. Taycosama seems to have accepted this invitation only to lull the suspicions of his rival, whom he soon after waylaid and took. He then threw him into prison, and at last allowed him only that sole consolation of Japanese pride, the liberty of dying by his own hand. This savage tyrant soon after caused thirty-one of the favourite wives of the deceased, with their children, to be led out and publicly executed. This deed struck the people with deep horror and pity, especially as many of them were the daughters of persons of distinction; and in execrating the cruelty of the present monarch, they almost forgot that of his predecessor.

Taycosama, on being applied to, refused to revoke the order of his predecessor against the missionaries, but he did not take any active steps to enforce it; and they found, that by keeping very quiet, they could still maintain their place. Ill fortune, however, decreed, that at this moment a detachment of Barefoot friars arrived from the Philippines. These new recruits, besides being quite ignorant of Japan, by no means possessed the prudence and address of the Jesuits. The latter strongly represented to them, that the only tenure on which they could remain, or have any success in Japan, was by avoiding every public exhibition of themselves and the ceremonies of their religion. The lofty mind of the Barefoots, however, held in utter disdain any such compromise. They immediately began publicly preaching, and celebrating the Catholic rites, without any regard to the remonstrances made by the governor. At this very crisis occurred another most unfortunate incident. A Portuguese vessel having been taken near Orudo, was found to contain a quantity of arms. This induced, on the governor's part, a very strict examination, from which the captain extricated himself pretty tolerably. The Japanese officer being thus impelled by curiosity to make inquiries respecting Portugal, the captain began a boastful account of its dominion, and the vast extent of its recent conquests. This drew out an inquiry, by what means so many and so distant regions had been subjected to its sway? The captain was so ill advised as to answer, that it was by sending missionaries, who converted a large proportion of the people, after which an armed force was landed, and being joined by these converts, soon made themselves masters of the country. This notice appeared to the governor so serious, that he lost not a moment in transmitting a full report of it to Taycosama. The rage of that chief then knew no bounds. He began with ordering every missionary to be instantly sent out of the country: then recollecting how vain every order to that effect had hitherto proved, he declared, that since he could not make them depart this kingdom, he would at least make them depart this life, and directed that the whole should be instantly put to death. Gradually cooling, however, he listened to intercessions in their favour, and ordered only that six Barefoot friars, three Jesuits, and a few Japanese, should be crucified, and that twenty-four should have one ear cut off. All their seminaries and establishments were at the same time broken up; yet they still individually lurked; and the death of Tayco-sama, which soon after took place, enabled them again to lift up their heads. New persecutions, however, soon arose; and during a space of forty years, Japan furnished continual additions to the list of Catholic martyrs. Nieremberg has given a description of the tortures which they were made to endure. The first was that of the *jar*, which consisted in immersing the head up to the nose in a vessel of water, while the feet were kept suspended in the air. Another was the *stair*, the sufferer being then bound to a stair, with his head on the lowest step, while a species of funnel threw continually vast quantities of water into his mouth, at the same time, a board pressing on the stomach, caused its continual ejection. The left arm alone remained at liberty, to make the signal of recantation. The last torture was that of the *cave*, in which half the body, with the head lowest, was buried under ground, the feet being raised in the air; an arm, however, being still left in a condition to make the required movement. By this continued system of torture and death, continued for about forty years, (1590 to 1630), the Portuguese, and the religion which they taught, were completely rooted out of Japan. Even now, in all the seaports, it is annually renounced with the most frightful ceremonies, and by trampling under foot all the Catholic images.

Notwithstanding the awful denunciation now fulminated against the Portuguese, that nation, in 1640, sent an embassy, composed of seventy-four individuals, to solicit a renewed commercial intercourse. This body, on their arrival, were immediately seized and thrown into prison, till the Emperor's pleasure should be known. The courier sent to court returned with a fatal mandate; in pursuance of which, all the ambassadors, with the exception of thirteen, were immediately put to death. The magistrates then sent for the survivors, and having asked them if they would faithfully report at Macao what they should see and hear, proceeded thus: "You are then to inform your fellow-citizens, that henceforth the citizens of Japan will not receive either money, merchandise, or presents from them: you see we have burnt the very clothes of those who were executed. Let your people use any of ours that fall into their hands in the same manner; we consent to it; and desire you will think of us no more than if there were not such a nation as the Japanese in the world." They were then shewn the heads of the ambassadors and the others, fixed on poles, and a large chest containing their bodies, on which was a long inscription, ending with these words: "All this is set forth, as a memorial of what is past, and as an advertisement for the time to come. Hence-

" forward, so long as the sun shall shine upon the " earth, let not any Christian be so hardy as to " set his foot in Japan. And be it known to all " the world, that if King Philip in person, or the " great Xaca, (one of the first deities of Japan), " shall presume to break this ordinance, he shall " pay for it with his head."

THE Dutch succeeded the Portuguese in the trade of Japan; and being by no means so intent upon the maintenance of their own dignity when profit was at stake, they have ever since, alone of all the European nations, maintained some small portion of this commerce. In 1600 they formed a settlement at Firando, but were afterwards removed to Nangasaki, and their privileges reduced always within narrower and narrower limits. Every year their annual fleet was accompanied by an embassy to the imperial court with presents and homage. The narratives published by individuals who accompanied these, have been our only source of information respecting the interior of Japan. The first account is that published by Montanus respecting the mission of Frisius and Bronkhorst in 1649; but this narrative is a mere shapeless compilation from the writings of the missionaries, illustrated by plates which are entirely the manufacture of Amsterdam. This deficiency is well compensated by the intelligent narrative of the learned KAEMPFER, who about the end of the seventeenth century twice accompanied the embassy to Jeddo. At Nangasaki they were obliged to submit to various humiliations, having their arms taken from them, their persons searched, and seals placed upon all their effects. On the road, however, they were treated with the same respect as is paid to the princes and great lords, the people falling on their knees as they passed, and the peasantry often going aside and laying themselves flat on their faces. Each Prince, as they entered his territory, sent compliments to them, with four servants in black silk gowns to attend them in their passage through it. They offered also whatever horses the embassy might want, and supplied pleasure barges to convey them across the arms of the sea. In short, he says, all Japan may be considered as a school of civility and politeness. The gratification derived from these honours was much abated by the rigorous state of restraint in which they were held. They were never allowed to alight from their chairs unless on the most urgent necessity; and on arriving at the inn, were immediately conveyed to their apartment, where they remained as in a dungeon, every window or chink which opened a view into the country being carefully stopped up. The attendants insisted on not leaving them even while they obeyed the humblest calls of nature. Their tedium, however, was enlivened by the view of the vast crowds travelling on the roads. The principal highway resembled in this respect the streets of the most populous city in Europe. This was produced at once by the numerous population of the country, and by their great propensity to travel, either for attending the court, for trade and business, or for their numerous pilgrimages. The mission now visited Jeddo, the capital, a vast city, and built with greater regularity than is usual in Europe. For this, too ample opportunities were afforded by the frequent fires, which were continually laying whole streets, and even quarters, in ashes. The houses were indeed mere masses of combustible matter, the walls being built of wood, the interior mats and paper. There were many splendid palaces, which covered a vast extent of ground, and were surrounded by large court-yards, but had nothing imposing in their aspect, as, like other houses in this country, they had only one floor. The palace formed a species of fortified city in the heart of the general one, surrounded with a wall of freestone, and having the ornament of a lofty tower many stories high. The ambassadors were introduced into the audience hall, called the hall of a hundred mats. Kaempfer assures us, that the elevated throne, the steps leading to it, and the ranges of lofty columns, pompously described and delineated by Montanus, exist only in that writer's own imagination. The real ornaments are merely the beautiful white mats, with gold fringes, that are spread on the floor; the rich gilding; and the cedar, camphire, and other valuable woods, curiously carved, and often japanned, of which the walls are formed. The Emperor being seated in the interior, three nobles came and led in the resident, creeping on his hands and feet till he came within the proper distance. They then cried aloud, *Hollanda Captain!* on which he immediately struck his forehead against the ground, and immediately "crawled backwards "like a crab," without speaking or hearing a word. This "mean and short thing" was all their return for a journey of upwards of three hundred miles, and 20,000 dollars expended in travelling and presents. They were afterwards paraded in another large hall, for the purpose of being viewed by the Empress and other ladies of the court, who were seated behind lattices; for whose further entertainment they received directions to dance, which, though an exercise not very congenial to their habits, they performed to the best of their ability. Such being their only amusements at court, they felt no regret on being permitted to take their departure again for Nangasaki.

Kaempfer has given a full view of that extraordinary division of power which has been established between the Dairi and the Cubo, the ecclesiastical and military sovereigns of Japan. The Dairi appears to have been originally the sole ruler; but, supplanted by the ample means of influence which the military power carries along with it, he now resides in empty pomp at Meaco. That city is still a capital scarcely second to Jeddo. It is the seat of the most extensive commerce: the finest silk stuffs, with gold and silver flowers, the richest varnishes, the best painted papers, the most skilful works in gold, silver, and copper, are there carried on. The Dairi, by his numerous attendants, is treated as scarcely less than a god. He never sets his foot to the ground; even his hair and nails have a sacred character; and every utensil and dress which he has made use of is immediately destroyed, lest it should be profaned by application to any vulgar purpose. He enjoys only the revenues of the city of Meaco and a stipend from the Cubo, which is small and irregularly paid; but the zeal and pride of his followers, who look upon themselves as superior beings to the rest of their countrymen, enables a court to be maintained in a style of indigent splendour. Meaco is the centre of all the literature and science of Japan: that of geometry has made here the greatest progress.

Although the Cubo be the sole civil and military ruler, and exercises a power completely absolute, each of the provinces is swayed by a hereditary governor, supreme as to the internal concerns of his own district. The strictest precautions are employed to prevent their chiefs from becoming independent. They are all obliged to reside for half a year at the court, and to leave hostages in their absence. Although there can scarcely be said to be any republican constitution, yet the inhabitants of the cities, divided into wards, exercise among themselves a certain police jurisdiction. Punishment is administered with intense and awful severity, and in that undistinguishing manner which seeks the security of the government without any regard to the merit or demerit of the object. The parent is punished for the crime of the child, and the child for that of the parent; and the inhabitants of a street or district are made responsible for the conduct of every person within its limits. The people, on the contrary, place their pride in shewing daring hardihood and perfect coolness in the midst of torments. The grandees, when condemned to death, claim only the privilege of being allowed to terminate their own life.

An interesting view of the interior of Japan was communicated by Thunberg, who sailed in

1775 from Batavia with the annual Dutch commercial fleet. The voyage, he observes, is extremely dangerous, and the Dutch give up as lost one ship out of five that sails thither. On the 13th August they came in view of the high mountains of Niphon, and in the afternoon found themselves in the entrance of Nangasaki harbour. Fires were already lighted on the tops of all the surrounding hills to give notice of their approach. In sailing up the harbour a delightful view opened of the surrounding hills and mountains, cultivated to the very summit. On arriving in the harbour, the first operation was to collect all the Prayer-books and Bibles, to be delivered to the Japanese, and kept till their departure; a precaution insisted upon, lest any attempt should be made to introduce Christianity. A muster-roll of the crew was then drawn out, for the purpose of being delivered to the Japanese, who called it every morning and evening. Then the captain clothed himself in a stuffed silk coat, of such huge dimensions as to be capable of containing three persons of his own size; which was with the view of inserting, whenever he went on shore, a small stock of contraband articles. A boat was quickly seen approaching, containing the officers and searchers, who were received with every possible respect, seated on a bedstead prepared for the purpose, and liberally supplied with tobacco and brandy. The first thing they did was to produce an order just arrived from court, decreeing that the captain should denude himself of his present capacious vestments, and put on others fitted to his actual dimension. This order was reluctantly obeyed, to the great astonishment of some ignorant Japanese, who had imagined that the former swollen state was the natural and stationary size of a Dutch captain. The officers then began to institute a search still more rigorous than usual. They turned the pockets of all the officers and crew inside out, and passed their hands over their clothes, and through their hair. All the trunks and chests were emptied, and even the boards sounded lest they should be hollow. Iron pikes were run into the butter tubs and jars of sweetmeats, and a thick pointed wire through the cheeses. They broke even several of the eggs. At length the Dutch were allowed to begin landing their cargo on the island of Dezima, a small appendage to Nangasaki, forming an island at high water, but at low water a mere street of the town. They were kept there as in a prison, the gate being constantly guarded, and locked every night. Our author was struck with the gloomy situation of those who had their permanent abode in this place. They became as it were dead; they never heard a word of news respecting any other quarter of the world, and in time lost all curiosity concerning them. Even the faculty of the will became extinct from want of exercise, there being no other for them but that of the Japanese, according to which they must entirely square their conduct.

Botany was the favourite pursuit of Dr Thunberg; and he with great difficulty obtained permission to make a few excursions, but always attended with a numerous train, who at once encumbered his motions, and caused a heavy expense, as it was necessary to treat them all. After a stay of about six months at Nangasaki, the embassy set out for Jeddo, the capital. Their road lay chiefly along the coast, partly by land, and partly by water. Their land conveyance was in *norimons*, a species of sedan chairs made of bamboo. There is neither post-chaise nor wheel-carriage of any kind in the empire. The poor travel on foot; those in better circumstances have a horse, on which, by the aid of baskets, a whole family is sometimes conveyed; but the *norimon* is the exclusive conveyance of the great. Our author discommends much the great diligence shewn to supply even the smallest sea-ports with ladies who have renounced the first virtue of their sex. The houses destined for them were usually the handsomest in the town, and placed close to the temples. Persons under the sanction of government purchase girls to be trained for this criminal trade, which is not considered here in the same disgraceful light as elsewhere, and forms even no obstacle to a good marriage. The Dutch were not allowed to enter these haunts; but upon earnest application were accommodated during their stay with a temporary wife. The ornaments employed by these and other Japanese ladies consisted chiefly in painting their lips blue, and their teeth black, so that they appeared to Thunberg sufficient to make even a fond lover take French leave of his mistress.

Thunberg, in travelling through this new country, had cherished sanguine expectations of forming a rich collection of plants unknown in Europe. He was completely baffled, however, by the laudable industry of the Japanese farmers. All those plants of which he was in search were classed in their vocabulary as weeds, the extirpation of which was the object of their most strenuous efforts; which had been so successful, that he proceeded through the whole provinces without seeing one. The principal towns through which he passed were Osaka, the seat of commerce and pleasure. It is called the Paris of Japan, abounding with every luxury which the empire affords, and resorted to by many of the great, as the most agreeable place for spending their fortunes; while its commerce is so great, that the ground floor of almost every house is a work-shop. The next was Meaco, the ecclesiastical capital, which, though now supplanted in political importance by Jeddo, continues still the principal seat of literature, manufactures, and trade. Though Thunberg was here four days, he never obtained more than a distant view of the palace of the Dairi. At length they arrived at Jeddo, the capital and residence of the Cubo, or temporal monarch. They were immediately waited upon by five physicians and two astronomers, who having heard that the Dutch were bringing with them a doctor much more learned than any who usually attended their embassy, came in hopes of adding somewhat to their stores of information. The chief object of the celestial observers was to be enabled to calculate eclipses with greater precision; but Thunberg regrets that he was not able to give them very much information upon this point. He could better satisfy the physicians, who had many inquiries to make, not only respecting the European mode of curing diseases, but concerning the kindred sciences of natural philosophy, botany, and surgery. Their visits became very frequent; and our traveller, though almost wearied out by their endless succession of questions, spent many an agreeable hour in their company.

The ceremonies of audience passed in rather a less mortifying manner than during the time of

Kaempfer. They were ushered into an ante-chamber, where they were seated on the floor in the Japanese attitude, which would have been very painful had not their large silk gowns enabled them in some degree to extricate their legs from so incommodious a posture. In this position they were addressed and questioned by a number of grandees, who came up to them *incog.*; but their rank was betrayed by the reverence of the bystanders. They put many questions, particularly about the European mode of writing, of which it was necessary to afford them specimens either on paper or on their fans. They had even reason to suspect that the Emperor himself was among this number. At the end of the period the ambassador was led in, bowed his head to the ground, and immediately departed; however he walked both in and out, instead of creeping, as formerly.

Thunberg has analyzed with considerable care the character of this extraordinary nation. He considers *sense* as a very prominent feature. They despise those glittering ornaments which are so studiously worn throughout all Asia, and to a great extent in Europe, and seek only to be decently and substantially clothed. He adds, that *liberty* is the soul of the Japanese; a praise which we do not fully understand, as he immediately after ranks submission to their superiors as a feature equally prominent. The laws, however, are said to be administered with very rigid justice, and the whole nation to be distinguished for the observance of the strictest honesty. They have seldom or never attempted to conquer other nations, but defend their own with unconquerable valour. Their most unamiable quality is pride, which is said to rise to the highest pitch, both in the nation and in individuals. Connected with this is resentment, in which they are said to be *quite implacable*. They remain always cool, however, and conceal their enmity, without ever forgetting it, till the moment arrives when they can strike the blow. They are said to be generally of very courteous manners, and even of a good-natured and friendly disposition, when they are treated in a corresponding manner, and nothing is done by which their resentment can be roused. In superstitious habits, and in the extent of their pilgrimages, they appear almost to rival the Hindoos. The original national faith is that of the Sinto, who seem to possess lofty ideas of a Supreme Being, but mingled with various degrading superstitions. Here, however, as in all the east of Asia, the religion of Boodh or Fo is the most popular, and it is professed by the Cubo. In industry the Japanese are pre-eminent, particularly in agriculture, so that though a great part of their country consists of rugged mountains, they have contrived to cover almost every corner of it with good crops. They have tea like China, but of a coarser quality. Their manufactures of silk and cotton are extensive; but in the former they are excelled by the Chinese, and in the latter by the Hindoos. They excel both, however, in working metals, particularly copper and steel; and in lacquering and varnishing wood, called by us japanned work, they are not equalled by any nation in the world.

After Russia, by the extension of her vast Asiatic dominion to Kamtchatka and the Kuriles, became the neighbour of Japan, she naturally conceived the desire of opening some intercourse with so great and opulent a state. No disposition, however, appeared to relax in those rigorous restrictions, which admitted of no exception except the single and narrow one granted to the Dutch. In hopes of obtaining some relaxation of this rigid system, Captain Krusenstern, in 1804, set sail from Kamtchatka on an official mission. He was received with courtesy; but the treaty for his landing was protracted to a great length by the vexatious, and, as he conceived, insulting precautions which were insisted upon. Although a Dutch vessel was setting sail for Batavia, they were not allowed to send any letters, except one to the Emperor, and this they were required not only to shew, but to furnish a copy so exact, that every line should end with the same word. As the Dutch captains passed by, Krusenstern saluted them, and was much surprised to see them go on without looking or speaking; but he afterwards learned, that it would have been at their peril if they had done otherwise. The Russians, after a month's negociation, were allowed to continue to wear their swords; but this "small "triumph," as they call it, was alloyed by the necessity of delivering up all their fire-arms. By a pretence of sickness, Captain Krusenstern obtained a spot to walk upon; but it was only a hundred paces long, enclosed with a high bamboo wall, and guarded by two watch-houses. At length they were landed, and accommodated on a neck of land, almost surrounded by the sea, and watched as close as the seven towers at Constantinople. Every thing, however, which was wanted for provisions and repairs to the vessel, was liberally supplied. The negociations for permission to proceed to court were delayed for many months, the Japanese exaggerating the distance and the time necessary to receive an answer. At length it was announced, that two plenipotentiaries, with eight great lords, might be very shortly expected; and it was understood, though not fully expressed, that this was to supersede their proceeding into the interior. The plenipotentiaries, on their arrival, announced, as an irrevocable decision, that no Russian ship could be allowed to enter Japan. They refused the presents, on the ground that their acceptance would require a return, and that a Japanese ambassador must then proceed to Russia, which was contrary to their law.

SOME years after, a favourable opportunity appeared to open, when the Russians on the eastern coast of Asia saved a Japanese vessel from shipwreck, and enabled it to return to Japan. In hopes of taking advantage of the favourable dispositions which this tended to produce, Captain GOLOWNIN sailed to Matsmai, the principal town of Jesso, which is now almost entirely a Japanese island. There they were first allured on shore, then thrown into a miserable dungeon, and, though with some improvement of their quarters, detained in prison for many months. Golownin once effected his escape, but, after wandering through the island for a number of days, was taken and conveyed back to Matsmai. He found the coast cultivated and populous, but the interior consisting of wild, and almost inaccessible mountains. Matsmai, the capital, is a large town, containing about 50,000 inhabitants. At length orders arrived from the Emperor to send him back to Russia; but all extension of commercial privileges was of course out of the question. He found the Japanese nation imbued with the deepest jealousy of the Russians, and viewing with alarm the vast extension of their empire. National pride made them believe that the advances of the English by sea, and of the Russians by land, were made in concert, and had for their sole object finally to obtain possession of Japan. Every thing, therefore, which could tend to unveil the secrets of the country to either of these potentates, was guarded against with the most anxious precaution.

# BOOK VI.

## NORTHERN ASIA.

## CHAPTER I.

### THE TERRITORY OF CAUCASUS.

*General Remarks.—Engelmann.—Pallas, Klaproth, Guldenstedt, &c.—The Circassians.*

We come now to treat of the north of Asia, or Asiatic Russia; a region of vast extent, comprising a full third of the continent, but thinly peopled, and containing comparatively few objects to excite curiosity and admiration. The reason has been explained in the preface, why the voyages along the Northern Ocean, and even the journies along its shores, are not made to enter into the plan of the present work. Our attention is thus confined to the inland divisions of this vast territory. These may be divided into two parts;—the Caucasian provinces, or the regions situated between the Black Sea and the Caspian; and that vast tract, extending across the whole breadth of Asia, which is known by the name of Siberia.

The territories interposed between the Black Sea and the Caspian, consist of vast ranges of mountains towering over each other, interspersed with narrow but fertile valleys, but nowhere opening into any extensive plain. Its loftiest ridge, called Elbrus, covered with perpetual snow, stretches from sea to sea, terminating at Derbend, whose iron gate opens only a narrow passage to the invader or traveller. Both to the north and south of this limit, the mountains slope gradually downward, till it sinks on one side into the vast *steppe* or flat plain of the Kuban, whence the mighty ranges of Caucasus rise like a wall, and on the other decline into the comparatively level territories of Georgia, Aderbijan, and Shirvan, connecting itself, however, with the lofty chains of Armenia. The recesses of this mountain world have always been occupied by a race of proud and warlike chiefs, who have imbibed the full spirit of the feudal ages, and have yielded only a slight and precarious submission to the successive empires that have held the sceptre of Asia. Russia is the one which has gone farthest towards establishing her sway; yet, though her supremacy is owned, she is scarcely able to extract even tribute; and a chain of military posts upon the Terek and the Kuban, are necessary to protect her provinces from predatory inroads. This power, according to her laudable practice, has been at very considerable pains to know these appendages to her extended empire. The result of various official surveys have appeared in the elaborate works of Pallas, and other learned travellers. These consist chiefly of topographical and descriptive details, and, as such, will be speedily noticed. In the mean time, the best idea of the vicissitudes and adventures to be encountered in travelling through these rugged chains, may be formed from the relation of P. F. Engelmann, who, in 1785, escorted through it an embassy to Persia.

This expedition consisted, on the Russian side, of two officers and six Cossack soldiers, with two interpreters. The Persian ambassador was also there, with his train, and they had in all twenty-seven riders, and twenty-three pack-horses. From the ruggedness of the roads, they could attempt to travel only on horseback. They set out on the 14th January, a season when the difficulties of travelling must be felt in their utmost force. The embassy passed through the territory of the Little Kabarda, without experiencing much obstruction. Four days brought them to the foot of the mightiest snowy barrier of the Caucasus. Here, on the steep banks of the Terek on the northern side, and of the Araqui on the southern, a road had, within the last two years, been laboriously effected. It was bordered on each side by walls of rock, rising into pyramidal peaks of prodigious height, and leaving a space, which, at its greatest breadth, did not exceed 150 feet. By this route, however, waggons could pass in summer; but, in winter, the snow was drifted in the ravines to such a depth, as entirely to block up the passage; and the mountains could be crossed only by climbing on foot or on horseback over their highest ridges. These precipitous summits of Caucasus were held by a race called Ossetes, whose abodes resemble fortresses, defended by round towers. They have a language of their own, resembling none but the Persian, and are mere heathens, worshipping dogs and cats.—The embassy had not gone far, when they came to a narrow pass, which they found entirely blocked up by these banditti, demanding toll; but as there was a regular stipulation that every thing Russian should pass free, the chief refused to give them the smallest article. They then threatened to roll down huge fragments of rock, and discharged, in fact, a few shots, without, however, doing any injury. The chief, then, having an escort of 200 light horse, sent them by a circuit of nearly thirty miles, to take the mountaineers in the rear, who, as soon as they saw this manœuvre, retreated, and allowed the Russians to pass.

The expedition had now only to encounter the obstacles of nature, which consisted in five successive ridges, the loftiest of which was quite above the clouds. In ascending, they experienced the most sudden change of the climate and of nature. Hitherto the weather had been moderate, and the hills and cliffs being still decked in varied hues, had exhibited magnificent landscapes. In March, he thinks, the Caucasus must be quite a paradise, when the lofty woods which stretch along the sides and at the foot of the mountains, exhibit all their pomp of verdure. A very different scene was presented in winter, amid its snowy heights. They had now to pass the five ridges, each from two to three miles in breadth. The first was surmounted easily and cheerfully. They then passed the Terek, which, though rapid, stood in need of no bridge, except that of its own eternal ice, formed by the snows of year after year piled over each other, and which the most intense heat of summer never dissolved. Its existence is known only by the loud dashing of its waves, which is heard beneath. They came now to the second ridge, much more steep and difficult. Here, between two lofty walls of rock, one above and the other beneath, with a torrent rolling along its foot, there intervened only a path of from two to three feet broad. As they proceeded along it with trembling steps, a tempest of wind arose, and blew upon them an immense quantity of snow, in the midst of which the ambassador, his steward, and another rider, with their horses, went over the precipice, and sunk into the abyss. The party had not the least hope of their preservation; but, by the greatest good fortune, there happened a little beneath to be a projection of the rock, upon which they all three lighted. They could not at first be seen beneath the snow which covered them; but in the course of two or three minutes, they worked out their heads and shewed themselves. It behoved the whole party to stop and consider what was to be done. The Cossack and Ossetine guides, who had some experience in such cases, were let down by strong ropes, which they tied round the ambassador, and the other two afflicted sufferers, and thus drew them up to the road. The ambassador, to the agreeable surprise of all, was found without any injury, except the greatest possible terror. Even two of the horses were saved; and our author asserts, that if the third had acted with all the judgment which this animal usually displays, he might have extricated himself also. Engelmann, however, grievously laments his fate, on being detained thus long in this perilous station, amid so furious a tempest, which threatened every instant to hurl them all into the same abyss.

After passing this mountain with so much toil and anguish, the Russians found, rising out of it, another, which appeared still more formidable. This was the third and most elevated of the snowy peaks. In looking up, it appeared an impossibility that they should ever reach the summit. Riding was now out of the question; and they were happy in being able to scramble on foot, sometimes sinking to the middle in snow. At length, through much peril and misery, they reached this loftiest of the Caucasian summits. The country beneath was entirely hid; they saw nothing but an ocean of clouds, with wind and snow driving around them. Notwithstanding the excessive cold, fatigue obliged them to take an hour's rest. They began then to descend the southern side, which they found still excessively steep. When they were about half way down, three mules, who were carrying a service of plate to the King of Persia, fell down at once to some depth, but so that their heads still appeared above the snow. Two of them worked their way out, and safely regained the road; but the other, finding nothing to rest upon, rolled on to the top of a high precipice, and fell down into the bed of the river. The two boxes containing the plate rolled down to the right and left. One arrived entire at the top of a rock, about two hundred feet beneath, while the other was broken, and the gold and silver plates, spoons, and dishes, were seen dashing from rock to rock in wild confusion. It was impossible to stir from the road in search of them. The governor of Georgia, however, promised, as soon as the ceasing of the great snows should allow those on the ground to harden, that he would commit the task to some alert mountaineers; and these, in fact, found not only the entire box, but almost all the scattered pieces with which the broken one had been filled.

The embassy experienced no farther adventure, but about one in the morning arrived at the nearest Georgian village. The road, though not more than twelve miles, had cost them eighteen hours of travelling; and the village, though very poor, afforded a most welcome refreshment. After a day's rest, they set out for Teflis, the capital of Georgia. The road lay along the valley of the Araqui, which continually widened as they descended its stream, till it became three or four miles broad. It was covered with beautiful woods of beech, chesnut, apple, and pear, with an underwood composed partly of shrubs unknown to Europe. Through this wooded vale the Araqui flows in various branches, and the mountains rise on each side, interspersed to half their height with villages, having gardens often formed upon slopes so steep, that it seems inconceivable how any thing can grow upon them. Those belonging to the chiefs are surrounded by a wall, and defended with towers. The landscape, he says, is not surpassed by any thing in Switzerland and Italy. After travelling three days through this beautiful country, he came to Teflis. We are here quite on Persian ground, and in the tract of other travellers, so that it will be unnecessary to follow his less interesting progress to Khoi, where he quitted the embassy.

From the topographical and descriptive works above alluded to, of Pallas, Guldenstedt, Reineggs, Klaproth, and Bibertstein, we shall now proceed to take a general view of the tribes who people the steeps of Caucasus. The minute details, indeed, with which these works are filled, possess little interest, unless for those who come into closer contact than we do with these Asiatic races. In a general view, however, society presents here some very striking features. The leading nation of Caucasus is that of the Circassians, called by the Russians *Tcherkess*. This remarkable people present almost a complete picture of what Europe was during the height of the feudal ages. The distinction of ranks and the pride of birth are carried almost to as lofty a pitch. The state consists of the prince, the *uzdens* or nobles, and the vassals, who are considered nearly in the light of slaves. They consist partly of hereditary *serfs* or bondsmen, and partly of slaves taken in war. Their office is to till the ground, drive the large ploughs drawn by six or eight oxen, cut timber, build houses, and perform all other laborious tasks. The Uzdens owe nothing to their prince except military service, with some presents, chiefly of cattle, at his marriage, or any other leading era in his life. These chiefs seldom appear abroad, unless " clad in complete steel." Their arms consist of a sabre, dagger, and pistols, which they wear in the girdle; of a bow and quiver, which are fastened with straps to the thighs; of a helmet and arm-plates of polished steel; and over all a coat of mail, formed of polished steel rings. They never leave the house without the sabre; but if they quit their village, they must be equipped in full armour. They have also a breed of horses, whose training and genealogy are as carefully studied as those of Arabia. The race is declared by a peculiar mark impressed on the buttock, which it is death to counterfeit. The merits of these steeds, besides beauty, consist in fleetness, and capacity of enduring fatigue; qualifications which greatly fit them for those light and rapid excursions in which they are destined to engage.

The chiefs of Circassia employ themselves in no regular or pacific occupation, but spend their time in convivial parties, war, hunting, or predatory expeditions. They have proved ever most troublesome and precarious subjects to all those who obtained a nominal sovereignty over them. The Russians, after defeating them in several great battles, are now owned as their masters, yet do not attempt to interfere in their internal administration; and light as is this foreign yoke, it is still spurned at by the Circassians. They make frequent plundering excursions into the Russian territory, where they are only checked by the fortified line of the Terek. Those tribes who distinguish themselves by their fidelity to Russia, are said to suffer more from the consequent enmity of their neighbours, than they gain by this seemingly powerful alliance. The Circassians are estimated by Pallas at 1500 uzdens and 10,000 vassals capable of bearing arms. He considers them as the first light cavalry in the world. Probably, if they could remain at peace with their neighbours, whose character and habits are similar to their own, they might set the whole world at defiance; but their ever doing so is totally out of the question.

One quality for which the people of this region have long been renowned is *beauty*. This envied excellence is said to be possessed in a peculiar degree by the Circassian dames, who have been long the boast of the oriental harams. In tropical countries beauty is usually to be sought among the mountains, where the fine and varied tints of the temperate climates are substituted for the dark hue produced by the intense action of the sun. This effect indeed is often counteracted by the poverty and hard labour to which the tenants of these rude districts are subjected; but here the pride and power of the nobles exempt their families from all menial tasks, and leaves nothing which can injure the delicacy of their form and complexion. Every means of improving this natural gift is studiously employed. They are fed in the most sparing manner on milk and pastry, administered only in small quantities. Though not immured like other orientals, they are carefully protected from the injuries of the air; their feet are kept warm and dry by clogs, and their hands are covered with gloves or mittens. The consequence seems to be, that though the Circassians are not all beauties, the proportion is greater here than in most other countries. These Circassian fair, if I may judge from the descriptions given, and from the paintings of an admirable artist, are characterized by a softness and delicacy of complexion, such as in Europe we would almost consider as extreme; by fine black or auburn locks; and by a slender and elegant form. As the Circassians do not sell even their peasantry, much less those of higher rank, the seraglios of Persia and Turkey can be supplied only by the plundering expeditions carried on by these tribes against each other. Of these exploits, when successful, the unfortunate maidens are often the prize; and are then sold at a high price to the merchants, who carry them for sale to the eastern imperial cities.

In a society where such paramount importance is attached to the distinctions of rank, unequal marriages are naturally viewed with deep reprobation. The vassal who marries the daughter of an Uzden, or the Uzden who marries a Princess, incurs the penalty of death. Deep disgrace is also attached to the violation even of minor distinctions between the different classes of nobles. The peculiar care taken to train the female part of the society to those qualities which may render them agreeable to the other sex, does not seem to secure any corresponding degree of attention. Marriage is transacted by the parent or guardian; and the first year is characterized by an almost Spartan separation, the husband and wife living in separate houses, and seeing each other only by clandestine visits. Even after that period little social intercourse takes place between them; they do not even appear to each other's visitors. Education in the families of the Princes is arranged upon a most singular system. Immediately on the birth of a child it is delivered to a noble, who is supposed to be distinguished for merit and accomplishments, and on whom the whole charge of its training devolves, the parents never even seeing it till that is completed. His business is to make the daughter a complete beauty, and the son an accomplished robber; after which he presents them to the parents, taking care previously to provide the young lady with a husband of her own rank.

The law of hospitality, and the right of revenge, exist in equal force among the Circassians as in all other rude tribes. Their chief wealth consists in their flocks and herds, which they secure at night, by building their villages in the form of a square or circle, the interior of which forms a court for the cattle. The castle of the chief is built on an eminence, distinct from the village. Their fields are cultivated, though in a rude and clumsy manner; and bees are reared so successfully, that honey becomes even an article of export. The animal and vegetable productions are very various, according as they are found in the valleys, or in the different stages of the mountainous ascent; and the Caucasus thus affords an ample field for the labours of the botanist.

Although the Circassians form the prominent race, this region is divided among innumerable other tribes, differing in name, and in minute national peculiarities ; but the proud and warlike sway of the chiefs, the beauty of the females, and the rude and predatory habits of the whole society, appear to be nearly the same in all. The Ossetes, of whose dealings we have had some observation, inhabit the Elbruz, or snowy steeps of the Caucasus, rising above Circassia. They are considerably ruder, and the nobles have much less power. To the east, bordering on the shores of the Caspian, are the widely diffused nation of the Lesghis or Lesghians, a race of formidable barbarians, who have always been terrible to the Persian monarchy ; and it has been said, a Sophi is mad who will attempt to make war against them. Their women are said to be as beautiful as the Circassians, and have also the reputation of being heroines, like their reported Amazonian ancestors. Along the Black Sea, the ruling people are the Abasses, generally agreeing with the Circassians, but considerably ruder. The Truchmens, Nogais, and Kumuks, are Tartar tribes, who wander over the plains which extend along the foot of Caucasus.

One of the circumstances most characteristic of these numerous tribes, is the vast variety of their languages. There is not a people, however small, which has not a distinct one of its own. Sometimes the dialects of the two immediately contiguous, do not bear the slightest resemblance to each other. The original of each can often be found only at so great a distance, that it is difficult to conceive, how any communication could have existed. Some insist, that these are languages radically different from those that can be found in any other part of Europe or Asia. The true cause of this variety probably is, that the extraordinary natural strength of this region has rendered it an asylum, often to distant tribes, in the successive tempests of invasion by which this part of Asia has so often been desolated.

## CHAPTER II.

### SIBERIA—EARLY DISCOVERIES.

*First Discovery and Conquest by the Russians.—Bell.*

ASIA wants a temperate zone. But for this, her vast extent, and the early civilization of her southern empires, must have secured her from being so far outstripped by Europe in all the arts and pursuits of life. That part of her territory which, as to its place on the globe, would come under the above description, enclosed by enormous chains of mountains, elevated into bleak table lands, and deprived of all maritime communication, wants the means of raising itself to a high place in the scale of improvement. It has surpassed tropical Asia in arms, and has produced a continued succession of conquerors; but it has derived from that region all its arts and intellectual culture. Proceeding northward, as we now do, to the immense tracts bounded by the Icy Sea, the prospect becomes still more gloomy.

Nature, indeed, presents herself on an extended scale, but everywhere with a vast and dreary monotony. Endless frozen plains; rivers, whose broad and sluggish stream reflects only the dark pine forest; a few shivering natives, roaming through the woods in quest of prey: such is the only spectacle presented from one to the other of its distant extremities. In our eyes it is rendered still more dismal, by its being a land of exile. The victim of imperial resentment, imprisoned in its boundless wilds, is cut off, as it were, from all civilized and social existence. Yet the active genius of the Russian government has discovered treasures even in this lost and neglected portion of the globe. Mines of extraordinary value have been found in the bowels of its mountains; a beneficent nature has furnished to its animals defences against the cold, the richness and beauty of which human art cannot rival; and vast tracts are covered with such rich pasture, as to indicate, that at some future period they may support nations as populous as those which now inhabit the most improved parts of the Russian territory.

Russia, during the middle ages, was too frequently overrun by her eastern neighbours to think of carrying her arms into their territory. Even after their divided power had enabled her in some degree to consolidate her empire, the southern frontier was still closely pressed. It was from her northern province of Archangel that an opportunity first occurred of penetrating into Siberia. The Samoiedes of the Obi and Petchora came along the Wichida (Vitenegda) to its confluence with the Dwina, where they exchanged their furs with the Russians. Anika Strogonoff, who superintended some salt works in that neighbourhood, first planned expeditions into their own territory. Purchas, who, from a corruption of the first name, calls him *Oneeko*, gives some details of his early operations. He professes to derive them chiefly from Hakluyt, who "had not "attayned unto it without great paynes." It had been revealed to him by some friends at the Russian court, who had acted thus in direct opposition to the orders of their government, so that, if discovered, "doubtless it would cost them all "their lives." Oneeko, it is said, seeing the valuable furs brought by these rude visitors, became most desirous to know "from whence they "came, or what countryes they did inhabit, "easily conjecturing that great wealth was there "to be gotten. Accordingly, he sent a party, "with divers base merchandize, as small bells, "and other like Dutch small wares." For these they obtained a great value in furs, and carried on a very profitable trade. The natives, ignorant of bread, subsisted entirely on the flesh of wild animals, whom they killed with their arrows, and whose skins they wore with the furry side outside in summer, and inside in winter. They had neither towns nor villages, but lived peaceably in companies, under the government of their old men. Oneeko, having obtained the information sought for, continued the traffic for a series of years, "by meanes whereof the Oneekos grew "very mightie." They adorned their native town with handsome edifices, particularly with a large church built entirely of hewn stone; "finally, they knew no end of their goods." It being, however, an established proverb in Russia, that "he which hath no friends in court, is scarce to "be accounted in the number of the living," Oneeko was fortunate enough to obtain the protection and favour of Boris, brother-in-law, and ultimately successor to Theodore Ivanovitch, the reigning emperor. Having obtained access by suitable presents, he made a full declaration of the whole affair, stating the productions and situation of these newly discovered countries, and "how great riches might thence arise into the "empire of Moscovia." Boris, highly pleased with the intelligence, "grew into an ardent desire to set forward this business." He communicated the intelligence to the Emperor, who, not "sleeping about the matter," immediately fitted out an expedition, consisting chiefly of "cap-

"taynes and gentlemen of small abilitie," who were willing to engage in so remote and arduous an undertaking. These messengers penetrated into the country of the Samoiedes; and, on meeting the people, offered presents, "such as "were of small and almost no value to them-"selves, but which seemed so precious to the "other, that when the Moscovites were coming "affarre off towards them, they would stay for "them with great dancings and clapping of their "hands, and cast themselves down at the feet of "the givers, accounting them altogether as gods." The Russians penetrated beyond the Obi; in the course of which journey they saw "many "wild beasts of strange shapes, most cleere foun-"taynes, extraordinary plants and trees, pleasant "woods and Samoiedes of divers sorts; whereof "some did ride on elkes or *loshes*, some were "drawn on sleds by rein-deer, and others also "were drawn by dogs, which are equal to harts "for swiftness." They saw also many other things, "not before seene, and therefore to be "marvelled at." In the course of their inter-course with the natives they made much mention of their Emperor, "whom they wonderfully ex-"tolled, and made him little less than an earthly "god." They thus effected their object of exciting in the Samoiedes a desire to visit Moscow. A few of that people were without difficulty prevailed upon to accompany the Russians on their return. On seeing the "stateliness" of Moscow, viewing its magnificent shops, and hearing the sound of its numberless bells, "they were alto-"gether astonished, and thought themselves to "be in some mansion of the gods." They could not, it is added, "without a certain terror," view the Emperor himself as he proceeded along in state. Finally, they ate with the greatest satisfaction of the meats set before them by the Muscovites, and evidently preferred them to the "raw flesh, or fish dried in the winde, wherewith "they fed themselves at home." In short, they made no hesitation in agreeing, for themselves and their countrymen, to pay each two skins of sables, "which to themselves were of no value, "but were esteemed by the Muscovites as preci-"ous as jewels."

The Czar, not content with the access thus obtained into the interior of Siberia, determined to consolidate his dominion by erecting fortresses upon the Obi. These were easily formed by logs cut from the neighbouring forests, and the interstices filled up with earth. The colony was peopled by sending into these parts "murtherers, "traitors, thieves, and the scumme of such as "deserve death;" so that "offenders among the "Muscovites did no less tremble at the name of "Siberia, than do evill persons in London when "they are threatened with Newgate." Emigrants of this description were, it seems, so numerous, that in a short time "they did almost "make a pretie kingdom;" and their situation being understood to be by no means uncomfortable, the terror of this punishment was much abated, unless among the grandees, "who do as yet "very much loathe the name of Siberia."

The attention of the Russian government was still more strongly attracted towards this region by the romantic adventures of Yermack, the Cossack. Ivan Vasilievitch II. having extended his dominion as far as the Caspian, found the trade of his subjects with Persia and Bokhara much harassed by the predatory attacks of the Cossacks. He despatched, therefore, a large force against them. These wandering troops were attacked, routed, many of them slain, and the rest obliged to save themselves by flight. Among these last were 6000, commanded by Yermack, who, setting out in search of new settlements, penetrated beyond the Obi into the interior of Siberia. He there encountered Kutchum, Khan of the Tartars, totally routed him, took his capital, and found himself suddenly at the head of a great empire. He endeavoured to secure it by owning allegiance to the Czar, and governing as his viceroy. His proposition to this effect was gladly accepted; but he soon after fell into an ambush laid for him by the Tartars, was killed, and the empire which he had established entirely subverted. This adventure, however, communicated to the Russian court a knowledge of these countries, and also of the facility with which they could be subjugated, of which she was not slow to avail herself. Purchas in a subsequent notice observes, that "the inhabitants "that dwell on the west side of the river Obi "seek daily to discover more and more;" and that "certaine other cities have been builded, "and more are builded daily." The troops in garrison at Narim having received orders to prosecute discovery to the eastward, set out, and "travelling through certaine vast deserts (the "Barabenski steppe), through many faire coun-"treys, many woods and rivers, came to a new "nation called Tingoesi (Tungouses)." These people, it is said, "were deformed with swellings "under their throats, and in their speech they "thrattled like Turkey-cocks." They were gentle, however, and were easily persuaded by the Samoiedes to submit to the light dominion of the Russians, whose only demand consisted in a few furs. They stated their habitation to be upon the great river *Jenisce* (Yenisei), which rolled through a fertile country, and was bounded by high mountains to the east. The Russians soon penetrated to the Yenisei, and to some distance beyond it. Meeting with nothing remarkable, and being informed that powerful and formidable nations dwelt to the south, they returned ; leaving instructions with the Tungouses to prosecute discovery as far as they could. The Tungouses executed this commission with great diligence. The following year they discovered another great river, which they called Pisida, and which is probably the Angara. On the opposite side they found a people " of good understanding, well set, " with small eyes, flat faced, browne colour, and " enclining to tawnie." They understood nothing of their language, but could only remark the almost continual repetition of the syllables *om om*, and a frequent, as well as loud, tolling of brazen bells. These symptoms clearly point out the Mongols or Burats, and the ceremonies of the Shaman religion. These things being reported by the Tungouses, the Muscovite government fitted out a new expedition of seven hundred men, who in the following year penetrated to the banks of the Pisida. They there distinctly heard the tolling of the bells, and when the wind blew from the opposite side, could distinguish the noise of men and horses. Their courage failing for crossing the river, they returned to Siberia ; where being examined upon oath, they deponed, " that in the " moneth of Aprile they were very much de- " lighted with the exceeding faire shew of that "countrey; and that they had seen therein many "rare plants, flowers, fruits, trees, fowles, and "wild beasts." This report being conveyed to court, the Emperor Boris received it with great interest, and orders were given to prepare an embassy with presents, which might carry greater weight with it than the usual train of light Cossacks and Tungouses. This design, however, was interrupted by the violent civil wars which broke out in Russia. Purchas conjectures that this newly discovered country is the boundary of Cataia, and fears "the Muscovites will lose their labour "if they ever return thither." In fact, however, the progress of their arms and discovery was only for a short time suspended. Pushing on in a different direction, they reached the Lena, and descended its stream to the shores of the Icy Sea. In 1639, Dimitrei Kopilof reached the coast of the Eastern Ocean. Thus, in the course of fifty years, a few wandering Cossacks and hunters added to the Russian empire an extent of territory, comprehending about a fourth part of the circumference of the globe. Proceeding in another direction, and overcoming the first fear inspired by a view of the Mongols, they founded the towns of Irkutsk and Nertschinsk, and established a chain of posts along the Amour. Here, however, they came in contact with the provinces tributary to China;

and a series both of negociation and of military encounter ensued, before the boundaries of the two empires were finally settled.

We shall now survey the state of these regions in the beginning of the last century, as exhibited in the faithful narrative of Bell, who passed through it in accompanying the embassy of Ismailoff to the court of China. The embassy proceeded from Petersburg to Moscow, and thence along the Oka and Volga to Kazan. In the country beyond Kazan, the most striking circumstance was the quantity of honey produced from bee-hives formed out of the hollowed trunks of trees. He has seen above a hundred in one village. Passing through Klinof and Kaygorod, he came to Solikamskoi, a large and populous town on the eastern bank of the Kama, now included in Siberia. Near this town were numerous rocks of salt, the property of Baron Strogonoff. The mineral was obtained by digging pits in the mine, and allowing them to fill with water, which was afterwards evaporated like sea-water. Elsewhere, they discovered the spots where the salt rivulets discharged themselves under ground into the rivers, and by an ingenious machinery contrived to block up the passage, and obtain the water for evaporation. He was much struck by the construction of the vessels called *lodias*, in which the salt is conveyed to Moscow. They are often larger than a British first-rate, flat bottomed, without a nail in the construction, with one mast and one sail. Six or eight hundred men are required to steer this huge machine, which, in ascending the Volga, must often be artificially dragged on. In this neighbourhood also were excellent iron mines, and specimens of that singular mineral asbestos. It is said to have been discovered by a huntsman, who wished to use the flakes as wadding to his gun ; but finding the gunpowder produced no effect, tried it in the fire. Astonished to find it proof against that element, he conceived it possessed by the devil, and carried it for remedy to the priest. All the exorcisms of that learned person proving of no avail, the matter was so widely talked of, that it came to the ears of some one who understood the qualities of the substance.

After leaving Solikamskoi, our traveller began to ascend the Ourals, usually considered the boundary between Europe and Asia. He found them about forty miles broad, but not nearly so high as those he had seen in Persia, and other parts of Asia. They are covered with tall firs, larches, birch, and other trees of a northern climate. After fifteen hours employed in passing them, he came into a rich and cultivated country, and in the evening reached Verchaturia, the custom-house between Russia and Siberia. Ten per cent is here levied on all money and merchandise passing through; an impost which, after all Mr Bell's justification, appears to us very heavy and injudicious. The embassy now proceeded by Epantshin and Tumen, and in a few days came in sight of Tobolsk, capital of Siberia. This city is situated on a high bank at the confluence of the Irtysch and the Tobol, and with its white walls and gilded cupolas, makes a fine appearance. It is fortified with a strong brick wall, and garrisoned by five or six thousand regular troops. It was the abode of many Russian merchants, enriched by the fur trade, and by that with China; and contained a considerable number of what were called Tartar streets, where that nation enjoyed the free exercise of their trade and religion. It serves also as a prison to a number of Swedish officers, who after being taken at the battle of Pultowa, were distributed in the different towns of Siberia, and particularly here. Unless in distance from their native country, their lot was mild, as they had free liberty to walk about, and could hunt and fish in the finest sporting country in the world. A number also amused their solitude with the arts and sciences, particularly music and painting, in which several are said to have become eminent proficients. The great rival to the Russian power was then the Kontaysha of the Kalmucs, whose dominion, broken and divided, has since ceased to be formidable. He could then, it is said, muster 100,000 horse. These people lived all in tents, roving from place to place, and commiserating those who were confined to one place of abode. The Kontaysha received the Russian deputies in his tent, seated them on mats, and entertained them with tea.

After leaving Tobolsk, the travellers saw only Tartar villages, in which the houses were built of wood and moss, with a large square hole, stopped up with ice, serving for a window :—in the inside a large bench, covered with mats or skins, on which the whole family sat during the day, and slept during the night. After travelling upwards of three hundred miles, they came to Tara, where preparations were to be made for passing the steppe of Baraba, a large marshy plain, full of lakes, and overgrown with tall woods of aspin, willows, and other aquatics. It affords, however, considerable room for hunting and fishing. A guard was necessary to secure them from the predatory incursions of the Kalmucs. The inhabitants lived in most miserable huts, half sunk below ground, and wore nothing but long coats of sheep skin, without even a shirt. They are much addicted to the Shaman superstitions, and have numerous diviners, particularly of the female sex. One whom they visited, a handsome young woman, produced the *shaytan*, a piece of broad wood cut into a rude resemblance of the human head, adorned with various silk and woollen rags. She then brought forth a small drum, with many brass and iron rings. Having performed for some time on this instrument, accompanied with a dismal song, in which the neighbours joined in chorus, she sat down, and declared herself ready to deliver her oracles. They put several questions; and considerable address was shewn in investing her answers with a degree of ambiguity, which might save her credit in any event.

After about a fortnight spent in passing this dreary plain, the embassy reached the Obi, and found a wooded country, diversified, about the villages, by corn and pasture. In five days they arrived at Tomsk, situated on an eminence upon the banks of the river Tomm, and in a fertile and pleasant country. To the south is a range of hills, beyond which is an extensive plain, covered with numerous tombs, erected seemingly in honour of departed warriors, and marking, as he supposes, the site of numerous battles. It is become a regular trade at Tomsk to go and dig these tombs, where they find not only armour and the trappings of horses, but gold, silver, and even precious stones. These have evidently been deposited according to the ancient custom of burying with deceased chieftains all his most precious effects. After leaving Tomsk, they came to a large river, Tzulimm, which they ascended on the ice; seeing for six days neither house nor inhabitants, but only tall firs rising like pyramids, and spreading their branches so wide as to render the woods almost impassable. The Tzulimm Tartars are a poor, ignorant, harmless race, living in huts half sunk under ground, with a fire in the middle, round which are benches, where the whole family eat and sleep. Eleven days after leaving Tomsk they came to Yeniseisk, a large and populous place on the great river Yenisei, and containing an excellent market for furs. The animals chiefly caught are white hares and black foxes, also a species called *piessi*, with a thick, soft, downy fur, which is much valued in China. Quitting Yeniseisk, they proceeded along the Tongouska, the chief tributary of the Yenisei. Here they found the Tungouses, who are described a brave, active, honest people, and their females virtuous. They have no permanent abodes, but range through the woods and along the rivers; and whenever they incline to fix, put together a few spars in a conical form, leaving a hole at the top for the smoke. Their employment is hunting, and their arms bows and arrows, with which they will attack the fiercest creatures, and even bears. They have light wooden shoes five feet long, with which they are able to walk in the deepest snow without sinking. The most valued animal is the sable, whose fur is so delicate that it is spoiled by the least wound or hurt. It is therefore pursued till it seeks shelter on the top of a tree, at the foot of which the hunter spreads his nets, then kindles a fire, the smoke of which the sable being unable to endure, drops down, and is caught in the net.

We shall not pause upon our traveller's hearsay accounts of Yakoutsk and Kamtchatka, which have since been fully explored by personal observation. He left the banks of the Tongouska for those of the Angara, where he found the Burats, a hardy pastoral people, with a breed of large horned cattle, and broad tailed sheep. They were formerly subject to the Mongol government, but now live quietly under the Russians, though they have not yet learned from them to till the fertile soil which they inhabit. The embassy came then to Irkutsk, a fortified town of 2000 houses, situated in a country abounding in game. They had intended to cross the Baykall upon the ice; but the heat was now so intense, and all the rivers beginning to open, that though assured it was still safe, they durst not venture themselves on the surface of so great a sea unless in ships. They determined to remain at Irkutsk till its navigation should be possible. At this place Bell was introduced to a celebrated Shaman, who was also a

Lama, and whose wonderful performances he was desirous to see. This great personage, however, pronounced himself unable to do any thing in a Russian house where there were images, and they were obliged to repair to a Buratsky tent in the suburbs. Here this learned man was found smoking tobacco, and for half an hour after their arrival he remained seated on the floor without any movement. He then began singing and beating with sticks, in which last operation the whole audience joined in chorus. Next he began writhing his body into the most distorted positions, till working himself up to a state of fury, he foamed at the mouth, and trode on the fire with his naked feet. When quite exhausted, he uttered three tremendous shrieks, after which he sat down perfectly cool, and declared himself ready to answer any question that might be put to him. The whole exhibition appeared to Mr Bell a complete and manifest cheat; an impression, however, very different from that which was received by the Burat spectators.

As soon as the Baykall was judged navigable, the embassy left Irkutsk to embark below the cataracts of the Angara. This being the only outlet for this immense lake, the water rushes tempestuously between high rocks, with a roaring like that of the sea in a storm. Our author does not conceive the whole world can contain a more awful scene than is here presented. Only a narrow passage is left on the eastern shore between the rocks and the land. The pilots and sailors who navigate the Baykall mention it always with the deepest reverence, calling it the Holy Sea, and the mountains that surround it the Holy Mountains; and they have tales of the disasters which overtook those mariners who named it in a less respectful manner. It is about 300 miles long, and 50 broad, bordered on every side by lofty mountains, wooded on the south, but to the west still covered with snow. Being overtaken by a violent gale, and seeing a bay, the shore of which appeared covered with shells or white sand, they steered into it for shelter. They were somewhat dismayed to find that these seeming shells or sands were all ice; and it was needful to set all hands to work with poles and boards to prevent the planks from being cut by the floating fragments. The rattling of the loose cakes caused at first considerable dismay; but at length the vessel was safely moored upon the solid body of the ice, and they got out and walked upon it. Next day the wind becoming favourable, they left their station, and reached the mouth of the river Selinga. They then sailed up to Oudinsk, where they left their barks, and proceeded by land. Being wetted in passing a river, they entered a tent, and were refreshed with tea prepared in the Thibetian fashion, by pouring it over a paste, so as to make it both meat and drink. In a few days they reached Selinginsk, a town of 200 houses, most injudiciously situated on a barren and sandy spot that produces nothing. Here we may pause, as the narrative now links itself with that which we have already given of the journey to China.

## CHAPTER III.

### SIBERIA—RECENT TRAVELS.

*Messerschmidt.—Gmelin.—Pallas.—Sievers.—Schangin.*

RUSSIA, in her first expeditions into Siberia, had any thing in view rather than the extension of knowledge, or the scientific exploration of the vast provinces thus easily added to her empire. Purchas, in enumerating all the new and striking natural objects to be found in these regions, repeatedly taunts the Muscovites as "negligent "searchers into such things," and "men that "care for nothing but gaine." This reproach, however, was fully wiped off in the course of the eighteenth century, when they set to Europe the example of scientific expeditions, conducted with the most liberal means, and on the most extensive scale.

THE first of these missions did not, either in its means or result, answer the expectations which might have been formed from its author. The traveller employed was DANIEL MESSERSCHMIDT, a remarkable and highly endowed individual, whose exertions in the cause were certainly very extraordinary. He studied at Halle, and acquired a most profound and extensive learning, which included not only all the established branches of science, but even the oriental languages. In 1716 he repaired to St Petersburg; and in 1719 entered into an engagement with Peter the Great to travel seven years through Siberia upon the small annual stipend of 500 rubles (not quite L. 80). He performed this vast journey almost alone, traversing most of the districts surveyed by future travellers, and several which none but himself has visited. He attended with almost superfluous punctuality to every point of his instructions. After spending the whole day in travelling and collecting objects of natural history, he sat late at night, and often till next morning, writing his journal. When any accident interrupted his travelling occupations, he wrote epigrams, songs, sonnets; while at other times he penned theological meditations, particularly on the Apocalypse. He made his collections of natural history without any assistance except that of some Russian boys, whom he occasionally hired for that purpose. Besides giving elaborate drawings and descriptions of animals and plants, he stuffed and otherwise preserved as many of these as possible. His ornithology alone, deposited in the academical library, amounts to eighteen closely written octavo volumes. He observed the altitude of the sun at every place of importance; and seems in no degree to have overlooked any branch of science except mineralogy. All these merits and acquisitions became unavailing towards his own welfare, through a wayward and hypochondriac disposition, which rendered him gloomy, solitary, mistrustful, and harsh, towards those whom he conceived to have in any degree failed towards him. These defects were less conspicuous during the first years, when he had for a companion Captain Tabbert, who afterwards, under the title of Baron Strahlenberg, wrote a good account of Northern Asia. His letters express the deepest affliction at the recal of this gentleman. "I separated myself, says he, "with many tears from the virtuous, honourable, "and faithful Tabbert, my only friend and sup"port. I am now left wholly abandoned, with"out society or aid." He continued, however, for five years longer to prosecute alone his journeyings through these wild regions; but in this savage solitude the peculiarities of his temper gained always new strength. Repeated complaints of his conduct were sent to the chancery of St Petersburg, and were too readily listened to. On reaching that capital he experienced a very different reception from that which he conceived due to him; and an inquiry was even instituted into his conduct, which terminated, however, in his entire acquittal. He might now have obtained a situation in some of the learned institutions; but, disgusted with the treatment which he had met with, and having unfortunately married a wife of the same rash and violent temper with himself, who fostered all his discontents, he withdrew entirely to Dantzic. Disappointed, however, in his expectations there, he again returned to St Petersburg, where he died in a state of almost entire poverty and desertion. His manuscripts have remained in the imperial library, and have been largely used by subsequent travellers, while he himself was almost entirely forgotten. Pallas, his illustrious successor in the career of discovery, has undertaken to bring his merits before the public, and has also published some extracts from his journals. One of them contains his journey from Mangasea, the most northerly town on the Yenisei, up the Nishnaia Tungouska. He had intended to proceed down the Yenisei to the Northern Ocean, but was assured that the season (June) was too late for such a journey. In descending the river the Tungouses frequently came out to him in little boats, composed of the rhind of the birch or the larch tree. He describes them as a brownish people, having a somewhat flat face, with various figures often painted on it, and wearing short leathern garments fitted to their shape, and very neatly sewed. These people pleased him much by their lively, frank, and honest deportment. Their *yourts*, or summer huts, consist merely of poles put together in a conical form, and roofed with the bark of the birch tree. Their winter abodes are more elaborate. These consist of one apartment, with windows filled up with expanded bladder instead of glass. The smoke escapes by a hole in the roof, which, for greater heat, is covered with dry grass. In a corner stands an oven, which serves at once to bake bread and warm the inmates. The latter, for their farther accommodation, have placed round the room broad benches, on which they sit, eat, and sleep, and beneath which the provisions are deposited. When the oven is first heated, the room is filled with an intolerable smoke throughout, unless for three feet immediately above the floor; so that the family, by lying along the benches, can keep themselves clear of it. In a short time it rises so high that they can stand upright without being involved in its atmosphere. There is also an outhouse for the dogs, where a fire is often kindled; yet these animals are sometimes frozen to death. The most severe cold lasts from the middle of December to the middle of January, during which hunting is impossible; but afterwards, by the use of snow-shoes, they can go out. Two sable skins sell from thirty to forty rubles; and when each man in the company has got one, they consider themselves as provided for the year.

In another of his long peregrinations, Messerschmidt traversed Daouria, and particularly examined the Dalai Nor, or Holy Lake, the source of the Argoun. It is eight geographical miles long and five broad, deep sunk in a bed of mountains. The ground upon its banks is clammy, and so soft that a man can scarcely ride over it. The water is thick, and has a whitish appearance as if soap had been dissolved in it. Sixteen pounds contain upwards of an ounce of a heavy, calcareous, and saltish *residuum*. In a recess of rock in one of the surrounding hills, he found a large bell, six cups, and a box with earth and dust, all composed of metal, with a small bundle of Tungut writings wrapped in a cotton cloth. The whole apparatus appeared to mark the place of deposit for the mortal remains of a Lama. In a plain at some distance he found numerous stone pillars, exceeding the human size by one half. At a distance they appeared like statues, but, on approaching, proved to be mere fragments of rock standing upright. Of the same kind he supposes may be the petrified army reported to exist in the steppe of the Kirghises.

This first scientific attempt to explore Siberia, the result of which was not altogether honourable to its author, was followed up afterwards on a much grander and more extensive scale. Though this new undertaking, however, was due to the spirit created by Peter, it was set on foot, not by him, but by one of his least distinguished successors, the Empress Anne. Its primary object was to explore Kamtchatka, a part of the Russian Asiatic dominions which was then very imperfectly known. The mission, however, received instructions, in the first instance, to traverse and survey Siberia; and from particular circumstances, the functions of the greater part of them terminated here. There was employed on this occasion a band of learned and ingenious travellers, such as the world had never before seen despatched on a similar mission; GMELIN, a physician, chemist, and botanist, of the first eminence, and to whom we are indebted for the fullest narrative of this important journey; Muller, who had already distinguished himself by a collection of original pieces relative to the history of Siberia and Tartary; de Lidele de la Croyere, and his brother, sons to the celebrated geographer of the same name, and who were intrusted with the care of making the astronomical observations; Behring, so celebrated for his discoveries in the eastern seas of Asia; Steller, also an eminent mariner and naturalist, and distinguished by his voyages to Kamtchatka and America; Kracheninikow, whose history of Kamtchatka is also valuable, with several other Russian learned men, and two German artists. They departed from Petersburg in August 1733.

As the first part of the journey through Siberia was by the same route followed previously by Bell, and afterwards by Pallas, we shall only stop to mark some of its most prominent features. At Kasan they first saw the Tartars, who in this quarter are all Mahometans, and have temples for the exercise of their religion. They practise polygamy, but their wives are not confined, and shewed a great inclination to have conversed with the strangers, had they known enough of their language. A number of Tartars newly enrolled were seen taking the oath in the following manner. They placed themselves on their knees while it was reading to them, after which they kissed the Koran, and had two naked swords presented to them, with a bit of bread at the point of each, which they received and eat. The import was understood to be, a wish that this morsel of bread might occasion their death, if they did not faithfully serve the Czar. Upon the whole, he says, they are humane, obliging, good people, very different from the ideas which are attached in Europe to the name of Tartar.

Immediately before passing the frontier of Siberia, the academical travellers saw the immense cave of Kungur, about four miles long, and two broad, formed by nature in the calcareous rock. In one place a rivulet flows through it, in another there is a pretty large lake; and on one spot grass and flowers are seen growing. It is not continuous, but composed of numerous passages communicating with each other; and the party spent nine hours, and several times lost themselves, in going through it. This cave contains lodgings for a hundred men, formed at the time when the Russians sought refuge from an incursion of the Baschkirs. It did not appear, however, to Gmelin so remarkable as the grotto of Boman in the Hartz, or the *Nebel loch* in the duchy of Wirtemberg.

Soon after passing the boundary of the Ourals, the travellers came to Katherinenburg, a new city founded by Peter in 1723. It is the central point of all the founderies and forges of Siberia, and the residence of the Supreme College of Mines. He who wishes to obtain a complete knowledge of the modes of extracting metals from the bowels of the earth, needs only a due residence at Katherinenburg. There is not a house which is not built, nor an individual which is not employed by government. The police is very strict; and the labourers are prevented from indulging in their national habits of excessive intoxication, by a strict prohibition to sell brandy, unless on Sunday, and then only in limited quantities. On the way to Tobolsk, they saw the fair of Irbit; a most crowded scene, where there was scarcely a province or city in the Russian empire which had not its representatives.

Tobolsk was found a populous city, divided into two parts, the upper and lower, the latter of which is better supplied with water, but subject to inundation. One-fourth of the inhabitants were Tartars, and the rest Russians, either exiles or the sons of exiles. A man of a middling condition may live comfortably on the annual income of ten rubles, (about a guinea and a half); which, however, has the unlucky effect of producing most excessive indolence. The Tartars here too are Mahometans, but by no means so cleanly or comfortable as those of Kasan. They have only one apartment, where the whole family, not excluding the cows and sheep, take up their abode. Gmelin never saw so many cows in any city as in Tobolsk; they appeared wherever he turned; so that the cow, he thinks, would form a most proper armorial bearing for the capital of Siberia. Our travellers had an opportunity of seeing the state of the dramatic art in this region of the world. They witnessed the representation of a piece entirely similar to the ancient mysteries represented in Europe during the middle ages. The Devil, Adam, Death, and other similar characters, acted the principal parts.

From Tobolsk, our travellers did not, like Bell, cross the desert of Barabinski, but descended the Irtisch by Tara and Jamuscheva. Their greatest annoyance arose from the swarms of mosquitoes, which almost covered them, and by their stings caused the most insupportable pain. Even the cows, it is said, were sometimes so tortured by them, that they fell down dead. At Jamuscheva an alarm was excited by a vast conflagration spreading along the steppe, and threatening to attack the fortress; and all the women were prepared to meet it with tubs of water. It died away, however, of itself; and such fires were said to be by no means unfrequent. Near this place is a salt lake, which may be called a wonder of nature. The whole of the bed and banks is covered with saline chrystal; and when a quantity has been taken away, it is reproduced in a few days. The salt is beautifully white, of the most excellent quality in every respect, and might be sufficient to supply fifty provinces.

The travellers having viewed the remains of some ancient edifices at Sempalat, proceeded along the river to Oust Kamengorskaia, after which they struck across the steppe towards Yeniseisk. The Tartars who occupied this district were no longer Mahometans, but devoted to the system of Shamanism, which, among this ignorant people, seems to have degenerated into pure sorcery. The Kam, or Shaman, maintained his reputation by beating on a magic drum, throwing himself into the most hideous postures, and pretending to foretel the future. The road being dangerous, they sent only a detachment to observe the remarkable monuments at Ablaikit. These reported, that the edifices presented nothing remarkable, the principal one consisting merely of a great hall, in which, however, there was a large idol of earth, and sixteen smaller ones. One of them had four heads, and twenty-four arms. The most remarkable feature was the vast mass of manuscripts, with which they could have loaded twenty waggons, and they brought away a considerable number. The mission passĕd Kolivan, founded in 1725, and which contained the greatest forges in this part of Siberia. The next place of consequence was Kuznetsh, a small town of five hundred houses, without trade or industry. The natives caught neither game nor fish, though the country abounded in the one, and the river Tomm in the other. They had at their tables neither fruit nor vegetables, nothing but bread and meat. The travellers continued to ascend the Tomm to Tomsk, at the confluence of that river with the

Obi, a place of considerable trade with the Kalmucs and Bucharians, and a thoroughfare for the Chinese caravans; but the indolence of the inhabitants is still complained of, and imputed to the extreme cheapness of provisions.

The travellers now proceeded across an extensive plain to Yeniseisk. The Tartars here had all been converted by the diligence of the Archbishop Philophei, who sent round a body of Cossacks to drive in as many as could be found. These collected Tartars were then plunged, with or without their consent, into the river, on coming out of which, a cross was tied round their necks, and they were judged sufficiently Christians. The Russians excused themselves by their total ignorance of the language, from giving them any further initiation. In about ten days the party reached Yeniseisk, a town of about seven hundred houses, who might carry on a considerable trade, were they not so much addicted to indolence and drunkenness. It being now December, the cold was intense, and almost intolerable. The air felt as if frozen; thick ice was formed in the inside of the windows; and the mercury fell one day lower than they had ever observed it any where. Another great inconvenience was, that when the stove was heated, a sulphureous smell issued from it, which caused violent headachs. This did not prevent them from setting out on the 13th of January for Krasnoiarsk, a modern city of from three to four hundred houses, chiefly inhabited by a race of Tartar militia, called *Sluschivies*, who live in easy circumstances, being rich in cattle, and the country round abounding in sables and other animals that produce valuable furs. The ground is so rich, that it will yield five or six successive crops without manure. A considerable number of antiquities, some of gold and silver, are dug out from the tombs in the neighbourhood. Among the curiosities of Krasnoiarsk, are some very extensive grottos, and a painted rock, the figures on which, however, do not surpass what might be made by the hand of a peasant. The Tartars of this district shewed respect for Christianity, but obstinately refused to be converted, dreading the necessity of giving up horse-flesh, and adopting the Russian mode of life; which last they hold in such horror, that they know of no stronger malediction than this: "Mayest thou be condemned "to live like the Russians."

The mission proceeded from Krasnoiarsk to Irkutsk, where they did not stop, but immediately set sail on the Baikal. This sea was still considerably encumbered with ice; but by keeping along its northern shore, they effected their voyage in safety. On the banks of the Upper Selinga Gmelin found a Taischa, or prince of the Mongol religion, with his Gelum or priest. From them he obtained a full account of their belief, which appeared to him an illegitimate branch of the Roman Catholic. They assured him, however, that the Shamans, who imposed upon the ignorant inhabitants of those regions, formed a heresy which was disowned and condemned by all the more orthodox Lamas. The mission passed through Selinginsk, on which he adds nothing to the information of Bell, and proceeded to Nertschinsk. This place had once been of some importance, but was greatly declined, in consequence of the caravans to the Chinese frontier no longer passing through it. It was also cruelly oppressed by the Vaivodes, or Russian governors. The inhabitants seemed to seek consolation in every kind of drunkenness and debauchery, which had reduced them generally to a complete state of disease and wretchedness. From Nertschinsk Gmelin went to examine the Sawodes, or lead and silver mines of Argunsk. These had been opened in 1704, by three Greeks, who, though carrying on their operations very rudely, produced for several years the annual amount of from 40 to 60,000 libs. of silver. About 1730, however, a German called Heidenreick, sent to examine the works, not finding the indications of this metal usual in the German mines, declared that the veins were exhausted, and that nothing more of consequence could be expected. After, however, the works were abandoned, and the machinery allowed to go to ruin, new veins were discovered, and several during the stay of our author. They were on a plain surrounded by mountains, and many of them in soft earth, so that they could be easily worked.

During his stay in this neighbourhood, our author was present at exhibitions made by several eminent Shaman impostors. One of them began by stripping himself naked, after which he put a robe of skins, stuck all over with instruments of iron, particularly two large horns, on the shoulders. He then gave a lecture on the nature of demons, asserting that they formed a regular hierarchy, and rose above each other by various gradations. He now began the usual leaps and howlings, during which the academical audience were in considerable tremor, not for the devil, but for the sharp instruments with which he was begirt. They saw another, who was accustomed to run an arrow through his body, and to exhibit even the blood streaming from it. On being closely examined, however, he laughed, and frankly owned, that he merely thrust the arrow into the front of his vestment, then drawing his body somewhat aside, carried it by a circuitous line till it was brought out at the back. As for the blood, it was clandestinely distilled from a vessel kept under his clothes for that purpose. Finding him so communicative, they urged him strongly to declare at once that he knew nothing of any devils, and had not the least idea what sort of beings they were; but this overture he positively rejected, insisting that he could still command a limited number, though he had not now, as in his youth, a hundred and twenty ready to obey his bidding.

Gmelin now retraced his steps to Yeniseisk, with the view of proceeding thence to explore the banks of the Lena. He proceeded first to Ilimsk, on the Ilim, a small and poor town, which, he says, may be called the dwelling of sloth. The inhabitants seemed to have no idea of any thing but drinking and sleeping. Though the country abounded in game, they had never thought of taking any, unless by the easy processes of spreading nets, and digging ditches. The soil, however, was so fruitful, that the labour of the Russian exiles rendered provisions cheap and plentiful. The Tungouses in this neighbourhood are poor, their whole property consisting in rein-deer, of which individuals have flocks of from five to fifty. They hunt chiefly with arrows, and sometimes entrap wild animals, by imitating the cries of their young. Their boats are formed of pieces of bark sewed together; the smallest contain one, and the largest four persons. Their religion has nothing of that tincture of Shamanism which predominates in the countries around the Baikal. Its only objects are idols roughly formed of wood, to which they pray for success in the chase, giving them, when successful, a share in its fruits. Their general principle, indeed, is to keep the flesh and skin for their own use, and present the bones only in offerings; but in cases of peculiar good fortune, they will treat their gods with a draught of the blood. Should the chase fail, the idol suffers the blame, and is often treated in consequence with the utmost harshness and contumely.

From Ilimsk the travellers departed for Istkut, on the Lena, at its junction with the Kuta. They passed in their way salt springs called Oserko, which supply all this part of Siberia. A pound of water here yielded about an ounce and a half of salt. The woods were filled with the most extraordinary multitude of squirrels, who were eagerly pursued by the natives for the sake of their skins. Istkut was a small fort and village, not differing from those formerly visited, except from the scarcity of liquor, in consequence of which that vehement passion for it which reigns throughout all Siberia, was more intensely displayed. Being brought from a distance, and only by government conveyance, the stock frequently ran out, when the arrival of a new supply produced a scene of rapture and furious indulgence. In general, it is laid down as a principle, that no Siberian misses any opportunity of getting drunk. They remained at Istkut till the Lena thawed, which was on the 4th May. On its banks they found goitres as prevalent, and of larger dimensions, than on the Alps. As they ascended, the villages became smaller and more thinly scattered, and it became more difficult to obtain refreshments. Their trouble was increased by their Tartar attendants, who, we presume, were impressed into their service by order of government, eagerly embracing every opportunity to desert. Even when prohibited from carrying their effects on shore, they chose rather to abandon all than to remain. Every one was prohibited, on pain of death, to afford them shelter, and every one afforded it; messengers were sent off in every direction, but none were overtaken. In examining the packages left by the runaways, Gmelin was surprised to find a small bag of earth forming an uniform part of their contents, and learned, on inquiry, that it was a portion of their native earth, the taste of which they imagined, even under a foreign sky, would preserve them from all the evils to which this sad change might expose them.

As the expedition passed the mouth of the Jtshora, the scene became still more gloomy. All traces of villages or regular habitations disappeared; stones no longer marked the distances from verst to verst; the mountains were bleak and rugged, and a thick and almost continual fog involved the air. The few Tungouses whom they espied, fled with the utmost speed, and hid themselves in the forests. Meantime, as the river was broad and deep, no difficulty was found in sailing up to Witim, an early founded but small village, of not more than twelve houses. They ascended the Witim, to see the beautiful mines of talc situated upon its banks. Their quality is so superior, that on their discovery the working of all those on the other rivers immediately ceased. This substance is used instead of glass throughout all Siberia, and to a great extent in European Russia. It is said to be often as clear, and is much stronger, resisting even cannon. It is split by the insertion of a knife into thin lamina, the value of which depends on their size. Those of an ell in length, are sold at from one to two rubles a-pound. The more usual size, however, is a quarter of an ell, when a ruble is paid for about four pounds. The party then continued to ascend the Lena, which grew always broader, and became subject to storms, which caused at one time apprehension of danger. At a place called Stolbi, they passed for twenty miles along a colonnade of mountains, presenting the varied forms of towers, castles, steeples, and pillars, with trees interspersed, which produced the most picturesque effect. Early in September they arrived at Yakutsk, where they found the depth of winter already fast approaching. On the 19th ice began to form on the Lena, and by the 28th the river was entirely covered, and could be passed on sledges. Ice is used here for a purpose not thought of elsewhere,—to warm the houses. It is found the most effectual mode of stopping up every chink and crevice, and is applied like a double glass to the outside of the windows. If the piece does not exactly fit, they have only to pour on water, which instantly freezes and fills it up.

Yakutsk is a small town, of five or six hundred wooden houses, an ample proportion of which consists of taverns. The soil is rich, but the climate unfits it for the culture of grain. A crop of rye, when sown, sometimes ripens and sometimes not. What indeed can be expected, where, in the end of June, the ground is still frozen three feet deep? Notwithstanding this, Yakutsk was once called the Peru of Siberia. This pompous title it owed to the abundance of sables, and to the exemption which its distance procured it from the exactions and restraints of government. Both these advantages were now sensibly diminished. The party spent the winter, as it were, imprisoned at Yakutsk, the season rendering it impossible to travel. It was indeed a period of darkness, since at nine in the morning day had scarcely broken, and before two in the afternoon the stars were visible. The natives took advantage of this gloom to enjoy abundance of sleep, scarcely rising, unless to their meals, and sometimes, when the day was very dark, never waking at all. Our travellers did not chuse to consign themselves so deeply to slumber; and though the gloomy season did not admit of much business, they found considerable amusement in the society of themselves, and of several merchants who were on their way to Kamtchatka; as well as in drinking punch, the established liquor of Yakutsk.

The natives of this region, who bear the name of Yakoutes, do not materially differ in appearance and habits from the other inhabitants of Siberia. Less active in the chase than the Tungouses, and not following the sables to so great a distance, they do not obtain their furs nearly so fine. They care little for bread, which is almost beyond their reach, and place their chief luxury in onions, garlic, and other roots. They eat also various berries, both fresh and preserved, which serve besides as an excuse for brandy as necessary to counteract their bad effects. Superstition, among these people, seems to subsist on a greater scale than among the Tungouses. Among other Shamans, held in high reverence, there was a young witch, who undertook to plunge a knife into her body without sustaining any injury. The academicians waited upon her to witness the exhibition. After beginning in the usual manner, by distorting her body, imitating the cries of different animals, and holding long discourse with unseen demons, she proceeded to the operation. She thrust the knife through her clothes, in a manner which altogether satisfied the believing Yakoutes; but she clearly discerned the full persuasion of the strangers, that her person was entirely untouched. She therefore appointed another rendezvous, when they saw her really thrust the knife into her body, cut out a portion of the *omentum*, roast it on the coals, and eat it. Struck, however, with consternation at her own wound, she frankly confessed, that this was the first time she had ever come to such an extremity, which was quite superfluous with reference to the Yakoutes; but that, mortified at her failure in deceiving them, she had summoned courage to take this step. She had trusted, moreover, to a doctrine held by many learned Shamans, that by eating a portion of her own fat, she would obviate any damage it might occasion. Finding this charm inefficacious, she put herself under their care; and having luckily struck no mortal part, a cure was in due time effected.

Circumstances, into the detail of which we shall not enter, prevented Gmelin from proceeding farther; and the remainder of his journey consisted chiefly in retracing his steps to St Petersburg.

A JOURNEY not less conducive to the interests of science was undertaken in 1769 by the learned and laborious Professor PALLAS, under the patronage of the Academy of Sciences. His travels in the Taurida and Caucasus have repeatedly appeared in an English dress; but the case is otherwise with his journey through Northern Asia, which is yet of at least equal interest. The variety and minuteness of the topographical and statistical details of which this learned author composes his narrative, render it not very easily susceptible of a regular analysis; and we must be content to catch, though in a somewhat unconnected manner, the most important of the particulars communicated in the course of it.

The journeys performed by M. Pallas in 1769 and 1770 embrace the line of the Ourals and the European frontier. It was only in 1771 that he undertook to penetrate into the extremities of Siberia, to supply the deficiencies of Gmelin, and observe the changes that have occurred since the time of that traveller; as also to survey the southern provinces, the limits of which had been recently fixed, and which were beginning to be settled and peopled. He begins with a description of the province of Isetsk, extending along the river Iset, which is about two hundred miles in length, and of equal breadth, and consists of a rich black soil, yielding the very best grain and pasture; yet it does not contain above 57,391 inhabitants. This thin population he ascribes partly to the great quantity of ground monopolized by the Cossacks, and partly to that consumed by the Baschkirs in the breeding of horses. This people have horses here in the greatest numbers and perfection, at which Pallas was astonished, when he saw the manner in which they were bred. The passion of the Tartars for koumiss, or fermented mares' milk, induces them to defraud the foals to a great extent of that which they ought to receive from their mother; and as they make no provision for winter food, the poor animals are often at that season left entirely destitute. They thrive, however, in spite of all, and many individuals possessed from two to three thousand horses, most of them from three to four hundred. They raised only so much oats and barley as was necessary to eke out their winter food, when the milk of their cattle failed.

Pallas, in penetrating though Siberia, did not take the high-road by the great cities of Tobolsk, Tomsk, and Yeniseisk. His object being natural history and the less explored parts, he proceeded along the great southern steppe, parallel to the Altai, and diversified by a chain of salt and bitter lakes. He reached the Tobol at the fortress of Zuerinogolosskaia, whence he intended to have traversed the fortified line of the Ischim to Omsk; but he was assured that the redoubts which defended it were in a very ruinous state, and quite unequal to defend the travellers from the frequent inroads of the Kirghises. He was obliged to take a circuitous route, descending the Tobol, and ascending the Irtysch. In considering the saline character of all the waters in this vast southern steppe, which extends to the Obi, Pallas can trace it only to the chain of mountains extending from the Oural through the land of the Kirghises, and joining itself to the Altai. In descending the Tobol, near its junction with the Ouk, he remarked an extensive distillery formed by Count Schouvalof, which had given rise to a village of three hundred houses. The process was very ill managed; the body of the still and the tubes were so little tight, and so much steam consequently escaped, that one could not remain near it a quarter of an hour without getting drunk, and a flame was produced on the approach of a lighted candle. Hence the spirit, though twice distilled, had not the same strength as one good distillation would have given it; and government, he thinks, ought to interfere in order to prevent such a waste of grain. In a fine country on the banks of the Korrassoun he saw many bones of elephants, some of very great size. Here too were a great number of open tombs, in which gold and silver ornaments had once been found; but every one had now been ransacked. This object of cupidity was said to have been the source whence the territory was first peopled; and however the emigrants might have failed in the search, its superb pastures, and lakes abounding with fish, must have amply indemnified them.

Pallas ascended the Irtysch to Omsk, situated at its junction with the Om. This city had just been transported to a new position, the fortifications of which were scarcely completed; and a handsome church and other public buildings were erected. He met a very inhospitable reception from the governor, who would scarcely give him a passport. However he now set out to continue his journey down the Irtysch. He passed along a great number of small saline lakes, some of which were completely saturated, and the bottom covered with a thick layer of the most pure and beautiful marine salt. Several, at a little distance, appeared completely white; yet Pallas contradicts the report as to any of them being covered with a crust of salt like ice. This, he says, is quite impossible in a lake at all agitated by the wind; and indeed the smallest flakes which he saw went immediately to the bottom. The neighbourhood of Koriakoffshoi, the principal military post on the line of the Irtysch, is distinguished not only by these lakes, but by a vast number of bones belonging to large animals, particularly to a buffalo of greater dimensions than is now found in any part of Asia. The country here presented a dreadful spectacle, being covered with the dead carcases of horses, which had died of a pestilential disease that had just been raging, and whose bodies the government took no pains to remove. He came to Semipalatnoi, or the Seven Palaces, ruins already described by Gmelin. They seem unworthy of their title, and are described as ill built, and evidently of Bucharian origin. Near this is the rendezvous of the trade carried on with the Asiatic merchants. Pallas saw a number from Taschkent and Little Bucharia, who brought bad cotton goods, and appeared less civilized than those of Great Bucharia. The most profitable trade is carried on with the Kirghises, who give their horses and cattle at a very cheap rate, for mere toys and trifles.

Pallas now proceeded by the rivulets of Schoulba and Ouba, along the foot of the Altai, that vast and rich chain which rises near the east of the Caspian, and under various names traverses first the whole breadth of Asia, then turning to the north runs parallel to the eastern shore of the continent, till it terminates at Behring's Straits. He considers it as the most considerable chain on the globe; and in its whole extent along the frontiers of Siberia it is eminently distinguished by metalliferous qualities. Our traveller was struck with the astonishing number of ancient works carried on by the unknown people who once inhabited these tracts. There is not a productive spot throughout the Altai where their traces may not be found. Hence were doubtless derived those numerous metallic ornaments and utensils buried in the tombs on the Irtysch. Descending that river, our traveller had an opportunity of surveying the ruins of Ablaikit, built by Ablai, a Kalmuc Prince. It bears marks of having possessed all the magnificence which could be given to it by an uncivilized people. The author counted forty-five idols, representing all that is most sacred among the Bourkans and the Kalmucs. Half of the figures were female; some of them were hideous, with inflamed features and countenances; others were monstrous, with ten faces and seven arms. They were variously formed, of copper, stone, and potter's earth. Fragments of writing were still found, but not in the same vast abundance as in the time of Gmelin. The edifice had been variously injured by the Russians and the Kirghises; and a squadron of cavalry, encamped near it, was just completing its destruction.

Mr Pallas now left the Irtysch, and after passing along the Altai, covered with perpetual snow, came to Kolivan, the earliest forge established in this part of Siberia. It was originally worked as a copper mine by an individual of the name of Denudoff; but the crown having learned that gold and silver were also produced, took full possession of it. It is now in a very languishing state, perhaps from the failure of wood, and is much surpassed by other forges in this district. The great scene of mining operations is now the Schlangenberg, or Serpent Mountain, so called from the multitude of that description of animals which are found there. This mountain is situated about sixty miles from the Irtysch, and a hundred from the Obi; and appears from the course of the rivers on both sides to tower above all the rest of the Altai. It may be considered as an enormous mineral mass; whenever its covering of slate rock is taken off, all the substances beneath are found to yield gold, silver, copper, and plumbago. Zinc, arsenic, and sulphur, are also abundant. Since 1746, when this great source of wealth was first discovered, the openings made into the mountain are almost innumerable, being guided in several instances by the example set by the Tchouds, or ancient inhabitants, some of whose workings reached sixty feet deep. To give an idea of the richness of the Schlangenberg, it is stated, between 1749 and 1771, to have produced 318 poods, or (at 36 pounds to each pood) 12,348 pounds of gold, and more than 324,000 pounds of silver. It still yields annually 36,000,000 pounds of mineral; and the veins already discovered would be sufficient to supply the same quantity for twenty years to come.

From the Schlangenberg Pallas proceeded north to Barnaoul on the Obi. If Schlangenberg be distinguished for the quantity of mineral substances, Barnaoul is not less so for the forges in which that substance is fused and refined. The minerals, with a few exceptions, are of difficult fusion, which renders the labour very extensive, and consumes an immense quantity of wood. Pallas now ascended the Obi to Tomsk. He found the country on the right, between the Obi and the Tomm, distinguished by high fertility, but unfortunately little inhabited, covered with forests of birch, and laid waste by hosts of field-mice. Tomsk is a large city, and a great emporium of the trade of Siberia. The ground on which it stands is very unequal, and there never was any thing so irregular as the line of its streets. They are narrow, winding, and running into each other; and the houses do not make the least attempt at a uniform line. A great part of the town had been consumed by fire, and never rebuilt; so that the ruins, and the cellars laid open, presented a shocking spectacle. Prevalent as drunkenness is in Siberia, Pallas never saw a town where it was so general as at Tomsk; and it leads, as elsewhere, to other species of debauchery, the diseases consequent on which had made dreadful havock here, as in the other towns of this region. Tomsk is the centre of the trade in brandy, or rather whisky, which is brought thither from the distilleries on the Tobol and the Iset, and thence distributed through the countries to the eastward.

From Tomsk nothing remarkable occurred till our traveller came to Knasnoiarsk. This town was not found at all changed from what it had been in the time of Gmelin. It had not increased, notwithstanding the fertility of the country round, and its favourable situation for trade. Indeed the vices of indolence and drunkenness appeared so rooted in the character of the inhabitants, as to give little hope of its prosperity. The foundation of these vices appeared to be the excessive cheapness of provisions. During his stay, oatmeal was sold from a halfpenny to three farthings a-peck, and had never been known to rise above three halfpence; an ox brought five shillings; a cow three; and an excellent horse was considered dear at ten shillings. This cheapness seems to arise partly from the want of a market, partly from the excessive luxuriance of the soil. It is said to be such, that manure is not only unnecessary, but destroys the grain. The climate is unfavourable for wheat; but oats, barley, and rye, produce most luxuriant crops. A large quantity of grain is exported to all the northern parts of Siberia.

M. Pallas travelled post from Krasnoiarsk to Irkoutsk, and spent only a few days in that city. He had a favourable passage across the Baikal, and was tracked up the Selinga, though with some difficulty, on account of the floating ice. At Selinginsk he found a very sensible change of climate. All the heights exposed to the south were cleared of snow, and the birds, which, in summer, had sought a warmer climate, were gradually making their appearance. Our traveller ascended the Selinga to Kiachta, the great scene of Chinese trade. It is situated in an elevated plain, surrounded by high, rocky, and wooded mountains. One of these, called the Eagle Mountain, is so near, that it overlooks both the Russian and Chinese towns; on which account the latter nation have had the art to obtain the cession of it. They have also secured for themselves a district abounding in vegetables, water, and fish; while on the Russian side there is nothing but sand and rock, and they cannot get a drop of good water for their tea unless by sufferance of their rivals. Every great commercial house in the empire has an agent at Kiachta; so that the society is pretty numerous, and the tone of manners more polished and sociable than in the other cities of Siberia. It would be very agreeable were it not for the endless urgency of the merchants to their guests to drink tea; their hospitality seeming to centre wholly in causing them to swallow the most enormous quantities of this liquid.

About a stone-cast from the wall of Kiachta is that of the Chinese city of Maimatshin. This place contains about two hundred houses enclosed with a wooden wall. The streets are straight, pretty broad, and kept very clean. The houses occupy a large space, having each a court-yard enclosed from the street. They are only one story high, built of timber and spars, plastered and painted white. The window-frames are large, but chiefly filled up with paper, only a pane or two of glass being afforded to admit the light. The roof is projecting, and each house is decorated with a flag. There are two pagodas, the ornaments of which are very splendid, and each house contains a recess covered with a silk curtain, in which are the *penates*, formed of finely painted paper. The Chinese merchants come to Maimatshin merely as travellers, and there are always at least two in company, one of whom remains while the other goes to China. They do not bring their families, no female being allowed to reside in the place; a privation for which the ladies of Kiachta are said to be at great pains to console them, more to their own profit than credit.

The trade between the two nations is carried on by the Chinese merchant coming to Kiachta, taking a view of the Russian merchandise, fixing on what he wishes, and stipulating what he is to give in return. The Russian then accompanies him to Maimatshin, and examines if the articles correspond exactly to the description which he had given. The Chinese take from the Russians skins, furs, cloths of various colours and qualities, a number of coarse manufactures, glass, and cattle; in return for which they give silk and cotton, both raw and manufactured, tea, tobacco, rhubarb, porcelain, and a variety of little trinkets and pieces of furniture. In bargaining, the advantage is said to be almost always on the side of the close, cautious, and artful Chinese, over the careless and babbling Russian. The trade, however, is of great benefit to the Russian empire, as it disposes of a large portion of surplus produce, which could with difficulty admit of transportation. It yields also a considerable revenue to the government, which imposes very heavy duties both on the exports and imports. The annual value of articles exchanged on each side is stated at between L.200,000 and L.300,000.

Pallas now performed a journey through part of Daouria, or Russian Mongolia, watered by the rivers Onon and Ingoda. This territory is inhabited by a race of Tungouses, much resembling the Mongols in their habits and external appearance. Of all the nations who inhabit the vast plains of the empire of Russia, these are the bravest, the most skilful in managing a horse, and in drawing the bow. In case of a limitary war they would form excellent light troops to oppose to the Mongols. They have been much reduced by contests with that people, who have the advantage in numbers; while the huntings by which they subsist, have been greatly injured by the increase of culture and population. They have Toions or princes, who collect the tribute from their subjects, and pay it to the Russian treasury. Sometimes, when ruined, the Tungouses come and hire themselves to work in agriculture or the mines, when they make good labourers. Pallas saw several exhibitions of their Shamans, particularly of the female sex, similar to those described by Gmelin; and observes in general, that superstition, throughout all Siberia, is radically one and the same.

Our traveller had here an opportunity of observing the *Dshiggetei* or wild horse, combining the qualities of that animal with those of the ass. Messerschmidt, by whom it was first observed, calls it the prolific mule. It differs from the mule, however, in many respects, having a light and slender form, and a superb covering of hair. Its mane and tail, indeed, resemble those of the ass, and its back is long and square. It is perhaps the swiftest animal in nature. The horse, in this respect, can bear no comparison, and it can be taken only by stratagem and ambuscade. The dshiggetei would, therefore, be extremely serviceable, could it be tamed by any process; but every attempt of this kind has hitherto failed, even when employed upon foals taken very young. Pallas saw also the *Argali*, or wild sheep, which seems to partake of the qualities of the goat, being covered with hair unless in winter, when a little wool is formed; and climbing rocks with the utmost agility. It is also excessively swift; but its young, when taken sufficiently early, are capable of being tamed.

Near the mouth of the Onon was found a considerable saline lake called *Zagan Noor*. Its bed consists of a black and tenacious clay, and on the surface floats a bitter salt, white as snow. All the surrounding plain consists of sand, detached probably from that great desert which extends between Russia and China, through the whole length of Western Tartary.

In 1786 P. Iwanowitch Schangin was sent by the Russian government to explore the loftiest regions of the Altai, situated between the Irtysch and the Katunia. The object was partly scientific, and partly to observe if there were any rocks of such beauty and value as might serve for the ornament of the imperial palace. Schangin spent the whole summer in exploring the banks of the Tscharysch, which takes its rise in these lofty regions, as well as of the numerous rivulets which concur in forming its stream. The task was attended with great labour and difficulty in regions where was neither path nor habitation, and where the track of wild beasts was often their best guide to the fords over the rivers. The wooded districts also swarmed with serpents, of which they often found in the morning several among their bed-clothes, though they appear to have been harmless, as none of the escort were bitten. Amid all these obstacles, our author completed his undertaking, and laid before the Russian government a complete mineral map of this remarkable district. The mountains on the right of the river, which were the highest, and covered with perpetual snow, consisted of granite; but those on the left were composed of porphyry, jasper, and serpentine, of which rocks they presented many beautiful varieties. They contained also rocks of a blue marble, and very large ultra-marine crystals.

Schangin indulges in few observations distinct from the immediate object of his mission. He gives, however, some account of the few Tartars who inhabit these wild and rugged regions. They are of middle stature, and not ugly; they have indeed the flat face of the Kalmucs, but with much better nose and eyes. It is supposed they may be a mixture of that people with the proper Tartar or Turkish breed race, who are extremely handsome. Some of the young females may dispute the palm even with the Russian beauties. Those advanced in years appeared to our author to form the ugliest sight he had ever beheld; which he imputes to their slovenly habits and perpetual drinking. The only occupations of these Tartars are hunting and breeding of horses. They have not the least idea of agriculture; and when offered bread, would scarcely taste it. They are a people of very few words, and appear neither to salute each other at meeting, nor to bid adieu at parting. They acknowledge a supreme being under the name of Kutai; but their chief worship is bestowed upon a piece of wood cut into the rude form of a head, which they place in the most conspicuous place of the hut, and call

*Ula-tai*, bedewing it occasionally with their favourite koumiss. Their huts consist merely of spars placed conically, and covered with felt or skins. The article which they are most anxious to purchase from the Russians is that of guns, for one of which they will give a horse worth fifteen rubles.

Schangin penetrated to the highest of the streams which form the Tscharysch, close to whose sources were others descending on the opposite side of the mountains, and forming the Katunia and the Buchturna, which falls into the Irtysch. Here they touched the extreme limits of the Russian frontier; and one of the mission having gone beyond the rest to fish in one of the streams, came upon a Chinese patrole of 35 men. They put many questions to him, pointing particularly to Schangin's tent, which was set up on a height at some distance; but the Russian knowing nothing of their speech, could give no reply. They then made a jeering comparison between his torn clothes and the comfortable silk dress which they themselves wore. At length the chief held out his tobacco pipe, when the Russian, actuated by an old antipathy of his nation to that substance, instead of accepting it, drew out a cross and held it before him; which caused a loud laugh from the opposite party. They then proceeded towards the tent; but on their approach, the Cossacks set up a loud cry *Kitaizi Kitaizi*, at which the Chinese took fright, and ran away, to the great regret of our author, who wished to have held some conference with these people.

The zeal of the Russian government for the improvement of its vast dominions, continued still unabated. In 1790 a new expedition was fitted out to examine whether rhubarb and other plants, now produced in perfection only upon the Chinese and Tartar frontier of Siberia, could not be advantageously transplanted into some part of the Russian territory. Sievers has given a lively narrative of this journey. They travelled at full speed from Moscow to Irkutsk, a distance of nearly 4000 miles, between the 13th February and the 26th April. The length of this period is ascribed to the bad roads, occasioned by the melted snow; for the journey has been known to be performed in less than a month.

Irkutsk is, next to Tobolsk, the largest city in Siberia, and contains 20,000 souls. It had been considerably improved in the course of the last twenty years. Besides several seminaries of education, it contained a small library and collection of natural history. It even supported a theatre, where were exhibited pieces of native production, that were pretty tolerable. The newest literature and music of Europe were transported thither by the military officers, who were continually going and returning.

Sievers now proceeded to sail across the Baikal. He was deeply struck with the appearance of the Angara, issuing out as by an immense mountain gate, four or five miles broad, and formed by the most stupendous walls of rock. He observes, that all the places round this sea are subject to slight earthquakes, and thinks it probable that its own deep bed must have been formed by some great convulsion of this nature. Its depth is such that, in the middle, a line of 400 fathoms has been let down without finding the bottom. Its water is the purest in the world, containing only a very small portion of calcareous earth, and so clear, that, at the depth of four fathoms, the smallest stones may be seen. The author had a delightful sail across it in a fine moonlight night. The appearance of the banks was continually changing, and presented successively deep meadows, immensely high walls of rock dipping into the water, high granite peaks, and smooth summits clothed with pines and verdure. As morning dawned, he found himself in the bay in which is situated the Possolskoi monastery, the usual rendezvous of the Russian embassies. The country was now peopled by a mixture of Russians and Mongols;

after some days spent in observing whom, he sailed up the Yenisei to Kiachta.

The observations of our author on Kiachta add nothing to the information of Pallas; but he formed an acquaintance with the *Bandida-Lama*, the great head, as to this part of Asia, of the religion of Boodh. He was allowed to enter the great temple, where he found about a hundred priests, clothed in red, and seated in successive rows. For the high priest there was erected a lofty and splendid throne, which he ascended only upon particular occasions, and behind which was the altar, on which were placed the images of the great gods, while those of inferior rank were arranged in rows along the walls. Before these august deities were placed brazen bowls with rice, brandy, and other victuals; and sometimes, on particular occasions, they were served with a hen, or even a sheep dressed whole. He confirms fully the report of Turner as to the immense extent of the system of noise on which these devout persons proceed. Bells, kettle-drums, trumpets eight feet long, huge sea-conchs, and other instruments, unite in producing a sound truly thundering and tremendous. Their worship is performed by putting both hands to their breast, and then falling flat on their faces. Their prayers are long, and were said to be put up for the welfare of all mankind, and of all the unfortunate, without difference of religion. The Lama gave our author an entertainment, at which were presented first tea, then milk-brandy, then a lamb newly killed and roasted on a wooden spit, then sour milk, and last of all tea again. He resided in a house built of wood in the Russian manner, surrounded by a number of felt tents to be used upon occasion.

Sievers now proceeded to fulfil the main object of his mission, by ascending the great ridge of the Yablonoy mountains, a continuation of the Altai, which rises at a little distance to the east and south. He found the country and people becoming gradually ruder. Even the Russians had betaken themselves, in a great measure, to a nomadic life, though the example of some Polish colonies had led them, and even the Mongols, to appreciate, in some small degree, the benefits of agriculture. At a village of Korokofskoi, he found himself at the farthest point to which waggons could travel, and was obliged to place all his baggage upon pack-horses, and lay in a stock of rye biscuit, the only provision which could be conveniently carried over these wilds. For two or three days, however, they still found inhabited spots, where they could rest for the night; but at length, in passing some Mongol huts, Sievers was warned, that he must bid adieu for some months to all human habitation. When night overtook them, his companions cut down branches of trees, and in half an hour built four houses sufficient to keep out the wind and rain, and to last for two or three years. Such is the system of all the hunters over these mountains; and the author, anticipating in his correspondent an objection to this waste of wood, assures him, that in this branch of the Yablonoy alone, there is as much timber as in all Germany. They caught here a great quantity of fish by a very simple process. Three men went by night to one of those deep ponds where the river has little current. One of them held a burning brand, by the light of which another struck the fish with a large cane, and handed it to the third. They now penetrated into the recesses of the Yablonoy by a road such as Sievers had never seen, and which struck him with dismay. Besides its ruggedness and steepness, it was crossed and encumbered by numberless trees, either withered with age, or torn up by the tempests. In the dreadful hollows which they had to cross, the cattle often sunk so deep in the mire, that they could scarcely be dragged out. In some part of the track along the two rivulets of Ossa and Kunalei, the scene was truly tremendous. Above appeared immensely high granite peaks, towering naked above the woods, with ranges of snowy summits over all; while beneath, the river was roaring in a deep cleft, along which they wound by a road excessively narrow. A pack-horse once fell, but was luckily caught by trees and saved. In general these animals proceed with surprising steadiness through these perilous paths. A great danger which besets the traveller is, that he may mistake one of the tracts made by wild beasts for the faint vestige of one which can alone lead him across these mountains. He is then soon involved in an inextricable labyrinth; yet if he has a hatchet, gun, powder and shot, he may procure for himself shelter and subsistence, till he can scramble to some human habitation; otherwise he must either perish or be devoured by wild beasts. Our author had with him a guide, who having hunted forty years through these Alps, was intimate with every track and recess through their wild and vast extent.

Through these tremendous steeps the travellers at length reached a spot marked by two warm baths, and where a decent cottage had been erected, which afforded them a most grateful shelter. These springs rise amid huge granite blocks, in an Alpine meadow, surrounded on every side by mountains, glaciers, and huge rocks having the form of ruins. They ascended next day the highest ridge, whence they beheld a vast range of rocky and snow-covered peaks, to which a thunder storm gave a terrible grandeur. He now began his descent, which he describes as a series of horror upon horror, so that what he had hitherto experienced appeared mere sport in comparison. They went first through a morass, which could not have been passable but for the great quantity of ice which still remained upon it. Our author deeply regrets that there was no painter's eye to observe the picturesque and varied forms of the immense cliffs reflected in its waters. The predominant form was that of a number of pyramids uniting into one summit, somewhat in the form of an apple; to which in fact the word Yablonoy makes allusion. The rest of their troubles were merely those of the former days on an augmented scale, and rendered more serious by the addition of an immense shower of rain. At length they arrived at a Simowie or cottage on the banks of the Tchikokan, which was to be the scene of some extensive botanical observations. It was a place so enclosed by high and wooded mountains, that they appeared as if at the bottom of a tower, and could see only a small portion of the sky. Here Sievers found the rhubarb growing in abundance, but refers to official communications for a full detail of his observations, only remarking, that the plant which grows on these high, cold, and wet spots, is rendered useless in medicine by the too great moisture of its root. These mountains were found rich in rare plants; but the animal world affords the chief motive which makes them an object of resort to the inhabitants of the neighbouring plains. Among their wild tenants he notices the Arctic bear, which is taken by the following process. A *fall*, or small wooden hut, is erected, in which a piece of carrion is placed. The door is made only three feet high; and when the bear stoops to enter it, the hunters throw on him from behind a machine composed of enormous wooden rollers, which crush him to death, without destroying the skin. Our author enumerates also several species of the stag, the musk cat, the wolf, the fox, the hare, the sable, the *dshiggetei*, the wild hog, the wolf, the squirrel.

It was formerly the custom among the Russian hunters to unite in associations, which chose as a commander the eldest and most experienced. This person appointed to each his task, rewarded those who did well, and belaboured with cudgels such as failed. Every morning at breakfast, it behoved each hunter to tell his dream, according to the chief's interpretation of which, he was either carried to the hunt, or left on guard. At present these grand associations have been given up, and such as are formed consist only in an agreement to share the fruits of their toil, which every one is left to carry on in the manner most agreeable to him.

From the Yablonoy, Sievers returned to Kiachta, and thence to the banks of the Irtysch. In 1792-3 he made an excursion into the steppe of the Kirghises, still for the purpose of discovering and examining the rhubarb, with a view to transplantation. There is no name more terrible in Asiatic Russia than that of the Kirghises, from their numerous predatory excursions which they make upon the frontier. Sievers, however, provided himself with a body of Cossacks and guides, to the number of twenty-two, who being well provided with fire-arms, could make head against two hundred Kirghises, a people of robbers rather than warriors. He had also Russian and Tartar passes from the governor of Tomsk, which were sufficient to secure him from any molestation on the part of the Princes. He found thus no difficulty in penetrating to the mountain Taragobatoi, near the lake of Nor Saisan, and the loftiest part of a chain branching from the Altai. The party had travelled more than a hundred miles ere they saw any trace of cultivation; and on their discovering a few acres under tillage, the Russians insisted that some of their countrymen must by some accident be there. The Kirghises, however, on being interrogated, declared that it was all done by themselves, and was even pretty common in this part of the steppe, though the manual labour was entirely performed by slaves, a genuine Kirghise considering any such occupation as far beneath his dignity. The plain beneath this great mountain range is considered by Sievers as the most delightful summer residence in the world. It displays the most rich vegetation, and at the same time enjoys the most magnificent alpine prospect. The snow which lies on the tops and in the hollows of the mountains, produces a coolness which prevents the production of noxious or troublesome insects.

Sievers sought here everywhere in vain for the genuine rhubarb, instead of which he was presented always with a spurious kind called *rheum Siberïum.* He had an opportunity, however, of observing the manners and character of the Kirghise horde. His impression was unexpectedly favourable, and he even prefers them to all the other Nomadic tribes of Asia. The Kirghise, he admits, like a wild beast, gives himself up to every natural instinct. He is inclined to thieving, and, like a child, wishes to have whatever he sees. The possession of herds above all appears to him to constitute supreme felicity. To obtain these he sets out on his robberies; to defend them, whenever it is dark he collects the whole in his *yourt,* takes his pike, and, alternately with others, rides round it during the whole night, accompanied by his dogs, who keep up a constant barking, to frighten the wolf. He stands in little awe of his prince, enters his court with few compliments, sits down and smokes his pipe. If any presents are brought while he is in the apartment, he expects a share, and will even help himself, if there should be a delay in offering it. Our author compares him to an English squire, according to the idea formed from Western in Tom Jones. His passion rages with the fury of a wild beast, but it is soon succeeded by gentleness and good humour. Sievers assures us, that by dint of courtesy, and a few presents, he found himself treated as the best of friends. He had only to enter a *yourt*, take his seat, draw out his pipe, present the landlord with a pennyworth of tobacco, and the lady with a thimble and two needles, and from that moment every thing in the house was his. The host would be his guardian in every danger, and the hostess treated him as if he had been a son. Drunkenness is by no means so prevalent as it generally is among the Asiatic Nomades. When offered brandy, they merely put it to their lips. Their favourite drink, as in the time of the earliest travellers, is *koumiss*, which our traveller extols as a most agreeable and wholesome liquor, and only slightly intoxicating.

F. G. Giorgi, who accompanied Pallas in his great expedition, afterwards drew up, from the observations then made, and from official documents, a general description of the Russian empire, the best of any yet published. From this work we shall extract the following statistical facts relative to Siberia.

Siberia is divided into two great governments, Tobolsk and Irkoutsk; the former of which includes all its western, and the latter all its eastern regions. Of these, Tobolsk, comprehending the vast tracts extending along the banks of the Obi, Irtysch, and Yenisei, includes the largest proportion of rich and cultivated land. By the enumeration of 1801, it contained 622,422 inhabitants, of whom 306,321 were male, and 316,098 female. Of these 2017 were Mongols, 17,236 Ostiaks, 273 Tschuwashes, 2936 Bucharians, 1993 Tungouses, 2581 Yakoutes, 3302 Samoiedes, 308 Jukagirs. This does not include the Cossacks, who are about 22,000, nor several tribes of the wandering Tartars.

The government of *Irkoutsk* includes some fertile territory on the southern frontier, and around the Baikal, but by far the greater portion consists of vast and frozen deserts. Its extent being vast, however, its population, in 1801, was found to be 451,934, of whom 208,793 are male, and 207,144 female. Among these there are, of Burats, 49,764 male, and 47,932 female; of

Mongols, 5713 male; Tungouses, 13,264 male, and 11,014 female; Yakoutes, 42,956 male, and 41,607 female; Jukagirs, 456 male, and 132 female; Koriaks, 900 male, and 779 female.

# APPENDIX.

LIST OF AUTHORITIES AND IMPORTANT WORKS RELATING TO ASIA.*

*N. B.—The Books mentioned under each Chapter after the mark ¶ are such as, though possessed of merit, it has not been consistent with the plan and limits of the work to analyze.*

## INTRODUCTION.

### CHAPTER I.—The Ancients.

Herodotus,† India, lib. iii. Scythia, lib. iv.

Curtius, Q. R. de Rebus Gestis Alexandri Magni.

Arrian, Expeditio Alexandri et Historia Indica. The last includes the Voyage of Nearchus.

Vincent, Dr, Periplus of Nearchus. 4to. London, 1797.

---

* In this list the object has been, to adopt such an arrangement as may exhibit the authorities on which each portion of the work was founded, without the necessity of loading the margin with references; and at the same time to exhibit a systematic Bibliography of Asia, or list of important works relating to the different regions of that continent.

† It is not conceived necessary to give the editions of the Classics, which may be found in any bibliographical work.

STRABO, India, b. xv.

DIODORUS SICULUS, b. ii. ch. 7. 12, 13.

ARRIAN, Periplus Maris Erythraei. By itself, and in Hudson's Geographi Graeci Minores.

VINCENT, Dr, on the Periplus of the Erythraean Sea. Vol. ii. 4to. London, 1805.

PTOLEMAEUS, Geographia—Bactriana, &c. b. vi. ch. 11, 12, 13. Scythia, b. vi. ch. 14, 15. Serica, b. vi. ch. 16. India, b. vii. ch. 1, 2. Sinæ, b. vii. ch. 3. Caravan route through Asia, b. i. ch. 12.

PLINIUS, Historia Naturalis, b. vi. chap. 17—22.

MELA POMPONIUS, b. iii. ch. 5, and 7.

D'ANVILLE, Antiquite Geographique de l'Inde. 4to.

——— Sur la Serique des Anciens, avec une carte.—Limites du Monde connu des anciens, avec une carte (Academie des Belles Lettres).

GOSSELIN, Geographie des Grecs. 4to. Paris.

——— Geographie des Anciens. Tom. iii. and iv. 4to. Paris, 1814.

## CHAPTER II.—THE ARABIANS.

ABOULFEDA, his great geographical work exists only in Arabic and in manuscript; the "Descriptio Mavarelnahar et Chorasmiae," by Gravius, and the Arabia (Arab. Lat.), are in Hudson's Geographi Graeci Minores; the Al Send and Al Hend (Hindostan) are translated by Thevenot in his collection.

EDRISI, Geographia Nubiensis Arab. Lat. per G. Sionitam et J. Hesronitam. 4to. Paris, 1619. The Arabic was printed at Rome, 1592.

EBN HAUKAL, Oriental Geography, translated by Sir William Ouseley. 4to. London, 1800.

IBN AL VARDI, BAKOUI, &c. See Notices et Extraits des Manuscrits du Roi de France. Tom. ii.

Anciennes relations des Indes et de la Chine de deux Voyageurs Mahometans qui y allèrent dans le neuvieme siecle, traduites de l'Arabe par l'Abbe Renaudot. 8vo. Paris, 1718.

BENJAMIN of Tudela, Itinerarium, ex versione Montani. 8vo. Plantin. 1575. Leyden, Elzevir, 1633.

——— In English. 12mo. London, 1783.

——— Extracts in Purchas, Harris, Pinkerton, &c.

## *BOOK I.*

## CHAPTER I.

ASCELIN and CARPINI. The narrative of their journeys was first printed in *Vincentii Burgundi Speculum Bibliothecae Mundi seu Speculum quadruplex*, 10 vols. fol. Argentorati, 1747. (There is a very early French translation in 5 vols. fol. under the title of *Miroir Historial*).

——— Opera dilettevole ad intendere, la qual si contiene doi Itinerarii in Tartaria. 4to. Venice, 1537.

——— An English translation of Carpini in Hackluyt, which wants, however, two chapters.*

——— A French translation in Bergeron Voyages (la Haye, 1735), contains the two chapters, as well as the relation of Ascelin.

## CHAPTER II.

RUBRUQUIS. The narrative of this traveller, partially published by Hackluyt, is given complete by Purchas in the beginning of his third volume, and copied or abridged in most of the subsequent collections.

---

* In the quotations throughout this work, even of foreign works, it has been not unusual to make use of the old English translations, the language of which possesses a force and *naivete*, which gives the spirit of these early narratives better than would easily be done in the English of the present day.

## CHAPTER III.

MARCO POLO, delle maraviglie del mondo da lui vedute o Viaggi, &c. fol. Venice, 1496. Ibid. 1508.

——— In German, Nuremberg, 1471.

——— In Spanish, with a treatise by Regio on the countries visited by Marco Polo. fol. Seville, 1720.

——— In French. 4to. Paris, 1556.

——— In English. fol. 1579.

——— Translated into English, with ample notes, by William Marsden, F. R. S. (the best edition yet published) 4to. London, 1818.

——— Inserted in the Italian collection of Ramusio; French translation in Bergeron; English translation in Purchas, Pinkerton, and several other collections.

## CHAPTER IV.

ODERIC de PORTENAU, de Mirabilibus Mundi. Inserted under the date of 1318 in the Acts of Bollandus, and in the Annals of Widingius; also, with a translation, in Hackluyt's collection.

MANDEVILLE, Sir John, A lytell Treatise or Booke, named Johan Mandeuyll, Knyht, born in Englande, in the towne of Saint Abone, and speaketh of the ways of the Holy Lande toward Jherusalem, and of Maruyles of Inde, and of other dyverse countries. London, 1499. 8vo.—1503, 8vo.—1568, 4to. —1684, 4to.—1725, 8vo.

——— In French, very rare. Lyon. Barth. Boyer. 1480.

——— Another. 4to. Paris. Jehan Bonfon. Goth.

——— In Italian. Venice, 1497. 1537. 1567.

——— In Spanish. Valencia. fol. 1540.

——— In Hackluyt, ed. 1589.

RICOLD de Monte Crucis, Voyages in Tartarie, traduits en Francais en 1351 par Jean le Long d'Ypres. This narrative, which M. Malte Brun seems to consider as unpublished, and probably as lost, I found, with several other curious ones, in the following rare work in the collection of John Rennie, Esq.

——— L'Histoire plaisante et recreative du Grand Empereur de Tartarie nomme le Grand Can. Fol. bl. l. 1528.

## CHAPTER V.—Age of Timur.

Clavijo, Historia del gran Tamerlan; ov Itinerario y narration del viage y relacion de la ambaxada que Ruy Goncales de Clavijo hizo por mandado del senor rey Don Henrique el Tercero, de Castille, en anno 1403, con discurso de Goncales Argova da Molina, y la vida del Tamerlan escripta por Paulo Jovio. Seville. fol. 1582. Very rare. Reprinted Madrid 1782.

Schildtberger, John. A short analysis in Forster's Discoveries in the North, p. 153—155. I have never been able to see the book itself, nor even its title and date in any catalogue.

Shah Rokh, embassy by. In the collections of Forster and Astley. More fully in Asiatic Annual Register.

——— Ambassades reciproques des Rois des Indes et de la Chine, en 1412; traduites du Persan, avec la vie de ces deux Souverains, et des Notes par M. Langles. Paris, 1788. 8vo.

## CHAPTER VI.—Southern Coasts.

Pinto, Fernan Mendez, Peregrinacam, en que da conta de muytas e muyto estranhas chusas que vio e ovvio no reyno da China, no da Tartaria, no da Sornam, que vulgarmente se chama Siam, no do Calaminham, no de Pegu, no de Martavan, e em outros muytos reynos e senhorios das Partes orientales. fol. Lisboa, 1614. Ibid. 1763.

——— In Spanish. Madrid, 1627. Valencia, 1645.

——— In Dutch. Amsterdam, 1653.

PINTO, In German. Amsterdam, 1671.
——— In French. Paris, 1645.
——— In English. fol. 1663.

SHARPEY and MIDDLETON. In Purchas's Pilgrims, vol. i.

——— Narrative of a Voyage to Arabia Felix, with an Account of the captivity of Sir Henry Middleton at Mocha. 8vo. This does not contain Sir Henry's own narrative, which is found only in Purchas.

GRANTHAM, Sir Thomas. Manuscript. Harleian. 4753. (British Museum).

ALBUQUERQUE Coelho, Antonio de, Governador e Capitao General da Cidade do Nome de Deos de Macao na China. Jornada que fez de Goa ate chegar a dita Cidade no anno de 1718. Escrita pelo Capitao Joao Tavarez de Velles Guerreiro. 12mo. Lisboa Occidental, 1732.

¶ LINSCHOTEN, Joan. Navigatio et Itinerarium in Indiam Orientalem, et descriptio totius Guineæ tractus, Loangæ, Angolæ, et Monomotapæ, insularumque S. Thomæ, S. Helenæ, Ascensionis, nec non insulæ Madagascar, situsque terræ firmæ a Bonæ Spei promontorio, usque ad mare rubrum. Hagæ, 1599. Amsterdam, 1614. Also in de Bry (Little Voyages), parts 2, 3, 4.

RHODES, P. Alexandre de, Voyages et Missions en la Chine en autre royaumes d'Orient. Paris, 4to. 1653, 1666, 1682.

HAMILTON, Alexander. A new account of the East Indies, giving an account of the situation, product, manufactures, laws, customs, religion, trade, &c. of all the countries and islands which lie between the Cape of Good Hope and the island of Japan. 2 vols. 8vo. Edinburgh, 1727. London, 1747.

Recueil des Voyages qui ont servi à l'etablissement et aux progres de la Compagnie des Indes Orient. des Hollandois, publié par Constantin. 5 toms. 8vo. Amsterdam, 1702–1706. 10 toms. 12mo. 1730.

## CHAPTER VII.—The Caspian.

Jenkinson, Johnson, &c. appeared first in Hackluyt, partly copied by Purchas, Pinkerton, &c. translated in Thevenot and Recueil des Voyages au Nord.

Cubero, Peregrinacion che ha hecho de la mayor parte del Mondo, D. Pedro Sebastiano Cubero. fol. Saragossa, 1688.

Beckewitz, Bruce. Memoirs of Peter Henry Bruce, containing an Account of his Travels in Germany, Russia, Tartary, &c. 4to. London, 1782.

Elton, Hanway, &c. Historical Account of the British Trade over the Caspian Sea, with a Journal of Travels from London through Russia, into Prussia, and back again through Russia into Germany and Holland; to which are added the Revolutions of Persia during the present century, by Jonas Hanway. 2 vols. 4to. London, 1753.

¶ Bell, John, of Antermony's, Travels from St Petersburg in Russia to several parts of Asia. 2 vols. 4to. Glasgow, 1763.

Histoire des Decouvertes faites par plusieurs savans voyageurs (Pallas, Gmelin, Guldenstedt, and Lepechin), dans plusieurs contrees de la Russie et de la Perse. 2 vols. 4to. Hague, 1779. 3 tom. 4to. Geneve, 1785—6.

## CHAPTER VIII.—From India overland.

Tenreiro, Antonio. The only copy of this narrative which I have seen is one appended to the folio edition of Mendez Pinto, published at Lisbon in 1763.

Bernardino, Fray Gaspar de Sao. Itinerario do India por Terra. 4to. Lisbon, 1611.

Godinho, P. Manuel. Relacao de novo camino que fez por terra e mar da India para Portugal, no anno 1663. Lisbon, 8vo. 1665.

Capper, James, Col. Observations on the passage to India through Egypt; also by Vienna through Constantinople to Aleppo, &c. 4to. London, 1784. 8vo. 1785.

CAMPBELL, Donald, of Barbreck. A Journey overland to India, partly by a route never gone before by any European. 4to. London, 1775.

TAYLOR, John, Travels from India by the way of Tyrol, Venice, &c. 2 vols. 8vo. London, 1799.

¶ IVES, Edward, Esq. A Voyage from India to England in 1754; also a Voyage from Persia to England by an unusual route. 4to. London, 1773.

JACKSON, John, Journey from India towards England, by a route commonly called overland; particularly between the rivers Euphrates and Tigris, through Curdistan, Diarbeck, Armenia, and Natolia, in Asia. 8vo. London, 1799.

## CHAPTER IX.—THIBET.

ANDRADA, Antonio, novo descubrimento do grao Catayo ou dos reynos de Tibet. 4to. Lisboa, 1626. I have only been able to find this and some similar narratives in the following work.

NIEREMBERG, Claros varones de la Companhia de Jesu, 6 tom. fol. Madrid, 1643, &c.*

GRUEBER and DORVILLE. Their narrative is inserted in Kircher's China Illustrata (fol. 1667), and in the fourth volume of Thevenot's Relation de Voyages curieux.

DESIDERI, Lettres edifiantes et curieuses, tom. xi.

---

* The titles of the volumes are fancifully varied, thus: Ideas de Virtud en algunos claros, &c. Firmamento religioso de Luzidos astros en algunos &c. Honor del gran Patriarca San Ignacio de Loyola, &c. (1645). Vidas exemplares y venerabiles Memorias de algunos, &c. (1647). The two last volumes are by Alonzo de Andrada, and are entitled Varones illustres in Santitad, Letras, y Zelo, &c. (1666—67). In the king's library I had an opportunity of picking out the grains of barley from this immense mass of Jesuit chaff.

HORACE DE LA PENNA, Relazione del Stato presente del gran regno de Thibet. 8vo. Roma, 1732.

## CHAPTER X.—CENTRAL ASIA.

PEGOLETTI. (In Forster's Voyages au Nord).

CHESAUD. (In Astley's Collection).

GOEZ. This narrative in the original Portuguese is given by Nieremberg, (see above). There is a Latin translation in the "Christiana expeditio apud Sinas" of Riccio. The analyses of Purchas and Astley are very slovenly and inaccurate.

GERBILLON, in Duhalde, Description Historique, &c. de la Chine.

## CHAPTER XI.

The materials for this chapter are generally derived from those already enumerated, particularly under the first chapter of the Introduction.

## *BOOK II.*

## CHAPTER I.—EARLY VOYAGES TO INDIA.

COSMAS INDICOPLEUSTES. In Montfaucon. Collectio Nova Patrum, Græcorum (2 tom. fol. Paris, 1705), Gr. Lat. A part of it (Gr. Fr.) in Thevenot's Collection.

CONTI, STO STEFANO. In Ramusio's Collection, tom. i.

ABDOULRIZACK. Translated with Notes by M. Langles in his Collection Portative des Voyages. 12mo. Paris, 1805.

BARTHEMA,—Ludovici, patricii, Romæ novum Itinerarium Ethiopiæ, Egypti, utriusque Arabiæ, Persiæ, Syriæ et Indiæ, citra ultraque Gangem. fol. No date, extremely rare.

——— Fol. Milan. 1511.

——— In Spanish (with the name). fol. Seville, 1576.

Barthema, in Ramusio, tom. i. English Translation, under the name of Vertomannus, in Willes and Eden's Decades, 4to. 1555.

## CHAPTER II.—Portuguese Discovery.

Di Barros, Decades IV. de Asia. fol. 1552, 1602. Continued by Couto, Decades V—XI. fol. (It is doubtful if the four last have been printed).

——— Reprinted in 15 vols. 12mo. Lisboa, 1777.

Castanheda, Fernan Lopez de, Historia de descobrimento e conquista da India por los Portugueses. 8 tom. fol. Coimbra, 1552—4.

——— Ital. by Ulloa. 2 tom. 4to. Venice, 1578.

¶ Faria y Sousa, Manuel, Asia Portuguesa. 3 tom. fol. Lisboa, 1666—75.

Osorio, Hieronymo, de Rebus Emanuelis Lusitaniæ regis virtute et auspiciis gestis. fol. Lisboa, 1575.

## CHAPTER III.—Portuguese Missionaries.

Guzman, Historia de las missiones che han hecho los religiosos de la companhia de Jesus, para predicar el Santo Evangelio en la India Oriental y en los Reynos de China y Japon. 2 tom. fol. Alcala, 1601.

Oriente Conquistado a Jesu Christo pelos Padres da companhia de Jesu da Provincia de Goa. 2 tom. 4to. 1710.

Cartas de la India. 1551, 1562, 1611.

Manrique, Itinerario de las missiones del India Oriental. 4to. Roma, 1653.

## CHAPTER IV.—English Embassies.

Mildenhall, Hawkins, Roe. In Purchas, vol. i. Roe more fully in Churchill's Collection, vol. i. and afterwards printed separately. 4to. 1540.

## CHAPTER V.—Miscellaneous Travels.

Bruton, William, Newes from the East Indies, or Voyage to Bengalla. 4to. London, 1638. Reprinted in Osborne's Collection.

Graaf, Voyages de, Amst. 12mo. 1719; and in Hist. Gen. des Voyages.

Mandeslo, Joh. Albr. Morgenlandische Reisebeschreibung, mit Adam Olearius Ammerkungen. fol. Schleswick, 1647.

——— French Translation. Amsterdam, 1727.

——— In English by Davies. fol. 1669.

Bernier, Francis, Voyages, contenant la description des Etats du Grand Mogul del Indostan, &c. 2 tom. 12mo. Amst. 1699, 1723, 1725.

——— In English, 1671—2. Inserted in Osborne and Pinkerton's Collections.

Tavernier, (J. B.) Voyage en Turquie, en Perse, et aux Indes. 6 tom. 12mo. Paris, (Hollande), 1692.

——— Utrecht, 1712.

——— In English. fol. London, 1678.

Hodges (William, R. A.) Travels in India during the years 1780, -1 -2 -3. 4to. London, 1793—1794. Translated with Notes by M. Langles in his Bibliotheque Portative des Voyages. Paris, 1805.

Niecamp, Jo. Luc. Historia Missionis Evangelicæ in India Orientali. 4to. Halle, 1747. Abridged from a German work on the same subject, in 13 vols. 4to.

¶ Thevenot (Jean) Voyage, contenant la relation de l'Indoustan, des nouveaux Mogols, et autres peuples et pays des Indes. 4to. Paris, 1684.

Dellon, Voyage aux Indes Orientales. Amsterdam. 12mo. 1699.

——— In English, with his account of the Inquisition at Goa. 8vo. 1699.

TAPP (David) Funfzehnjahrige Ostindianische Reise-beschreibung von 1667—1682. 4to. Hanover, 1714.

GROSE (John Henry) Voyage to the East Indies, begun in 1750, and continued till 1764. 8vo. London, 1766.—French translation. 12mo. Paris, 1758.

TIEFENTHALLER (P. Joseph) Historisch-Geographische Beschreibung von Hindostan, &c. herausgegeben von J. Bernouilli. 2 vols. 8vo. Berlin, 1786.

——— In French, with Anquetil du Perron's Recherches, and Rennel's map. 3 tom. 4to. 1785.

RENNEL (James) Memoir of a Map of Hindostan, or the Mogul Empire, with an Introduction illustrative of the geography and present division of that country, and a Map of the country situated between the borders of the Indus and the Caspian. 8vo. London, 1788.

——— In French from the 7th edition. 3 tom. 8vo. 1800.

## CHAPTERS VI. VII. VIII.—DESCRIPTION OF HINDOSTAN.

ASIATIC RESEARCHES; or Transactions of the Society instituted in Bengal, for inquiring into the history and antiquities, the arts, sciences, and literature of Asia. 12 vols. 4to and 8vo. Calcutta—London reprinted, 1799—1819.

ASIATIC ANNUAL REGISTER for 1799 and following years. 8vo. London.

Fifth Report of the Select Committee of the House of Commons on the affairs of the East India Company. Ordered to be printed 12th July 1812. 1 large folio volume.

Papers relating to the East India Company, ordered to be printed 3d and 13th June 1813. 2 vols. folio. Include Mr Grant's View of the State of Society among the Asiatic subjects of Great Britain, Mr Strachey's Reports, &c.

JONES (Sir William) Works. 8 vols. 4to. 1799—1801.

BUCHANAN (now Hamilton) Francis, M. D. A Journey from Madras through the countries of Mysore, Canara, and Malabar, for the express purpose of investigating the state of agriculture, arts, and commerce; the religion, manners, and customs; the history, natural and civil; and antiquities. 3 vols. 4to. London, 1807.

MILL (James) History of British India. 3 vols. 4to. London, 1818.

COLEBROOKE (H.) Remarks on the husbandry and commerce of Bengal. 8vo. London, 1806.

VALENTIA (Lord) Voyages and Travels. 3 vols. 4to. 4 vols. 8vo.

GRAHAM (Maria) Journal of a residence in India. 4to. Edin. 1812—1815.

——— Letters on India. 8vo. Edin. 1815.

WILKES (Col. M.) Historical Sketches of the south of India. 3 vols. 4to. London, v. y.

DUBOIS (Abbe) Description of the character, manners, and customs of the people of India. 4to. London, 1817.

WARD, View of the history, religion, and literature of the Hindoos. 2 vols. 8vo. 3d Edit. 2 vols. 8vo. 1817.

TONE on the Mahrattas, (in Asiatic Annual Register).

BROUGHTON (T. D.) Letters written in a Mahratta camp in 1809. 4to. London, 1813.

FITZCLARENCE (Lt. Col.) Journey from India to England. 4to. London, 1819.

MALCOLM (Sir John) Sketch of the Sikhs. 8vo. London, 1812. (Several papers on the subject in Asiatic Researches).

TYTLER (Alex. Fraser) Considerations on the present political state of India. 2 vols. 8vo. 1815.

BUCHANAN (Rev. Claudius) Christian Researches in Asia. 8vo. London, 1811.

HAMILTON (Walter) East India Gazetteer. 8vo. London, 1815.

HAMILTON, Geographical Description of Hindostan, 2 vols. 4to. London, 1820.

## *BOOK III.*

### CHAPTER I.—THE HIMMALEH.

HARDWICKE (Capt.) Narrative of a Journey to Serinagur. Asiatic Researches.

WEBB and RAPER, Journey to explore the sources of the Ganges. *Ibid.* vol. x.

COLEBROOKE (H.) On the height of the Himalaya mountains. *Ibid.* vol. xi.

MOORCROFT, Journey to the lake Manasarowara in Undes. *Ibid.* vol. xii.

Quarterly Review for February 1820.

FRASER (J. B.) Outline of his narrative in Edinburgh Philosophical Journal, No. 1.

### CHAPTER II.—THIBET.

BOGLE, Account of Thibet, containing a description of the manners, customs, religion, and commerce of the inhabitants, extracted from his papers by Mr Stewart. Philosophical Transactions, No. 67. part. 2. and Annual Register 1778.

TURNER (Samuel) An Account of an Embassy to the court of Teshoo Lama in Thibet, containing a narrative of a journey through Bootan and part of Thibet; to which are added, views taken upon the place by Lieutenant Samuel Davis, and observations mineralogical, botanical, and medical, by Robert Saunders. 4to. London, 1800.

### CHAPTER III.—NEPAL.

GIUSEPPE (Father) Account of Nepal, including the narration of its invasion by Purthi Nerain.—Asiatic Researches, vol. ii.

Kirkpatrick (Col.) An account of the kingdom of Nepal, being the substance of observations made during a mission to that country in the year 1793; illustrated with a map and other engravings. 4to. London, 1811.

Hamilton (formerly Buchanan) Francis, M. D. An account of the kingdom of Nepal, and of the territories annexed to this dominion by the House of Gorkha; with engravings. 4to. Edin. 1819.

## CHAPTER IV.—Countries west of India.

Forster (George) A Journey from Bengal to England, through the northern parts of India, Cashmire, Afghanistan, and Persia, and into Russia by the Caspian Sea. 2 vols. 4to. London, 1798. 8vo. 1808.

Elphinston (Mount Stewart) An Account of the kingdom of Caubul, and its dependencies in Persia, Tartary, and India. 4to. London, 1815. edit. in 2 vols. 8vo.

Pottinger, Travels in Beloochistan and Sinde. 4to. London.

Encyclopædia Britannica, Supplement, art. Caubul. As this article was contributed by the author of this work, he has taken the liberty to extract a few pages *verbatim*.

# *BOOK IV.*

## CHAPTER I.—Persia, (early).

Zeno (Caterino) Commentari del Viaggio in Persia e delle guerre fatte nell' imperio Persiano del tempo di Uxan Cassano, &c. 8vo. Venice, 1558.

Barbaro (Josafat) no separate edition.

Contarini (Ambrogio) Viaggio del Ambasciatore della signoria di Venetia al Uxan Cassan re di Persia, &c. 12mo. Venice, 1543.

The above three narratives are printed by Aldus in one

small 8vo volume, entitled, Viaggi fatti da Vinegia, &c. Venice, 1543–1545. They are also inserted in the collection of Ramusio.

SHERLEY, Sir Antony, Relation of his Travels into Persia. 4to. 1613. Also in Purchas.

DON GARCIA DE SYLVA, Commentarios de la Embaxada que del parte del Rey de Espana Don Phelipe III. hizo al Rey Scha Abas de Persia. Anno 1618. Ayscough MSS. (British Museum).

——— De Rebus Persarum Epistola. 1619. Spahani exarata. Antwerpiae, 1620. This letter does not contain any of the particulars in the above MS. narrative.

HERBERT, Thomas, A Relation of some years Travels into Africa and the Great Asia, especially the territories of the Persian monarchy, and some parts of the Oriental Indies, and Isles adjacent. fol. London, 1634, 1635, 1665, 1667.

——— In French, by Wiquefort. 4to. 1663.

OLEARIUS, Adam, Muskowitische oft begehrte Beschreiburg der neuen Orientalischen Reise an der Koenig in Persien, (with Mandeslo's narrative appended). Sleswig. fol. 1647. A more complete edition at Hamburg, 1690.

——— In French, by Wiquefort. fol. Amst. 1726.

——— In English. 4to. 1669.

CHARDIN, Chev. Journal du Voyage en Perse, et aux Indes Orientales, par la Mer Noire. fol. London, 1686. This edition contains only the journey from Paris to Ispahan. The description of Persia never appeared till the following:

Voyage de M. le Chevalier Chardin en Perse, et autres lieux de l'Orient. Amst. 10 tom. 12mo. 1711.

——— Le Meme. Amst. 4 tom. 4to. 1735.

——— Le Meme, augmentee des Notes, &c. par M. Langles. 10 tom. 8vo. avec des planches en folio. (The best edition).

BEMBO, Ambrogio—in Morelli, Dissertation respecting some learned Venetians who are little known. Ital. Venice. fol. 1804.

LEANDRO, Persia, overo secondo Viaggio di F. Leandro di Sto Cecilia carmelitano scalzo, dell' Oriente, scritta da medesimo. 4to. Roma, 1757.

¶ VALLE, Pietro della, Viaggi in Turchia, Persia, e India, (chiefly Persia). 4 tom. 4to. Roma, 1650, 1658, 1663.

BRUYN, Corn le, Journey through Muscovy to Persia and the East Indies, (In Dutch). Distinguished by its valuable plates representing cities and ruins.

——— In French. Amst. 2 vols. fol. 1718.

——— In English. 3 vols. fol. 1718.

FRANKLIN, William, Observations made on a Tour from Bengal to Schiraz, with a short account of the remains of the celebrated palace of Persepolis. 8vo. London, 1790.

BEAUCHAMP, Voyage en Perse. (Journal des Savans. 1790.)

## CHAPTER II.—PERSIA, (RECENT.)

MALCOLM, Sir John, History of Persia, from the earliest ages to the present time. 2 vols. 4to. 1816.

OLIVIER, Voyage en Perse. 2 vols. 8vo. Paris, 1807.

WARING, Scott, Tour to Schiraz. 4to. 1812.

MORIER, James, Journey through Persia, Armenia, and Asia Minor, to Constantinople, in the years 1808 and 1809. 4to. London, 1812.

MACDONALD KINNEIR, John, Geographical Memoir of the Persian Empire, accompanied by a map. 4to. London, 1813.

RICH, Claudius James, Memoir on the ruins of Babylon. 8vo. London, 1815.

¶ MORIER, (J.) Second Journey through Persia to Constantinople, between the years 1810–16; together with an account of his Majesty's embassy under Sir Gore Ouseley, Bart. 4to. 1818.

OUSELEY, (Sir William) Travels in various countries of the East, particularly Persia. vol. i. 4to. 1819.

## CHAPTER III.—Holy Land.

Arculfus—Willibald—Bernard—in Mabillon Acta Sanctorum Ordinis S. Benedicti. Seculum Tertium.

Bouldesell (William de) L'hystoire plaisante, &c. See under Ricold, page 491.

Brocquiere (Bertrandon de) Voyage, first published in the Memoires of the French Institute.

——— In English by Johnes, and in new edition of Hackluyt.

Breydenbach (Bern. de) Opus transmarinæ peregrinationis ad sepulchrum Dominicum in Hierusalem. fol. 1483. Mentz, 1486, 1541. Spire, 1502.

——— In French, 1484, 1489, 1517.

Baumgarten (Martin) Peregrinatio in Ægyptum, Arabiam, Palestinam, et Syriam. Nuremberg, 1621, 1673.

——— In English, in Churchill's Collection.

Georgewitz (Bart.) Voyage de la Sainte Cite de Jerusalem, avec les ceremonies des Turcs. Liege. 4to. 1600.

Aldersey (Laurence) in Hackluyt.

Sandys (George) Travels. fol. London, 1615, 1621, 1673; also in Purchas.

¶ Rosacio (Giuseppe) Viaggi de Venetia a Constantinopoli, e per mare e per terra insieme quella della Terra Santa. 4to. Venice, 1518, 1598.

Zuallardo, Devotissimo Viaggio de Jerusalem, fatto e descritto l'anno 1586, con disegni di Varii Luoghi di Terra Santa. 8vo. Roma, 1587, 1595.

Adrichomius, Theatrum Terræ Sanctæ. fol. Cologne, 1590.

Vera (Juan Caverio de) Viage de la Terra Santa y descripcion de Jerusalem, y del Sante Monte Libano. 8vo. Pampeluna, 1613.

Cotovicus (Joan) Itinerarium Hierosolymitanum et Syriacum. 4to. Antwerp, 1619.

Brocardus (Bonaventura) Palestina sive Descriptio Terræ Sanctæ.

Noe (Fr.) Viaggio de Venetia al Santi Sepolcro e al Monte Sinai. 8vo. Venice, 1638, 1676. Bassano, 1685.

Doubdan (M. J.) Voyage de la Terre Sainte, enrichie de figures. 4to. Paris, 1661.

Cheron (Anne) Agée de *quatre vingts* ans, Relation d'un Voyage, (a Jerusalem). Paris. 12mo. 1671.

Gonzales (D.) Reisen nach Jerusalem. 2 vols. 4to. Antwerp.

Morison (Sieur) Relation d'un voyage nouvellement fait au Mount Sinai et a Jerusalem. 4to. Toul, 1704.

Relandus (Hadrian) Palestina ex monumentis veteribus illustrata. 4to. Utrecht.

## CHAPTER IV.—Asiatic Turkey.

Eldred (John) in Hackluyt.

Biddulph (William) Travels of certain Englishmen into farre countries, Africa, Asia, Troy, Bithynia, &c. 8vo. London, 1609.

Pococke (Richard) A description of the East, and of some other countries. 3 vols. folio. 1743, 1745, 1748. (Reprinted in Pinkerton's Collection).

——— In French, 6 vols. 12mo. 1772.

Wood, Ruins of Palmyra, formerly called Tadmor in the Desert. fol. London, 1753.

——— Ruins of Baalbek, anciently called Heliopolis or Cœlosyria. fol. 1757.

Chandler (Richard) Travels in Asia Minor; or an account of a Tour made at the expense of the Society of Dillettanti. 2 vols. 4to. Oxford, 1774.

Clarke (Edward Daniel) Travels in various countries in Europe, Asia, and Africa, Part II. Sect. 1. 4to. London, 1812.

MACDONALD KINNEIR (John) Journey through Asia Minor, Armenia, and Koordistan, in 1813, 1814, with remarks on the marches of Alexander, and the retreat of the Ten Thousand. 8vo. 1818.

SEETZEN (Dr) In Malte Brun, Annales des Voyages.

BURCKHARDT (John Lewis) Travels in Nubia. 4to. London, 1819.

¶ LUCAS (Paul) Voyage au Levant, avec figures. 2 tom. 12mo. Paris, 1704.

MAUNDRELL (Henry) Journey from Aleppo to Jerusalem at Easter, A. D. 1697. 8vo. Oxford, 1703, 1707, 1714, &c. (In Pinkerton's Collection).

THEVENOT (Sieur) Voyage au Levant, &c. 5 tom. 12mo. Amst. 1725.

MARITI (Abate) Viaggio per l'isola de Cipro, per la Soria e la Palestina. 5 vol. 8vo. Turin, 1769.

——— In French, 2 first vols. 8vo. Paris.

——— In English, 3 vols. 8vo. 1791.

VOLNEY, Voyage en Syrie et en Egypt, pendant les annees 1783, 1784, et 1785, troisième edition, revue and corrigee par l'auteur, et augmentée. 2 tom. 8vo. 1800.

CHATEAUBRIAND, Itineraire de Paris à Jerusalem. 2 tom. 8vo. Paris, 1812.

## CHAPTER V.—ARABIA.

NIEBUHR (Carsten) Reisebeschreiburg von Arabien, aus eigenen Beobachtungen, und in Lande selbst gesammlten, Nachrichten. 4to. Copenhagen, 1772.

——— In French. 4to. Copenhagen, 1773. And at Amsterdam, (with the questions of Michaelis). 3 tom. 1776-80. This last edition is the best.

——— In English, 2 vols. 8vo. 1799; also in Pinkerton's Collection.

VALENTIA's (Lord) Voyages and Travels to India, Ceylon, Abyssinia, the Red Sea, and Egypt. 3 vols. 4to. London, 1809.

SEETZEN, In Malte Brun, Annales des Voyages.

BAHDIA, Travels of Ali Bey. 2 vols. 4to. London.

¶ LA ROQUE, Voyage dans l'Arabie Heureuse par l'ocean oriental et le detroit de la Mer Rouge. 12mo. Paris, 1716.

——— Voyage fait par ordre du Roi Louis XIV. vers le Grand Emir, Premier chef des Arabes du desert. 12mo. Paris, 1717. (This volume contains d'Arvieux's account of the manners of the Bedouins).

## *BOOK V.*

### CHAPTER I.—EASTERN INDIA.

CÆSAR FREDERIC, Travels through India. In the edition 1606 of Ramusio, and a translation in Purchas, vol. ii.

BALBI (Gasparo) Viaggio dell' Indie orientali. 8vo. Venice, 1590. In Ramusio and Purchas.

SYMES (Major Samuel) An account of an embassy to the kingdom of Ava, sent by the governor-general of India in the year 1795. 4to. London, 1800.

BUCHANAN (Dr Francis) On the religion and literature of the Hindoos. Asiatic Researches, vol. vi.

TACHARD (P.) Premier Voyage de Siam des P. P. Jesuites envoyes par le Roi aux Indes et a la Chine. 12mo. Paris, 1686.

——— Second Voyage. 12mo. Paris, 1689.

CHAUMONT (Chev. de) Relation de l'ambassade a la cour de Siam. 12mo. Paris, 1687.

LOUBERE, Description du royaume de Siam. 2 vols. 12mo. Amst. 1714.

BORRI, Christoforo, Relazione della nova missione dei Padri della Compania de Jesu nel regno de Cocincina. 8vo. Roma, 1631.

BORRI In French. 8vo. 1631.

——— In English. 4to. 1633.

BARROW, John, A voyage to Cochin-china in the years 1792 and 1793, containing a general view of the valuable productions and political importance of that flourishing kingdom, &c. 4to. London, 1806.

——— In French by Malte Brun. 2 vols. 8vo. Paris, 1807.

¶ HUNTER, William M. A. Concise account of the kingdom of Pegu, its climate, produce, trade, government, and inhabitants. 8vo. London, 1785.

TURPIN, Histoire civile et naturelle du Royaume de Siam, et des revolutions qui ont bouleversé cet empire jusqu'en 1770. 2 vols. 12mo. 1771.

CHAPMAN, Voyage to Cochin-china in 1778. Asiatic Annual Register 1801.

RICHARD (Abbé) Histoire naturelle et civile du Tunkin. 2 vols. 12mo. Paris, 1788.

## CHAPTERS II. III. IV.—CHINA.

The ANDRADAS and PIREZ. In Di Barros Decada iii. lib. vi.

MENDOZA, (Juan Gonzales de) Historia de las cosas mas notables, ritos y costumbres del gran reyno de la China, con un itinerario del nuevo Mondo. Rome, 1585. Venice, 1588.—Mendoza's description is drawn up from the report of the Augustines, Franciscans, and St Ignatius; and he has appended a narrative of their adventures.

RICCIUS et TRIGAUTIUS, De Christiana expeditione apud Siuas, suscepta ab societate Jesu. August. Vind. 1615. Lugdun, 1616.

——— in French, 1617.

——— Abridged translation in Purchas, vol. ii.

NAVARETE, Tratados historicos, politicos, &c. de la monarchia de China. fol. Madrid, 1676, (rare).

Dutch transactions and embassies in Astley's Collection, vol. iii.

NIEUHOFF, John, Embassy of the Dutch East India Company to the Great Tartar Khan, the Emperor of China, (in Dutch). Amst. 1665.

——— In French. fol. Leyden, 1665.

——— In Astley's and Pinkerton's Collections.

A relation of second and third Embassies from the East India Company into the empire of China, by Arnoldus Montanus and John Ogilvy. fol. London, 1670. Translated from Dapper in Dutch. fol. Amst. 1670.

LECOMTE (P. Louis) Nouveaux Memoires sur l'état present de la Chine. 2 vols. 12mo. Paris, 1696, 1700, 1702.

——— In English. 8vo. 1697—98.

Description Geographique, Historique, Chronologique, Politique, et Physique, de l'empire de Chine, et de la Tartarie Chinoise; enrichie des cartes generales et particulieres de ce pays. 4 vols. folio. Paris, 1735. 4to. Hague. 1736.

——— In English, under the title of General History of China, Chinese Tartary, Corea and Thibet, (with some additions). 4 vols. 8vo. 1741.

——— In German. Rostock. 4 vols. 4to. 1747.

Lettres Edifiantes et Curieuses ecrites des missions etrangeres. 26 tom. 12mo. Paris, 1780. Tomes 17. to 26. relate to China. The narratives of the persecutions are given in tomes 19. 23. 24.

MEMOIRES concernent l'histoire, les sciences, et les arts de Chinois, par les missionaires de Pekin, (chiefly P. Annot). 15 vols. 4to. Paris, 1775, &c.

First Russian Embassies, in Purchas, vol. ii.

ISBRAND IDES. Account of his great journey to China in the year 1692, from Moscow through Siberia, Daouria, and Great Tartary. By Adam Brand. (In German). Franckfort, 1697.

ISBRAND IDES, In French. 12mo. Amst. 1699.

LANGE (Sieur) Journal du Voyage de Moscow, a Pekin, et de sa residence a la cour de Chine, in 1721 et 1722. 12mo. Leyden, 1726.

BELL (John) Travels. See above, p. 493.

STAUNTON (Sir George) Authentic account of the embassy from the king of Great Britain to the Emperor of China, taken chiefly from the papers of Lord Macartney, Sir Erasmus Gower, and other gentlemen, in the several departments of the embassy. 2 vols. 4to. London, 1797. ed. in 3 vols. 8vo.

——— In French, by Castera. 4 vols. 8vo. Paris, 1798.

BARROW (John) Travels in China, containing descriptions and observations made and collected in the course of a short visit to the imperial palace of Yuenmien, and a subsequent journey through the country from Peking to Canton; wherein it is attempted to appreciate the rank which this extraordinary empire holds in the scale of civilized nations. 4to. London, 1804.

——— In French, by Castera. 3 vols. 8vo. with 4to atlas. Paris, 1805.

——— In German. 8vo. Hamburgh, 1805.

ELLIS (Henry) Journal of the proceedings of the late embassy to China. 4to. London, 1817. 2 vols. 8vo. 1818.

MACLEOD, N. Narrative of a voyage in his Majesty's ship Alceste to the Yellow Sea, &c. 8vo. 1817.

HALL (Captain Basil) Account of a Voyage of Discovery to the west coast of Corea, and the Great Loochoo island; with an appendix containing charts and various hydrographic and scientific notices. 4to. London, 1818; 12mo. 1819.

ABEL (Dr Clarke) Journal of Travels in the interior of China, and of a voyage to and from that country. 8vo. London, 1818.

¶ SEMEDO, Relazione della grande monarchia della China, Roma, 1643. In English, fol. London, 1655, 1670. In French, Lyons, 4to. 1667.

Kircher (Athanasius) China monumentis sacris et profanis, necnon variis naturæ et artis spectaculis illustrata. fol. Amst. 1670.

Grozier, Description Generale de la Chine. 4to. Paris, 1785. 2 vols. 8vo. 1787.

——— In English, 2 vols. 8vo. London, 1788.

Braam (Van) Proceedings of the Dutch embassy to China. 2 vols. 8vo.

De Guignes. Voyage. 3 tom. 8vo. Paris.

## CHAPTER V.—Japan.

Gusman, Oriente Conquistado, and Nieremberg, see above, p. 496.

Account of the embassies of the Dutch East India Company to the Emperors of Japan (in Dutch). fol. Amsterdam, 1669.

——— In English, by John Ogilvy. fol. London, 1670.

——— In French. Amsterdam. fol. 1680.

Kaempfer (Engelbrecht). The History of Japan, containing an account of the ancient and present state and government of that empire, translated from his original manuscript in High Dutch, never before printed, by I. G. Scheuchzer. 2 vols. fol. London, 1728.

——— In French. 2 toms. fol. Haye, 1729. 3 toms. 12mo. Amsterdam, 1732.

——— Also in Pinkerton's Collection.

Thunberg (K. P.) Travels through Europe, Asia, and Africa, during the years 1770 to 1779 (in Swedish). 4 vols. 8vo. Upsal, 1788—93. The two last volumes relate to Japan).

——— In English. 4 vols. 8vo. London, 1794.

——— In French, with Notes by Langles and Lamarck. 2 vols. 4to. 1796.

Krusenstern, Voyage round the World, in the years 1803 to 1806. Russian original. 3 vols. 4to. with folio Atlas.

——— In English, by Hopner. 2 vols. 4to. London, 1813.

GOLOWNIN (Captain) Recollections of Japan. English translation. 2 vols. 8vo. 1818.

¶ CARON (Fran.) Description of Japan, in reply to different questions put in 1636 by Philip Lucas (in Dutch). Hague, 4to.

——— In Thevenot, Astley, and Pinkerton's Collections.

CHARLEVOIX (Pere) Histoire du Japan. 3 toms. 4to. Paris, 1736; also in 6 toms. 12mo.

## *BOOK VI.*

### CHAPTER I.

ENGELMAN, Reise von den nordlichen Seite des Kaukasus bis nach Choy in Persien, in Jahr 1785, (Pallas's Neue Nordische Beytraege, vol. ii.)

PALLAS (P. S.) Bemerkungen auf einer Reise in die Sudlichen Statthalterschaften des Russischen Reichs. 2 vols. 4to. 1796, 1799.

——— In French, 2 vols. 4to. with coloured plates. Leipsic, 1799.

——— In English, 2 vols. 4to. London, 1801.

GULDENSTEDT (John Antony) Reisen durch Russland und in Caucasischen Gebirge, (edited by Pallas). 2 vols. 4to. Petersburgh, 1787, 1791.

KLAPROTH, Julius Henry, Reise in den Caucasus. 3 vols. 8vo.

——— In English, by Schoberl. 4to. London.

REINEGGS, Historical and Geographical Description of the Caucasus. English translation, 2 vols. 8vo. 1807.

ELLIS, Memoir of a Map of the countries between the Black Sea and the Caspian. 4to. London.

### CHAPTERS II. III.—SIBERIA.

First discovery and conquest, in the latter part of Coxe's History of Russian Discoveries, 4to. London, 1780; and in Purchas, vol. ii.

BELL, see above, page 493.

MESSERSCHMIDT, (Daniel Gottlieb), Nachricht von siebenjahriges Reise in Siberien, (Pallas, Neue Nordische Beytrage, vol. iii.)

GMELIN, (Joh. George) Reisen durch Sibirien von den Jahr 1743 bis 1733. 4 vols. 8vo. Gottingen, 1751 and 1752.

——— In French, abridged by Keralio. 2 vols. 12mo. Paris, 1767. Also in Histoire Gen. des Voyages, tom. xviii.

PALLAS, (P. S.) Reisen durch verschiedenen provinzen des Russischen Reichs in den Jahren 1768 bis 1773. 3 vols. 4to. Petersburg, 1771, 1773, 1776.

——— In French, 5 toms. 4to. with fol. Atlas. Paris, 1788.

——— Le Meme, avec des Notes, par Langles et Lamarch. 8 toms. 8vo. Paris, 1794.

SCHANGIN, (P. J.) Merkwurdige Reise in den hochsten Altaische Gebirge, (Pallas Nordische Beytrage, vol. vi.)

SIEVERS, Briefe uber Sibirien (Ibid. vol. vii.)

GIORGI, (I. G.) Geographische, Physicalische and Naturhistorische, Beschreiburg von den Russischen Reichs. 3 vols. 4to. Konigsberg, 1799—1801. 9 vols. 8vo.

¶ CHAPPE D'AUTEROCHE, (Abbé), Voyage en Siberie, faite par ordre du Roi en 1761, contenant les moeurs, les usages des Russes, et l'etat actual de cette puissance, la description geographique et le nivellement de la route de Paris a Tobolsk, &c. 3 vols. 4to. with fol. Atlas. Paris, 1768.

DE LISLE, M. Journal d'un Voyage fait en 1740 a Beresow en Siberie, aux depens de la cour imperiale. (Hist Gen. des Voyages, tom. xviii.)

LEPECHIN, (Ivan) Journal of Travels through different provinces of the Russian empire, made between the year 1768 and 1771 (in Russian). 4to. Petersburgh, 1771.

——— In German. 3 vols. 4to. 1774.

GIORGI, J. G. Bemerkungen aufeiner Reise in Russischen Reich von 1772 bis 1774. 2 vols. 4to. Petersburg.

# INDEX.

THE END.

# ERRATA.

## VOL. I.

| | | | | |
|---|---|---|---|---|
| *Page* 82, *line* 13, | from bottom, for | *Tartars* | read *Fathers.* |
| 118, 2, | | *instruments* | read *vestments.* |
| 122, 13, | from top, for | *mighty* | read *nightly.* |
| 272, 15, | | dele *so*, and insert it next line after *me.* | |
| 342, 14, | | *Medea* | read *Medusa.* |
| 405, 4, | from bottom, for | *evening* | read *morning.* |

## VOL. II.

| | | | |
|---|---|---|---|
| 139, 6, | from bottom, after *of* add *the mode of.* | | |
| 149, 5, | from top, | dele *partly.* | |
| 212, 13, | for | *fine* | read *five.* |
| 240, 14, | | *artisans* | read *Africans.* |
| 245, 2, | | *offered* | read *afford.* |
| 259, 12, | | *entry* | read *victory.* |
| 332, 5, | | *dust* | read *dirt.* |
| 348, 6, | | *aptness* | read *openness.* |
| 409, | lowest line, | 70 | read 50. |

## VOL. III.

| | | | |
|---|---|---|---|
| 120, 7, | from top, for | *second* | read *sacred.* |
| 133, 4, | | dele *good.* | |
| 186, 6, | from bottom, for | *Arabio* | read *Asiatic.* |
| 259, 11, | | *executed* | read *excited.* |
| 440, 6, | | *Lidele* | read *Lisle.* |

---

## DIRECTIONS TO THE BINDER.

Map of Asia to front Title Page, Vol. I.

Oriens secundum Ptolemæum, Vol. I. p. 481.

Map of Hindostan, to front Title Page, Vol. II.

Western Asia, the same, Vol. III.